ENVIRONMENTAL ETHICS AND PHILOSOPHY

ENVIRONMENTAL ETHICS AND PHILOSOPHY

N. Ghai
J.S. Negi

CYBER TECH PUBLICATIONS
4264/3, Ansari Road, Daryaganj, New Delhi-110002 (India)
Ph.: 011-23244078, 011-43559448 Fax: 011-23280028
E-Mail: cyberpublicationsdelhi@yahoo.com
Website: www.cybertechpublications.com

ENVIRONMENTAL ETHICS AND PHILOSOPHY

N. Ghai, J.S. Negi

First Edition 2011

Published by :

G.S. Rawat for **Cyber Tech Publications**
4264/3, Ansari Road, Daryaganj, New Delhi-110002 (India)
Ph.: 011-23244078, 011-43559448 Fax: 011-23280028
E-Mail: cyberpublicationsdelhi@yahoo.com
Website: www.cybertechpublications.com

CONTENTS

Preface

1. Introduction 1
2. Environmental Information 26
3. Liability for Environmental Damage 67
4. International Trade and Competition 135
5. Financial Resources, Technology and Intellectual Property 217
6. Foreign Investment 254

Bibliography 270

Index 271

Preface

An environmental impact assessment describes a *process* which produces a written *statement* to be used to guide decision-making, with several related functions. First, it should provide decision-makers with information on the environmental consequences of proposed activities and, in some cases, programmes and policies, and their alternatives. Secondly, it requires decisions to be influenced by that information. And, thirdly, it provides a mechanism for ensuring the participation of potentially affected persons in the decision-making process.

Since environmental impact assessments were first established in the domestic law of the United States under the 1972 National Environmental Protection Act, they have been progressively adopted in a very large number of national legal systems. Internationally, environmental impact assessments are required under numerous international conventions and in EC law, in the requirements of various multilateral development banks, and in various non-binding instruments adopted at the regional and global level. Principle 17 of the Rio Declaration states that: environmental impact assessment, as a national instrument, shall be undertaken for proposed activities that are likely to have a significant adverse impact on the environment and are subject to a decision of a competent national authority.

The mandatory language of Principle 17 is consistent with the view that environmental impact assessments are now required by general international law, particularly in respect of environmentally harmful activities which may have transboundary consequences, and if only to meet a state's obligation to ensure that activities within its jurisdiction and control 'respect the environment of other States or of areas beyond national control' without first having assessed the transboundary environmental consequences of potentially harmful activi-ties. The language of Principle 17, however, is general, and does not provide the detail as to the minimum requirements which states need to satisfy.

Environmental impact assessments emerged internationally after the 1972 Stockholm Conference and are now an established international and domestic legal technique for integrating environmental considerations into socio-economic development and decision-making processes.

—Author

1

Introduction

Environmental impact assessments emerged internationally after the 1972 Stockholm Conference and are now an established international and domestic legal technique for integrating environmental considerations into socio-economic development and decision-making processes. An environmental impact assessment describes a *process* which produces a written *statement* to be used to guide decision-making, with several related functions. First, it should provide decision-makers with information on the environmental consequences of proposed activities and, in some cases, programmes and policies, and their alternatives. Secondly, it requires decisions to be influenced by that information. And, thirdly, it provides a mechanism for ensuring the participation of potentially affected persons in the decision-making process.

Since environmental impact assessments were first established in the domestic law of the United States under the 1972 National Environmental Protection Act, they have been progressively adopted in a very large number of national legal systems. Internationally, environmental impact assessments are required under numerous international conventions and in EC law, in the requirements of various multilateral development banks, and in various non-binding instruments adopted at the regional and global level. Principle 17 of the Rio Declaration states that: environmental impact assessment, as a national instrument, shall be undertaken for proposed activities that are likely to have a significant adverse impact on the environment and are subject to a decision of a competent national authority.

The mandatory language of Principle 17 is consistent with the view that environmental impact assessments are now required by general international law, particularly in respect of environmentally harmful activities which may have transboundary consequences, and if only to meet a state's obligation to ensure that activities within its jurisdiction and control 'respect the environment of other States or of areas beyond national control' without first having assessed the transboundary environmental consequences of potentially harmful activi-ties. The language of Principle 17, however, is general, and does not provide the detail as to the minimum requirements which states need to satisfy. To a certain extent the details relating to common approaches are reflected in the instruments described in this chapter and in the international cases which have arisen since Principle 17 was adopted: New Zealand's application to the ICJ concerning the resumption by France of underground nuclear testing (1995), the case concerning the Gabcikovo-Nagymaros project (1997), and the dispute between Ireland and the United Kingdom concerning the MOX plant (2001). These cases indicate an increasing recognition that international law requires the preparation of a prior environmental impact assessment before a state engages in, or permits, an activity which may have serious adverse impacts on the environment. Other developments, described below, reflect the growing role of strategic environmental assessment (of programmes and plans) and risk assessments associated, in particular, with foodstuffs.

NON-BINDING INSTRUMENTS

The Principles of the 1972 Stockholm Declaration do not expressly identify environmental impact assessment as an instrument of national or international policy. However, the rationale underlying environmental impact assessment can be identified in the principle that 'rational planning constitutes an essential tool' for reconciling development and environment needs, and that planning 'must be applied to human settlements and urbanisation with a view to avoiding adverse effects on the environment and obtaining maximum social, economic and environmental benefits for all'. An earlier draft of the Stockholm Declaration contained a draft Principle 20 which would have provided the elements of a clearer commitment to environmental impact assessment. The proposal set out in draft Principle 20 was not agreed at Stockholm following the objections of several developing countries, which maintained that the obligation to consult, dependent upon a prior determination that activities or developments could lead to significant adverse effects on the environment, might be abused by developed states to impede projects by developing countries. UN General Assembly Resolution 2995 (XXVII) (1972) partially revived draft Principle 20 by providing that technical information on proposed works should be supplied to other states where there is a risk of significant transboundary environmental harm, but that this information should be received in good faith and not used to delay or impede the development of natural resources.

Subsequent non-binding instruments developed the approach underlying draft Principle 20. Principle 5 of the 1978 UNEP draft Principles of Conduct proposed that: states should make an environmental impact assessment before engaging in any activity with respect to a shared natural resource which may create a risk of significantly affecting the environment of another state or states sharing that resource.

Whilst Principle 5 was innovative, it did not provide any detail on how the assessment should be carried out, who should participate in it, and to what purpose it should be put. This gap was partly remedied by the 1982 UNEP Conclusions of the Study on the Legal Aspects Concerning the Environment Related to Offshore Mining and Drilling within the Limits of National Jurisdiction, which provided more detailed guidance on the appropriate modalities for carrying out an environmental impact assessment. Support for environmental impact assessment is found in a range of other acts of international institutions adopted after the Stockholm Conference, including in relation to development assistance. The 1982 World Charter for Nature supports the 'exhaustive examination' and 'assessment' of activities likely to pose a significant risk to nature or which may disturbnature, and requires that activities should not proceed or should minimise potential adverse effects on the basis of the findings of the assessment or examination. By 1986, the Experts Group on Environmental Law of the World Commission on Environment and Development had identified environmental impact assessment as an 'emerging principle of international law', taking the view that states planning to carry out or permit activities which may significantly affect a natural resource or the environment should make or require an assessment of their effects before carrying out or permitting the planned activities. In 1987, UNEP prepared guidelines on the nature and extent of the obligation to carry out an assessment. The UNEP Goals and Principles include three related objectives in ensuring the 'environmentally sound and sustainable development' of planned activities: ensuring that environmental effects should be taken into account before decisions are taken to allow activities to be carried out; providing for the implementation of national environmental impact assessment procedures; and encouraging reciprocal procedures for notification, information, exchange and consultation on activities likely to have significant transboundary effects. The Principles, which propose bilateral, regional or multilateral arrangements, reflect a minimum set of standards which have been broadly endorsed and are reflected in state practice, at the national level and in binding international instruments.

UNCED and the ILC

References to environmental impact assessment abound in Agenda 21. It calls on all countries to 'assess the environmental suitability of infrastructure in human settlements', ensure that 'relevant decisions are preceded by environmental impact assessments and also take into account the costs of any ecological consequences', integrate environmental considerations in decision-making at all levels and in all ministries, and ensure the transparency of and accountability for the environmental implications of economic and other policies.Agenda 21 also endorses 'comprehensive analytical procedures for prior and simultaneous assessment of the impacts of decisions', including their environmental impacts and the assessment of 'costs, benefits and risks', and the systematic application of techniques and procedures for assessing environmental impacts.

Environmental impact assessment is also encouraged in specific Agenda 21 programmes, including deforestation, atmospheric protection and energy use, fragile mountain ecosystems, conservation of biological diversity, management of biotechnology, protection of oceans and seas, protection of freshwater resources, management of toxic chemicals, solid wastes and sewage, and radioactive wastes. Agenda 21 endorses the need for individuals, groups and organisations to participate in environmental impact assessment proce-dures. The WSSD broadly confirmed UNCED's requirements. Article 7 of the ILC's draft Articles on the Prevention of Transboundary Harm from Hazardous Activities draws upon the output of UNCED, and in particular Principle 17 of the Rio Declaration. Article 17 provides that:

Any decision in respect of the authorization of an activity within the scope of the present articles shall, in particular, be based on an assessment of the possible transboundary harm caused by that activity, including any environmental assessment.

The ILC's commentary to its draft Articles notes that the requirement of assessment of adverse effects of activities has been incorporatedin many international agreements, and that the practice of requiring an environmental impact assessment 'has become very prevalent' in order to assess whether a particular activity has the potential to cause significant transboundary harm.

TREATIES AND OTHER BINDING INSTRUMENTS

A number of treaties and other binding instruments include provisions requiring the performance of an environmental impact assessment in specified circumstances. The 1985 EC Directive on Environmental Impact Assessmentled the way in providing international guidance on the nature and extent of an environmental impact assessment and the use to which it should be put, an approach subsequently adopted and extended in the 1991 UNECE Convention on Environmental Impact Assessment in a Transboundary Context (1991 Espoo

Convention), and in the 1991 Protocol on Environmental Protection to the Antarctic Treaty. But these were by no means the first instruments supporting, in general terms, the use of environmental assessment. The 1974 Nordic Environmental Protection Convention required an assessment of the effects in the territory of one party of activities carried out in the territory of another party: the Convention allows authorities to require an applicant for a permit to carry out environmentally harmful activities to 'submit such additional particulars, drawings and technical specifications' as are deemed necessary for evaluating the effects in another state. The UNEP Regional Seas Conventions include general language on environmental impact assessment, as does the 1982 UNCLOS (see below).

Article 14(1) of the 1985 ASEAN Agreement similarly limits the extent of the obligation to carry out an environmental impact assessment, requiring that the contracting parties: undertake that proposals for any activity which may significantly affect the natural environment shall as far as possible be subjected to an assessment of their consequences before they are adopted, and they shall take into consideration the results of their assessment in their decision-making process.

Many other international agreements addressing specific environmental media or particular activities provide for express or implied general obligations on environmental impact assessment. Such agreements include those governing the Antarctic, atmospheric emissions of nitrogen oxide, occupational health, asbestos use, transboundary movements of waste, transboundary watercourses, industrial accidents, the energy sector, public participation, and mining on the seabed of the high seas. For some early conventions which did not include provisions on environmental impact assessment, such as the 1971 Ramsar Convention, the parties have subsequently adopted guidelines. The 1985 Vienna Convention and its 1987 Montreal Protocol do not expressly require that the development of replacement technologies for prohibited ozone-depleting substances be subject to an environmental impact assessment; this will limit the effectiveness of those treaties.

The convoluted language of the 1992 Climate Change Convention appears to require an impact assessment of the measures taken to mitigate or adapt to climate change on a range of factors including the environment, and requires all parties to: take climate change considerations into account, to the extent feasible, in their relevant social, economic and environmental policies and actions, and employ appropriate methods, for example impact assessments, formulated and determined nationally, with a view to minimizing adverse effects on the economy, on public health and on the quality of the environment, of projects or measures undertaken by them to mitigate or adapt to climate change.

1982 UNCLOS

The 1982 UNCLOS requires the prior assessment of the effects of activities on the marine environment. Under Article 206:

When states have reasonable grounds for believing that planned activities under their jurisdiction or control may cause substantial pollution of or significant and harmful changes to the marine environment, they shall, as far as practicable, assess the potential effects of such activities on the marine environment and shall communicate reports of the results of such assessments at appropriate intervals to the competent international organisations, which should make them available to all states.

The authoritative Virginia Commentary describes the obligation as being 'simi-larto therequirementsof some nationalenvironmental legislation,forexample, the United States National Environmental Policy Act (NEPA) of 1969, to prepare environmental impact statements in respect of actions likely to affect the quality of the environment in a significant way', its purpose being to ensure that such activities may be effectively controlled, and to keep other states informed of the potential risks and effects of such activities. The Virginia Commentary describes prior assessment as 'an essential part of a comprehensive environmental management system, and is a particular application of the obligation on States, enunciated in article 194, paragraph 2, to "take all necessary measures to ensure that activities under their jurisdiction or control are so conducted as not to cause damage by pollution to other States and their environment"'.

Article 206 has been the subject of an international dispute between Ireland and the United Kingdom. In October 2001, Ireland brought proceedings against the United Kingdom under UNCLOS concerning the authorisation by the United Kingdom of a new nuclear plant to manufacture mixed oxide (MOX) fuel. Ireland claimed, *inter alia,* that the United Kingdom had violated the obligation set forth in Article 206 of UNCLOS, in particular for authorising the plant on the basis of a 1993 Environment Impact Statement which failed to assess the potential effects of the operation of the MOX plant on the marine environment of the Irish Sea, including in relation to international movements of radioactive materials to be transported to and from the MOX plant, and which had not been updated to take into account the factual and legal developments which had occurred between 1993 and the plant's authorisation in 2001. In December 2001, ITLOS prescribed provisional measures but declined to suspend the operation of the plant, as Ireland had requested, pending the constitution of the arbitral tribunal which would address the merits. In this regard, Judge Mensah expressed the view that: none of the violations of the procedural rights arising from the duty to . . . undertake appropriate environmental assessments are 'irreversible' in the sense that they cannot effectively be enforced against the United Kingdom by decision of the Annex VII arbitral tribunal, if the arbitral tribunal were to conclude that any such violations have in fact occurred.

A different – but minority – view was expressed by ad hoc Judge Szekely, to the effect that the inadequacy of the 1993 Environmental Impact Statement justified more extensive provisional measures, 'since the environmental impact assessment is a central tool of the international law of prevention'. The merits phase is likely to address, among other issues, the extent of the obligations flowing from Article 206, including the relationship between that provision and other applicable environmental assessment obligations.

EC law

Council Directive 85/337/EEC on the environment was the first international instrument to provide details on the nature and scope of environmental assessment, its use, and participation rights in the process. Despite the limitations which have become apparent since it entered into force in July 1988, the Directive has served as a model for subsequent legal instruments, from which practical experience in implementation can be discerned. The Directive was adopted unanimously by the (then) ten EEC member states and requires them to take 'the measures necessary to comply with [the] Directive by 3 July 1988'.In 1997, the Directive was significantly amended by Council Directive 97/11/EC, which member states were required to bring into force by 14 March 1999. In 1999, the Commission published guidance on the assessment of indirect and cumulative impacts, and two years later on the screening and scoping of projects. Also, in 2001, the EU adopted Directive 2001/42/EC on the assessment of the effects of certain plans and programmes on the environment.

DIRECTIVE 85/337/EEC (AS AMENDED)

The 1985 Directive had a lengthy gestation period. Its origins lay in the EEC's 1973 First Environmental Action Programme, which identified the need to implement procedures to evaluate the environmental effects of certain activities at the earliest possible stage. The EC Commission's first proposal was in 1980, and it required a further five years, including lengthy deliberations at the European Parliament and the Economic and Social Committee, before the European Council adopted the proposal in 1985. Since the EEC Treaty had, at that time, no express provision for the adoption of environmental legislation, the Directive was based upon Articles 100 and 235, and for this reason its primary objective was stated to be economic rather than environmental: to approximate national laws on environmental assessment in order to remove disparities IMPLEMENTING INTERNATIONAL PRINCIPLES which could create unfavourable competitive conditions and affect the functioning of the common market. By contrast, the amending Directive 97/11/EC is firmly rooted in attaining environmental objectives, in a precautionary context.

Directive 85/337/EEC requires the environmental assessment 'of public and private projects which are likely to have significant effects on the environment', excluding projects serving national defence purposes or projects whose details are adopted by a specific act of national legislation, since these were expected to undergo an appropriate assessment during the legislative process. Article 2(1) of the Directive provides that: member states shall adopt all measures necessary to ensure that, before consent is given, projects likely to have significant effects on the environment by virtue, *inter alia,* of their nature, size or location are made sub ject to an assessment with regard to their effects.

'Significant effects on the environment' are not defined by the Directive. Member states may, in exceptional cases, exempt a specific project in whole or in part from the Directive, subject to compliance with the obligation to inform the public and the EC Commission of the reasons for the exemption. Article 4 divides projects subject to assessment into two classes: certain projects which are presumed to have 'significant effects on the environment' and for which assessments are mandatory (Annex I projects), and other projects for which assessment is not presumed to be necessary but will be required if they are likely to have 'significant effects on the environment' (Annex II projects). Annex I originally listed nine categories of projects which were subject to a mandatory assessment, including crude-oil refineries, thermal power stations of over 300 megawatts and nuclear power stations, radioactive waste disposal and storage installations, certain iron and steel works, integrated chemical installations, construction of motorways, express roads and long-distance railway lines, trading ports, and waste disposal installations. Directive 97/11/EC has extended the list to twenty-one categories of project, including certain projects previously listed in Annex II (for example, reprocessing of nuclear fuels and certain agricultural projects).

Annex II projects were originally subject to an assessment 'where member states consider that their characteristics so require'. Directive 97/11/EC has revised Article 4 of Directive 85/337/EEC so as to permit a member state to make that determination either by a 'case-by-case examination' or on the basis ofthresholdsor criteriasetby themember state, orby applying both procedures, and the member state must take into account the selection criteria set out in a new Annex III.

The list of illustrative projects in the original Annex II was lengthy, and is now even lengthier. It includes projects as diverse as car racing tracks, theme parks, the construction of ski-lifts, and the rubber industry.

The assessment process is defined in Articles 5 to 10 of Directive 85/337/EEC. The assessment is to include:

1. the supply by the developer of information set out in Annex IV (formerly Annex III), in an appropriate form;
2. consultation with authorities likely to be concerned by the project;
3. provision of information to, and consultation with, the public concerned;
4. provision of information to, and consultation with, other member states likely to be affected;IMPLEMENTING INTERNATIONAL PRINCIPLES
5. the obligation that information gathered must be taken into consideration in the development consent procedure; and
6. provision of information by the competent authority to the public when a decision has been taken.

By Article 10 full respect is to be given to the limitations regarding industrial and commercial secrecy and safeguarding of the public interest which are imposed by national regulations, administrative provisions and accepted legal practices. The Annex IV (formerly Annex III) information to be provided in accordance with Article 5 includes a description of the project (including physical characteristics of the whole project, land use requirements, production processes, residues and emissions resultingfrom the operation of the project), an outline of the main alternatives where appropriate, the aspects of the environment likely to be significantly affected, and measures to limit adverse environmental effects.

APPLICATION OF THE DIRECTIVE

Differences in the interpretation of the Directive by member states, the Commission and private persons have resulted in many disputes between individual citizens and their governments, and between the EC Commission and the member states. It has been said that the Directive attracts more complaints to the EC Commission than any other environmental Directive. The Commission has published two reports on the implementation of the Directive, in 1991 and 1997. These have addressed a broad range of concerns, relating to matters such as:

- the extent to which the Directive applies to projects which were initiated and for which planning permission was sought, or partially granted, before 3 July 1988 (the date of entry into force);
- the definition of Annex I projects;
- the extent to which EC member states have a discretion in determining whether to subject Annex II projects to an environmental assessment; and
- the adequacy of implementation by member states, including the failure to ensure that environmental assessments be recorded in writing.

The resolution of these interpretative issues has to a certain extent been assisted by a developing jurisprudence from the ECJ, although the number of cases is not large. Even before the amendments introduced by Directive 97/11/EC, the ECJ has sought to limit the extent of the discretion which may be exercised in relation to Annex II projects, requiring the discretion to be informed by the principles laid down in Article 2(1). The Court has also ruled that entire classes of projects may not be excluded and that in determining whether an assessment is required pursuant to Article 4(2) it is necessary to have regard to a project's location or nature and the cumulative effect of a series of projects, so that generally applicable *de minimis* thresholds are inadequate.The Court has confirmed that modifications to Annex II projects maybe subject to assessment where they may have significant effects on the environment.There has also been considerable national litigation over the Directive, before the courts of various member states, including early support for the view that the obligations set out in the Directive are sufficiently clear to be directly effective.

DIRECTIVE 2001/42/EC AND STRATEGIC ENVIRONMENTAL ASSESSMENT

In the 1990s it became apparent that the assessment of projects alone did not ensure that potential environmentally harmful activities would necessarily be prevented, and that underlying policies and plans which would give rise to individual projects were not being assessed adequately, if at all, for their environmental effects. EC Directive 2001/42/EC is the first international instrument to impose binding obligations, requiring member states to ensure that 'an environmental assessment is carried out of certain plans and programmes which are likely to have significant effects on the environment', and is to be domestically implemented by 21 July 2004. The Directive is likely to inspire changes elsewhere: a Protocol on strategic environmental assessment is being negotiated under the 1991 Espoo Convention (see below), and the World Bank and other multilateral development banks have been informally making use of, and considering the adoption of an instrument on, strategic environmental assessment.

Under the EC Directive, an assessment is to becarried out forall programmes prepared in specified areas or which require an assessment under Article 6 of the 1992 Habitats Directive, unless they use only small areas at local level and entail minor modifications, in which case an assessment is only required where the member state determines that it is likely to have a 'significant environmental effect'. Plans and programmes relating to national defence, or civil emergency or financial or budget matters are not subject to the Directive. The assessment is to be carried out during the preparation of a plan or programme and its adoption or submission to a legislative procedure. It requires the preparation of a report which identifies, describes and evaluates the likely significant effects, and must include the information referred to in Annex I, including reasonable alternatives. The Directive provides for consultations involving relevant authorities and the public which may be affected or which have an interest in the plan or programme, as well as transboundary consultations with potentially affected member states and their public. By Article 8, the environmental report and opinions resultingfrom the various consultations are to be taken into account during the preparation of the plan and programme and before its adoption. The Directive also requires that certain specified information be made available to consultees and, innovatively, that the member state monitors the significant environmental effects of the implementation of the plan or programme 'to identify at an early stage unforeseen adverse effects, and to be able to undertake appropriate remedial action'.

1986 Noumea Convention

Article 16 of the 1986 Noumea Convention requires each party to assess, within its capabilities, 'the potential effects of [major projects which might affect the marine environment] so that appropriate measures can be taken to prevent any substantial pollution of, or significant harm within, the Convention Area'.On 21 June 1995, New Zealand filed proceedings at the ICJ challenging France's resumption of underground nuclear tests, on the ground, among others, that the tests violated France's obligation to carry out a prior assessment of their impacts on the environment, in accordance with Article 16. New Zealand also asserted that customary international law required an environmental impact assessment to be carried out 'in relation to any activity which is likely to cause significant damage to the environment, particularly where such effects are likely to be transboundary in nature'. The approach was endorsed by four South Pacific states and Australia, which had sought to intervene in the ICJ proceedings.In response, France did not deny the existence of obligations under the 1986 Noumea Convention or customary law, but rather stated that too much should not be read into the 1986 Convention or customary law, and that environmental assessment requirements permitted a considerable 'margin of appreciation' to states as to the manner in which they sought to avoid causing damage. As the Court found that it did not have jurisdiction to entertain the application, the arguments were not addressed by the majority. Two dissenting opinions, however, reflected an emerging recognition of the potential place of environmental assessment in customary law. Of particular note is Judge Weeramantry's opinion that the requirement to carry out an environmental impact assessment was 'gathering strength and international acceptance, and has reached the level of general recognition at which [the ICJ] should take notice of it'. As described below, that opinion appears to have informed the Court's decision two years later in the case concerning the Gabcikovo-Nagymaros project.

1991 Espoo Convention

The 1991 Espoo Convention was adopted under the auspices of the UNECE, and in several aspects it imposes more onerous requirements than the 1985 EC Directive on which it is based. It came into force on 10 September 1997, and commits parties to take all appropriate and effective measures to prevent, reduce and control significant adverse transboundary environmental impacts from proposed activities. The Convention requires that parties of origin must notify affected parties of certain proposed activities which are likely to cause a significant adverse transboundary impact, and requires discussions between concerned parties. The Convention defines 'impact' broadly to include: any effect caused by a proposed activity on the environment including human health and safety, flora, fauna, soil, air, water, climate, landscape and historical monuments or other physical structures or the interaction among these factors; it also includes effects on cultural heritage or socio-economic conditions resulting from alterations to those factors.

A 'transboundary impact' is defined as: any impact, not exclusively of a global nature, within an area under the jurisdiction of a party caused by a proposed activity the physical origin of which is situated wholly or in part within the area under the jurisdiction of another party.

The party of origin is required to ensure that, in accordance with the provisions of the Convention, an environmental impact assessment is undertaken 'prior to a decision to authorise or undertake a proposed activity listed in Appendix I that is likely to cause a significant adverse transboundary impact'. Appendix III provides guidance for determining the environmental significance of activities not listed. The assessment procedure must allow public participation in the preparation of the documentation, ensure an opportunity to the public living in areas likely to be affected to participate in procedures, and ensure that the opportunity provided to the public in the affected country is equivalent to that provided to the public of the party of origin.

The Convention requires transboundary co-operation. Under Article 3, the party of origin must notify any of the seventeen proposed activities listed in Appendix I which is likely to cause a significant adverse transboundary impact, as early as possible, to 'any partywhich it considers may be anaffected party' and no later than when informing its own public. The notification must include information on the proposed activity, its possible transboundary impact, and the nature of the possible decision, and should allow a reasonable time for a response as to whether the affected party will participate in the procedure. Where the affected party decides not to participate, the operational provisions of the Convention will not apply, and the party of origin can decide on the basis of its national law and practice whether to carry out an assessment.

Once the affected party decides to participate in the procedure, and after it has received information relevant to the proposed activity and its possible significant transboundary impact, it must promptly provide the party of origin, at its request, with reasonably obtainable information relating to the potentially affected environment under its jurisdiction, where such information is necessary for the preparation of the environmental impact assessment. Where a party considers that it is likely to be affected by a significant adverse trans-boundary impact of a proposed activity listed in Appendix I, and it has not been notified in accordance with Article 3(1), an exchange of 'sufficient information' must take place at the request of the affected party 'for the purposes of holding IMPLEMENTING INTERNATIONAL PRINCIPLES discussions on whether there is likely to be a significant adverse transboundary impact'. If the parties agree that such an impact is likely, the provisions of the Convention are to apply. If there is no such agreement, any such party may submit the question to an inquiry commission established under Appendix IV unless another method of settling the question is agreed. Concerned parties must ensure that the affected party's public is informed about the proposed activity and is provided with an opportunity to make comments or objections to the competent authority of the party of origin.

The documentation to be submitted to the competent authority of the party of origin must contain the information required in Appendix II, which is more comprehensive than that required by the original Annex III to the 1985 Directive. This includes, but is not limited to, descriptions of: the proposed activity and its purpose; reasonable alternatives and the 'no-action alternative'; the environment likely to be significantly affected and its alternatives; the potential environmental impact, its alternatives and an estimation of its significance; and mitigation measures. Indications should also be given of predictive methods, underlying assumptions and relevant environmental data used, gaps in knowledge and uncertainties, an outline for monitoring and management and any plans for post-project analysis, and a non-technical summary with appropriate visual presentations. The documentation must be provided to the affected party and distributed to its authorities and public in areas likely to be affected, and the comments of those authorities and that public are to be submitted to the competent authority of the party of origin 'within a reasonable time before the final decision is taken on the proposed activity'.

Under Article 5, consultations must take place between the party of origin and the affected parties concerning the potential transboundary impact and measures to reduce or eliminate the impact. These may relate to alternatives to the proposed activity (including the 'no-action alternative' and mitigating measures), otherforms of mutualassistance, and anyother appropriatematters. In taking the final decision on the proposed activity, the parties must take due account of the outcome of the environmental impact assessment, including the documentation, as well as the comments received under Articles 3(8) and 4(2) and consultations under Article 5. The party of origin must inform the affected party of the final decision and the reasons and considerations on which it was based. If new information which could have materially affected the decision becomes available to a concerned party after-the decision was made, that party shall inform other concerned parties and, as requested, hold consultations on revision of the decision.

A further innovation of the Convention is the provision of requirements on post-project analysis and follow-up. Concerned parties must decide, at the request of any one of them, whether and to what extent a post-project analysis is to be carried out, including surveillance of the activity and a determination of any adverse transboundary impact. The objectives of a post-project analysis are set out in Appendix V; they include monitoring compliance with authorisation conditions and the effectiveness of mitigation measures; a management review; and verification of past predictions. Where the post-project analysis establishes reasonable grounds for concluding that there is a significant adverse transboundary impact or factors which may result in such an impact, the concerned parties must consult on 'necessary measures' to reduce or eliminate the impact.

The Convention also provides for bilateral and multilateral co-operation to implement its provisions in accordance with the elements set out in Appendix VI, and on the development of research programmes. Institutional arrangements include an annual meeting of the parties, which is charged with keeping the implementation of the Convention under review, with the assistance of the secretariat. In 2001, an Implementation Committee was established, and on 21 May 2003 a Protocol on strategic environmental assessment was adopted in Kiev.

A number of more general provisions of the Convention are also relevant to the further development of international law in relation to environmental assessment, information and co-operation. Concerned parties must enter into discussions, at the request of any such party, on whether a proposed activity not listedinAppendixI is likely to cause a significant adversetrans boundary impact, and therefore should be treated as if so listed. Appendix III provides general guidance to assist in the determination of the environmental significance of activities not listed in Appendix I, by virtue of one or more criteria, including its size, location and effects. The Convention does not affect parties' rights under national laws, provisions or practices to protect information the supply of which would be prejudicial to industrial and commercial secrecy or national security, and does not affect the right of a party to implement more stringent measures. Moreover, the Convention does not prejudice 'any obligations of the parties under international law with regard to activities having or likely to have a transboundary impact'.

1991 Antarctic Environment Protocol

Article 8 of the 1991 Antarctic Environment Protocol (which supersedes the environmental assessment provisions under the 1988 CRAMRA) requires prior assessment of the impacts of activities on the Antarctic environment or on dependent or associated ecosystems. The detailed obligations take a different approach from the 1985 EC Directive and the 1991 Espoo Convention. They establish a range of procedures, the use of which will be dependent on whether the activity is expected to have (a) less than a minor or transitory impact; or (b) a minor or transitory impact; or (c) more than a minor or transitory impact.This approach is similar to that recommended in paragraph 11 of the 1982 World Charter for Nature. The assessment must be:

applied in the planning processes leading to decisions about any activities undertaken in the Antarctic Treaty area pursuant to scientific research programmes, tourism and all other governmental and non-governmental activities in the Antarctic Treaty area for which advance notice is required under Article VII(5) of the Antarctic Treaty, including associated logistic support activities.

Assessments are also required for any change in activity, including an increase or decrease of intensity, the decommissioning of a facility, or otherwise.

Annex I to the Protocol sets out a five-stage procedure for carrying out the assessment.

1. In the preliminary stage, the proposed activity is considered in accordance with national procedures, and, if the activity is determined to have less than a minor or transitory impact, the activity may proceed.
2. If the activity will have a minor or transitory impact or more, an Initial Environmental Evaluation will be prepared, which should contain sufficient information to assess whether the activity will have more than a minor or transitory impact. The information should include a description of the proposed activity, including its purpose, location, duration and intensity, and a consideration of any alternatives and impacts, including cumulative impacts. If this evaluation indicates that a proposed activity is likely to have no more than a minor or transitory impact,

the activity may proceed subject to compliance with appropriate procedures, including monitoring of impacts.

3. If this evaluation indicates a likelihood of more than a minor or transitory impact, a Comprehensive Environmental Evaluation must be prepared, and must include descriptions of the proposed activity, the initial and predicted future environment reference state, and methods and data used to forecast impacts. The Comprehensive Evaluation will also include an estimation of likely and direct impacts; indirect or second order and cumulative impacts; mitigation measures; unavoidable impacts; effects on the conduct of scientific research; gaps in knowledge and uncertainties; a non-technical summary; and a contact person or organisation.
4. The draft Evaluation is to be made publicly available, circulated to all parties and forwarded to the Protocol's Committee on Environmental Protection, with a ninety-day comment period and at least 120 days before the next Antarctic Treaty Consultative Meeting. The proposed activity may not proceed until the draft Evaluation has been considered by the Antarctic Treaty Consultative Meeting on the advice of the Committee, within a maximum period of fifteen months from the date of the draft's circulation.
5. A final Evaluation must address comments received and be circulated to all parties and made publicly available at least sixty days before the commencement of the proposed activity. The decision on whether to proceed with a proposed activity must be based on the Comprehensive Evaluation and other relevant considerations. Procedures will be put in place to assess and verify the impact of activities following the Comprehensive Evaluation, including the monitoring of key environmental indicators.

Biodiversity and risk assessment

The 1992 Biodiversity Convention requires parties to identify 'processes and categories of activities which have or are likely to have significant adverse impacts on the conservation and sustainable use of biological diversity, and monitor their effects through sampling and other techniques' and to require environmental impact assessment of proposed projects that are likely to have 'significant adverse effects on biological diversity'. Article 14 also requires parties to promote notification, exchange of information and consultation on activities under their jurisdiction or control which are likely to significantly and adversely affect the biological diversity of other states or areas beyond the limits of national jurisdiction, and to provide for immediate notification in any case of imminent or grave danger or damage.

The sixth conference of the parties endorsed draft guidelines for incorporating biodiversity-related issues into environmental impact assessment legislation and processes and in strategic environmental assessment, and urged parties and other governments and organisations to apply the guidelines in the context of their implementation of Article 14(1) of the Convention.

The Guidelines provide considerable detail as to the context of an environmental impact assessment (following the approach set forth in other international instruments), and the conditions under which assessments must and should be carried out.

The 2000 Biosafety Protocol to the Convention requires 'risk assessments' to be carried out in respect of import decisions relating to living modified organisms, in order to identify and evaluate the possible adverse effects of living modified organisms on the conservation and sustainable use of biological diversity, taking also into account risks to human health.

The risk assessments are to be carried out in a 'scientifically sound manner, in accordance with Annex III and taking into account recognized risk assessment techniques', and may be carried out by the exporter. Annex III identifies the methodology to be applied in carrying out a risk assessment, including:

(a) An identification of any novel genotypic and phenotypic characteristics associated with the living modified organism that may have adverse effects on biological diversity in the likely potential receiving environment, taking also into account risks to human health;

(b) Anevaluation of the likelihood of these adverse effects be ingrealized...;

(c) An evaluation of the consequences should these adverse effects be realized;

(d) An estimation of the overall risk posed by the living modified organism based on the evaluation of the likelihood and consequences of the identified adverse effects being realized;

(e) A recommendation as to whether or not the risks are acceptable or manageable . . . ; and EIAs); and Decision VI/7 (endorsing guidelines for incorporating biodiversity-related issues into environmental impact assessment legislation and processes and in strategic

(f) Where there is uncertainty regarding the level of risk, it may be addressed by requesting further information on the specific issues of concern or by implementing appropriate risk management strategies and/or monitoring the living modified organism in the receiving envi-ronment.

World Bank and other multilateral lending institutions

Many international organisations, including multilateral development banks, have developed their own environmental impact assessment procedures, of which the most widely studied is that adopted by the World Bank in 1989.World Bank Operational Directive 4.01 was adopted in 1989, its objective being to ensure that the development options adopted were sound and enduring from an environmental perspective and that environmental consequences were recognised at an early stage in the project cycle and included in the project scheme. The Operational Directive was the subject of significant criticism, including the failure to provide for a 'no-action alternative' whereby the project may be stopped because the environmental risks are too great to allow the project to proceed at all, and its silence as to mandatory requirements concerning the provision of information to local populations and their right to participate in the environmental impact assessment process. In 1999, the policy was converted into a new format, now reflected in Operation Policy (OP) 4.01 and Bank Procedures (BP) 4.01, which have sought to address these and other issues.

By OP 4.01, the World Bank requires environmental assessment (EA) of projects proposed for Bank financing to help ensure that they are environmentally sound and sustainable, thereby improving decision-making. EA is described as a process, which: evaluates a project's potential environmental risks and impacts in its area of influence; examines project alternatives; identifies ways of improving project selection, siting, planning, design and implementation; and includes the process of mitigating and managing adverse environmental impacts throughout the implementation of the project.

It is premised on the Bank's preference for 'preventive measures over mitigatory or compensatory measures, whenever feasible'. The borrower is responsible for carrying out the EA, which may comprise one or more of an environmental impact assessment (EIA), a regional or sectoral EA, an environmental audit, a hazard or risk assessment, and an environmental management plan (EMP).The Bank is responsible for environmental screening of each proposed project to determine the appropriate extent and type of EA, and classifies the proposed project into one of four categories.

A proposed project is classified as Category A if it is 'likely to have significant adverse environmental impacts that are sensitive, diverse, or unprecedented', and will normally require an EIA (or a comprehensive regional or sectoral EA). A proposed project is classified as Category B if its potential adverse environmental impacts are site-specific, if few of the impacts are irreversible, and if mitigatory measures can be designed more readily than for Category A projects.

The scope of EA for a Category B project will be narrower than for a Category A project. A proposed project is classified as Category C if it is likely to have minimal or no adverse environmental impacts. A proposed project is classified as Category FI if it involves investment of Bank funds through a financial intermediary, in subprojects that may result in adverse environmental impacts. Environmental assessments are also required for special project types. Category A and B projects must be subject to public consultation.

The adequacy of the application of OP 4.01 is reflected in the fact that thirteen of the twenty-three requests filed at the World Bank Inspection Panel by July 2001 alleged inadequate environmental assessments. In some cases, the Panel found no violations, but in others the Panel found violations which led or contributed to a decision to withdraw financing, or other proposed remedial actions.

Gabcikovo-Nagymaros Case

The developments described in this chapter, which largely took place in the late 1980s and early 1990s, provided the background to one aspect of the dispute between Hungary andSlovakiaconcerningtheconstruction oftwo barrages onthe River Danube. A central part of Hungary's case was that the two parties to the 1977 Treaty had failed, by 1989, to adequately assess the project's impact on the environment, in particular the impacts on freshwaters and biodiversity.The ICJ considered that Hungary was not entitled (in 1989) to suspend construction on its part of the project, or (in 1992) to terminate the 1977 Treaty, and that the 1977 Treaty therefore remained in force between the parties. However, the Court recognised that the project's impact upon, and its implications for, the environment were a key issue, and that the impact and implications were considerable, and ruled that Articles 15 and 19 of the 1977 Treaty prescribed 'a continuing – and thus necessarily evolving – obligation on the parties to maintain the quality of the water of the Danube and to protect nature'. Noting that 'vigilance and prevention are required on account of the often irreversible character of damage to the environment and of the limitations inherent in the very mechanism of reparation of this type of damage', the Court ruled that: the Parties together should look afresh at the effects on the environment of the operation of the Gabcikovo power plant. In particular they must find a satisfactory solution for the volume of water to be released into the old bed of the Danube and into the side-arms on both sides of the river.

The Court has, in effect, read into the two provisions of the 1977 Treaty a requirement that the parties carry out a continuing environmental assessment of the project's impacts on the environment. The rationale behind the Court's approach is reflected in the Separate Opinion of Judge Weeramantry, who was in the majority and a member of the Court's drafting Committee. Developing his Opinion in the 1995 New Zealand nuclear tests case, Judge Weeramantry states:

> In the present case, the incorporation of environmental considerations into the Treaty by Articles 15 and 19 meant that the principle of EIA was also built into the Treaty. These provisions were clearly not restricted to EIA before the project commenced,

but also included the concept of monitoring during the continuance of the project . . . Environmental law in its current state of development would read into treaties which may reasonably be considered to have a significant impact upon the environment, a duty of environmental impact assessment and this means also, whether the treaty expressly so provides or not, a duty of monitoring the environmental impacts of any substantial project during the operation of the scheme.

Moreover, according to Judge Weeramantry, the 'principle of contemporaneity' in the application of environmental norms supplemented his observations regarding continuing assessment and provided the standard by which the continuing assessment is to be made:

It matters little that an undertaking has been commenced under a treaty of 1950, if in fact that undertaking continues in operation in the year 2000. The relevant environmental standards that will be applicable will be those of the year 2000.

CONCLUSIONS

The judgment in the *Case Concerning the Gabcikovo-Nagymaros Project* indicates the extent to which the concept of environmental assessment has developed and become established since the first edition of this book. A b road range of international instruments now establishes general obligations requiring prior environmental assessment of projects which may cause environmental harm; a smaller number set forth more detailed criteria for the conduct of such assessments, whether in particular geographic areas, to protect particular resources, or in respect of particular categories of activities. The EC's experience under the 1985 Directive identifies some of the difficulties associated with environmental impact assessments, and as other regions and organisations formalise similar arrangements they could usefully draw upon the lessons learned in the EC. As noted in the introduction to this chapter, there is considerable support for the view that environmental impact assessments are required as a matter of customary law, particularly in respect of activities which may cause transboundary effects. Most multilateral development banks now require some form of environmental impact assessment, and they are now required by international law also to assess the environmental consequences of potentially damaging projects into which they consider putting financial resources.

In the past decade, the limitations of the first generation of project-related environmental impact assessments has become apparent, and this has translated into a second generation of instruments revising earlier approaches and establishing strategic environmental assessments of programmes and plans. In respect of projects, the critical issues remain: the scope of the impacts to be assessed; the type of projects to be covered; the availability of information to the public and their participation in the process; and the requirement that the statement be taken into account *before* authorisation is granted. The unwillingness of states to subject themselves to what they consider to be unnecessary

and intrusive environmental assessments remains a problem, as illustrated by the differences between the United Kingdom and Ireland over the need to carry out an assessment on a nuclear reprocessing plant which led to the adoption of a Recommendation on the matter by PARCOM in June 1993, and a similar dispute in 2001 concerning the quality of the assessment of the MOX plant. The decision of the UNEP Legal Experts Group, in 1993, to add to the Montevideo Programme a new programme area to promote the widespread use of environmental impact assessment procedures by governments and international organisations reflected the need to elaborate international criteria establishing generally agreed minimum standards.

2

Environmental Information

INTRODUCTION

Improving the availability of information on the state of the environment and on activities which have adverse or damaging effects are well-established objectives of international environmental law. Information is widely recognised as a prerequisite to effective national and international environmental management, protection and co-operation. The availability of, and access to, information allows preventative and mitigation measures to be taken, ensures the participation of citizens in national decision-making processes, and can influence individual, consumer and corporate behaviour. Information also allows the international community to determine whether states are complying with their legal obligations.

Environmental impact assessment, addressed in chapter 16, is one important technique for acquiring environmental information. International agreements and practice have developed other techniques for ensuring that states and other members of the international community are provided with information on the environmental consequences of certain activities. Legal obligations developed with early treaty obligations requiring parties to provide information to the depository, or to other parties, on measures to implement commitments. Since then, environmental information has gradually emerged as a central issue of international environmental law. Principle 2 of the 1972 Stockholm Declaration called for the 'free flow of up-to-date scientific information and transfer of experience'. The 1982 World Charter for Nature broadened the scope and extent of obligations relating to information, calling for the dissemination of knowledge of research, the monitoring of natural processes and ecosystems, and the participation of all persons in the formulation of decisions of direct concern to the environment.

By the mid-1980s, numerous treaties addressed public education, information exchange and consultation. The Seveso accident in 1982 and the Chernobyl accident in 1986 focused attention on the need to improve the provision of information in emergency situations and, towards the end of the 1980s, eco-labelling and corporate environmental auditing and accounting had become issues addressed by law at the international level. By the time of UNCED in 1992, numerous treaties and other international instruments included substantive obligations relating to information: particularly noteworthy are the 1986 IAEA Notification Convention, the 1989 Basel Convention, the 1991 EC Directive on Environmental Information and the 1992 Industrial Accidents Convention. Notably, no fewer than four of the Rio Declaration's twenty-seven Principles are concerned with improving the provision of, and access to, environmental information. The Rio Declaration calls for: exchanges of knowledge (information); individual access to environmental information; public awareness; notification of emergencies; and prior and timely notification of certain potentially hazardous activities. Chapter 40 of Agenda 21, entitled 'Information for Decision-Making', recognises that the need for information arises at all levels, from senior decision-makers at international levels to the grass roots and individual level, and to that end calls for the development of two programme areas: to bridge the 'data gap' and to improve information availability. The UNEP Legal Experts Group has also agreed a new programme area to promote public awareness, education, information and public participation, including the development of national rules, laws and standards.

The period since the first edition of this book has seen numerous significant developments which consolidate and, in some respects, develop existing techniques. The 1998 Aarhus Convention establishes a Europe-wide regime, clarifying and, in certain respects, developing the EC rules. The 1998 Chemicals Convention is largely concerned with issues related to the access to, and exchange of, information; and other agreements, such as the 1997 Kyoto Protocol, the 2000 Biosafety Protocol and the 2001

POPs Convention, include prominent commitments to ensuring appropriate flows of information. The commitment to ensuring the adequacy of information is affirmed by the WSSD Plan of Implementation, and were reflected also in a trend to allow arbitration proceedings concerning international environmental matters to be open to the public.

A detailed consideration of relevant international instruments identifies at least nine separate but related techniques concerning the provision and dissemination of information. These provide for or require:

1. information exchange;
2. reporting and the provision of information;
3. consultation;
4. monitoring and surveillance;
5. notification of emergency situations;
6. public right of access to environmental information;
7. public education and awareness;
8. eco-labelling; and
9. co-auditing and accounting.

The examples cited in the following sections are intended to be illustrative rather than exhaustive, given the large number of instruments and examples of state practice relating to informational matters. The overlap between the obligations relating to information exchange, consultation, reporting and notification is often evident, and it is important to bear in mind that these different areas are interrelated, as reflected in many recent international environmental agreements. In addition to the multilateral instruments which are cited, there are many others which are not mentioned as well as literally hundreds, if not thousands, of bilateral instruments which also contribute significantly to the law in this area.

In this regard, the recently adopted ILC draft Articles on the Prevention of Transboundary Harm adopt, as a central element, requirements relating to information, and may be seen as 'codifying' general practice, in particular as reflected in treaty requirements. They provide that, where an assessment of risk has taken place and indicates a risk of causing significant transboundary harm, the state of origin shall provide the state likely to be affected with timely notification of the risk and the assessment and shall transmit to it the available technical and all other relevant information on which the assessment is based.

The draft Articles then propose that the states concerned shall enter into consultations, at the request of any of them, with a view to achieving acceptable solutions regarding measures to be adopted in order to prevent significant transboundary harm or at any event to minimize the risk thereof.

The states concerned are to seek solutions based on an equitable balance of interests, in the light of the factors set out in draft Article 10. The state of origin should not take any decision on authorisation pending the receipt, within six months, of the response of the state likely to be affected, and if the consultations fail to produce an agreed solution the state of origin must take into account the interests of the state likely to be affected. The draft Articles also provide for procedures in the event that there is no notification, require the exchange of timely information while the activity is being carried out, and call for information to be provided to the public likely to be affected by that activity, and to ascertain their views.

INFORMATION EXCHANGE

The general obligation to exchange information is found, in one form or another, in virtually every international environmental agreement. 'Information exchange' can be characterised as a general obligation of one state to provide general information on one or more matters on an *ad hoc* basis to another state, especially in relation to scientific and technical information. 'Information exchange' may be distinguished from specific obligations to provide regular or periodic information on specified matters to a specified body (reporting) or to provide detailed information on the occurrence of a particular event or set of events, such as an accident or emergency or proposed activity (notification). 'Information exchange' of a general nature is endorsed by Principle 20 of the Stockholm Declaration and by Principle 9 of the Rio Declaration, which supports exchanges of scientific and technical knowledge as a means of strengthening 'endogenous capacity-building for sustainable development by improving scientific understanding'. Other relevant texts include: Principle 7 of the 1978 UNEP draft Principles of Conduct, which calls for the exchange of information based upon the principle of co-operation and the spirit of good-neighbourli-ness; Article 5 of the 1986 Legal Principles of the WCED Legal Experts Group, which supports the exchange of information between states upon request, and in a timely manner, concerning transboundary natural resources; Article 12 of the ILC's draft Articles on Prevention of Transboundary Harm; and the WSSD Plan of Implementation.

Under environmental treaties, the obligation to exchange information can be a requirement between states, between states and international organisations, and between international organisations and non-state actors. By way of an early example, the 1949 Inter-American Tropical Tuna Commission was granted the power to request information from 'official agencies of the contracting parties, and any international, public, or private institution or organisation, or any private individual'.

Many other international organisations are required to facilitate and encourage the exchange of information, which dates back to some of the earliest international environmental agreements. The 1933 London Convention requires information exchange on the adoption of certain implementation measures, including import and export. The 1940 Western Hemisphere Convention requires parties to 'make available to all the American Republics equally through publication or otherwise the scientific knowledge resulting from . . . co-operative effort'.

Information exchange can be required in respect of general and undefined matters or in relation to specific matters. Examples of the former include the obligation to exchange information on: general scientific, research and technical matters; helping 'align or co-ordinate' national policies; research results and plans for science programmes; appropriate technologies; relevant national records; national legislation; implementation; relevant national authorities and bodies; and even the availability of professors and teachers.Examples of more specific requirements include information exchange on: aspects of pest and plant diseases; catches and migratory movements of fish; tuna fisheries; pollution from land-based sources; the conservation of species of wild flora and fauna; archaeological excavations and discoveries;environmental modification techniques for peaceful purposes; the protection of nuclear material; certain environmentally harmful activities; forest management, research and development; and the conservation and sustainable use of biological diversity.

Several later conventions established more detailed rules on the type of information to be exchanged. The 1982 UNCLOS requires the exchange of scientific information and other data relevant to the conservation of fish stocks, on marine scientific research, and on marine pollution. Article 8 of the 1979 LRTAP Convention requires the exchange of 'available information', through an executive body and bilaterally on emissions data at periods of time to be agreed upon of: certain air pollutants; major changes in national policies and general industrial development; control technologies for reducing air pollution; the projected cost of the emissions control; meteorological, and physico-chemical data relating to processes and effects; and national, sub-regional and regional policies. Article 4 of the 1985 Vienna Convention requires the exchange of 'scientific, technical, socio-economic, commercial and legal information', as further elaborated in Annex II to that Convention, as well as information on alternative technologies. The 1987 Montreal Protocol calls for information exchange on best technologies, possible alternatives to controlled substances and products, and costs and benefits of relevant control strategies.

A widespread concern about the limited effectiveness of the traditional language on information exchange has resulted in the adoption, in some conventions of more focused language. The 1992 Climate Change Convention, for example, calls on parties to promote and co-operate in 'the full, open and prompt exchange of relevant scientific, technological, technical, socio-economic and legal information related to the climate system and climate change, and to the economic and social consequences of various response strategies'. A number of conventions have established more formal institutional arrangements and procedures for information exchange. Examples include the establishment of a documentation service, an information service,and even a permanent committee of information. International organisations may also play a role in ensuring information exchange. They may be required to prepare an annual report, or to keep parties 'abreast of . . . theoretical and practical work', or to convene international information exchange confer-ences. Notwithstanding a greater willingness of states and the private sector to seek to improve flows of information, it is unclear how effective these general obligations to exchange information have been.

The apparently limited effectiveness of many of these earlier obligations was often due to the reluctance of states to share information which might have commercial value, and the obligation, usually raised by developed countries, to ensure respect for intellectual property rights. Under the Biodiversity Convention, this issue was addressed explicitly for the first time, although the language finally agreed may have raised more questions and uncertainties than it re-solved. Increasingly, agreements have therefore included express provisions on confidential information. The 2000 Biosafety Protocol, for example, requires information to be submitted to the clearing-house mechanism established under the Convention '[w]ithout prejudice to the protection of confidential in-formation'. Similarly, under the 1998 Chemicals Convention, the exchange of information is on condition that parties 'shall protect any confidential information as mutually agreed'.

REPORTING AND PROVISION OF INFORMATION

The obligation to report or to notify certain information on a regular or periodic basis, outside the context of an emergency situation or the occurrence of a particular event or activity, is a regular feature of international environmental agreements. At least four types of reporting or information provision requirements are used in international environmental agreements. First, the provision of a periodic report provided by an international organisation to the parties to a treaty; secondly, a requirement that parties provide a periodic report to the institutional organs or to other parties to that treaty; thirdly, a party (or state) may be required to provide information to another party (or state) on the occurrence of a certain event or activity; and, fourthly, a treaty may allow for a report to be presented by a non-governmental actor to a party to a treaty, which may be subject to onward transmission by the latter.

Reports by organisations

Some environmental treaties require one or more of the institutional organs to provide regular reports to its parties. This technique is used to inform all the parties of relevant measures being taken under the Convention, or to provide information on the activities of the organisation itself to ensure accountability. An early example is the 1949 Inter-American Tropical Tuna Convention, which requires the Inter-American Tropical Tuna Commission to 'submit annually to the government of each high contracting party a report on its investigations and findings, with appropriate recommendations'. Other conventions provide that reports should be submitted every two years, or for the transmission of 'periodic reports' or publications, or at such time as the institutional organ 'may consider necessary'. The 1990 Articles of Agreement establishing the European Bank for Reconstruction and Development requires the Bank to provide an annual report on the environmental import of its activities. Occasionally, the institutional organ might be required to report to another international organisation; this approach is reflected in the work of the UN Commission on Sustainable Development, which receives reports from relevant organs, organisations, programmes and institutions of the UN system dealing with various issues of environment and development to enable it to monitor the progress of the implementation of Agenda 21 by analysing and evaluating reports submitted by other international organisations.

Reports under treaties or other agreements

The second type of reporting obligation arises where a party to a treaty is required to provide a periodic report to the institutions established under the treaty or to other parties to that agreement. These reporting requirements, which increasingly require detailed and regular information, are used to provide information on the implementation of treaty commitments. The 1933 London Convention was among the first, requiring parties to 'notify the Government of the United Kingdom . . . of the establishment of any national parks or strict natural reserves, . . . and of the legislation, including the methods of administration and control, adopted in connexion therewith', as well as measures adopted in regard to the grant of certain licences. Similar reporting requirements exist for authorisations of licences for the killing and taking of living resources; on the construction of certain installations or projects and worksor proposed expeditions; statistical information concerning catches; or the establishment of quotas.

Often, parties must provide progress reports on implementation measures and their effectiveness, and other relevant national legislation, including the adoption of import restrictions. Parties may also be required to report infrac-tionsof conventions bypersons withintheirjurisdiction andthe penaltiesthey impose, as well as information on persons liable to contribute to a pollution fund established in accordance with the terms of a convention. Increasingly, parties are being called upon to provide inventories or statistics of their natural and cultural resources or of the production of certain chemicals or prod-ucts, and to report on their emissions and discharges and the consequences thereof.

In fulfilment of the functions of the UN Commission on Sustainable Development, governments are required to provide information on activities they undertake to implement Agenda 21, the problems they face, and other environment and development issues they find relevant. Parties to a treaty can also be required to report on particular situations or events, including the existence of certain hazardous facilities; the transit of hazardous substances;the actions they take in relation to certain pollution incidents; substances dumped into the marine environment; the existence of evidence suggesting that unlawful dumping may be taking place; incidents or accidents involving oil or other harmful substances; the discharge of land-based pollutants;and accidents involving hazardous waste. Other examples of specific reporting requirements arise upon the occurrence, outbreak and spread of pests and diseases, on inadequate oil disposal facilities at ports, and on conservation measures concerning fish stocks.

The 1992 Climate Change Convention and its 1997 Kyoto Protocol illustrate the extent to which reporting requirements have become increasingly detailed and onerous. Reporting, which is described as 'the communication of information related to implementation', is a central technique for ensuring implementation of the 1992 Climate Change Convention. All parties must publish and make available to the conference of the parties 'national inventories of anthropogenic emissions by sources and removals by sinks of all greenhouse gases not controlled by the Montreal Protocol', and communicate to the conference of the parties 'information related to implementation'. These reports must include a general description of steps taken or envisaged to implement the Convention and 'any other information the party considers relevant to the achievement of the objective of the

Convention and suitable for inclusion in its communication including, if feasible, material relevant for calculations of global emission trends'. The EC and parties which are members of the OECD are additionally required to include in their communications a detailed description of the policies and measures that they have adopted to implement their specific commitments under the Convention and a specific estimate of the effects that the policies and measures they have taken will have on anthropogenic emissions by its sources and removals by its sinks of greenhouses gases. All developed country parties must provide information on the provision by them of 'new and additional financial resources', other assistance, and the transfer of and access to environmentally sound technologies and know-how. The

Kyoto Protocol adds the additional burden on Annex I countries of reporting the progress made towards reaching greenhouse gas reduction commitments.Differentiated timeframes are adopted for providing the communication. Developed country parties were required to provide their initial communication within six months of the Convention's entry into force; all other parties were required to provide their initial communication within three years of entry into force, except for least-developed countries which may make their initial communication available at their discretion. Developed country parties are currently in the process of submitting their third communications. Other innovations of the 1992 Climate Change Convention include the possibility for two or more parties to make a 'joint communication' provided that such a communication includes information on: each individual party's fulfilment of its obligations; rules on confidentiality; the provision to developing countries of financial resources 'to meet the agreed full costs incurred . . . in complying with' their reporting requirements; and the establishment of a subsidiary body for implementation to consider information provided by parties in accordance with Article 12. The Convention and its Protocol thus reflect a more comprehensive effort to address reporting.

Reports of events other than emergencies

The third situation requiring the provision of information or a report (closely connected to the obligation to consult) arises on the occurrence of an event other than an emergency situation.

Examples include the construction of an installation or advance notice of activities which may entail significant environmental risk. In such circumstances, the state in which the activity is taking place may be required to provide information either directly to states which may be affected or to an appropriate intergovernmental organisation. The need for the provision of such information has been widely recognised by the international community since the mid-1970s. In 1972, UN General Assembly Resolution 2995 recognised that co-operation towards implementation of the 1972 Stockholm Declaration will be effectively achieved if official and public knowledge is provided of the technical data relating to the work to be carried out by states within their national jurisdiction, with a view to avoiding significant harm that may occur in the environment of the adjacent area.

The 1974 OECD Recommendation on Principles Concerning Transfrontier Pollution similarly provides that: [p]rior to the initiation in a country of works or undertakings which might create a significant risk of pollution, this country should provide early information to other countries which are or may be affected.

Similar provisions exist in the 1978 UNEP draft Principles of Conduct,the 1986 WCED Legal Experts Group Report, and Principle 19 of the Rio Declaration. Several treaties require the provision of information on the construction of certain installations, including the siting of hazardous installations or the conduct of hazardous activities near border areas. The 1980 Agreement Between Spain and Portugal on Co-operation in Matters Affecting the Safety of Nuclear Installations in the Vicinity of the Frontier provides in Article 2 that: [t]he competent authorities of the constructor country shall notify the neighbouring country of applications for licences for the siting, construction or operation of nuclear installations in the vicinity of the frontier which are sub mitted to them . . .

Article 3 requires comments by the neighbouring country to be taken into account before the licence is issued.

Is the provision of prior information regarding certain hazardous activities now required by customary international law? The 1982 ILA Montreal Rulesand the 1987 IDI Resolution on Transboundary Air Pollution suggest that customary law does and should require states planning activities which might entail a significant risk of transfrontier pollution to give early notice to a state likely to be affected and to enter into good faith consultations at the request of such a state. Principle 19 of the Rio Declaration appears to restate that obligation in unequivocal terms, and this is also now confirmed by the 2001 ILC draft Articles on Prevention of Transboundary Harm.

Information to and from non-state organisations

A fourth type of reporting requirement, which may be considered to be in an emerging stage of development, relates to obligations allowing, or requiring, non-governmental actors to report certain information to states, possibly for onward transmission to other parties or to the agreement's institutional organ, or to provide informational reports to organisations. The UN Commission on Sustainable Development is mandated to 'receive and analyse relevant input from competent non-governmental organisations, including the scientific and private sector, in the context of the overall implementation of Agenda 21'. Although this falls short of actually entitling non-governmental actors to provide reports, it clearly envisages a role for them in providing inputs which will, in all likelihood, resemble reports.

CONSULTATION

The international community has recognised the importance of information on activities and other circumstances which could affect the interests of states in relation to shared natural resources. Typically, this is provided for in international agreements by two related commitments: a requirement to provide information to potentially affected states on particular activities, and a requirement to engage in consultation. The latter presupposes the provision of certain information. The obligation of states to consult with each other in the context of the conduct of certain activities has been recognised by international courts and tribunals, and is reflected in many international environmental instruments, as well as in Article 9 of the ILC's draft Articles on Prevention of Transboundary Harm. In 2001, the ITLOS prescribed provisional measures ordering Ireland and the United Kingdom to co-operate and, for that purpose, to 'enter into consultations forthwith' to exchange further information on the possible consequences for the Irish Sea arising out of the commissioning of the MOX plant, to monitor the risks or the effects of the operation of the MOX plant for the Irish Sea, and to devise measures to prevent pollution of the marine environment which might result from the operation of the MOX plant. The order was premised on 'prudence and caution' and the duty to co-operate under Part XII of UNCLOS.

Principle 19 of the Rio Declaration reflects what many states have recognised as required practice in terms which reflect an obligation of customary international law: states shall provide prior and timely notification and relevant information to potentially affected states on activities that may have a significant adverse transboundary environmental effect and shall consult with those states at an early stage and in good faith.

Environmental treatieshaverequired consultation to take place between anum-ber of different actors, including between two or more states; between a state and an international organisation; between a state and a non-governmental actor; between two or more international organisations, and between an international organisation and a non-governmental actor. Many institutional arrangements established by environmental treaties, such as conferences or meetings of parties, serve as fora for consultations between parties. Specialised institutional arrangements for environmental treaties have included a special Consultative Committee and a ConsultativeCommitteeofExperts.

The obligation to consult arises in many circumstances. As a general matter, consultation has been required on the implementation of an agreement, or on 'all problems of common interest' raised by the application of a particular convention. Consultation can also be required as part of the process for the peaceful settlement of disputes, including by removing doubts concerning the fulfilment by a party of its treaty obligations.

A second type of situation calling for consultation arises when the activities of one state are likely to affect the environment or the rights and interests of another state. Thus, a state may be obliged to enter into consultations when, for example, pollution caused by the activities of one party to an agreement is likely to affect adversely the interests of another party to that agreement; or when there is a question of the 'permissibility of environmentally harmful activities which entail or may entail considerable nuisance' in another party; or where a party is 'actually affected by or exposed to' a significant risk of pollution.

A third category of situations requiring consultation arises over the use of sharednatural resources.Thus, consultation canberequiredgenerallyinrespect of shared resource issues, as well as in the following specific situations: to avoid infringement of the rights and interests of states where natural resource deposits (such as wetlands) lie across two or more jurisdictions; where there are plans 'to initiate, or make a change in, activities which can reasonably be expected to have significant effects beyond the limits of national jurisdiction';where a party 'intends to establish a protected area contiguous to the frontier or to the limits of the zone of national jurisdiction of another party'; where certain commercial activities may harm wildlife; and for the dissemination of information on environmental impact assessments.

A fourth category of situations requiring consultation arises in times of emergency. Consultations may be required: to ensure that appropriate action is taken in emergency situations; prior to the issue of a special permit to permit the marine dumping of hazardous wastes and other matters in emergen-cies; and to minimise the radiological consequences of a nuclear accident.Consultations are also required between a party and the most representative organisations of employers and workers to implement national policies on protection of the working environment and in applying the provisions of relevant conventions.

The obligation to consult in such situations is now widely recognised by customary international law, and the failure to engage in consultation may violate the principles of good faith and international co-operation under international law. This view is supported by the *Lac Lanoux Arbitration*, was further elaborated upon by the ICJ in the *Fisheries Jurisdiction* cases, and was reflected in the order of ITLOS in the *MOX* case.

Prior informed consent

The obligation to consult is closely linked to the principle of 'prior informed consent' (PIC). This principle has achieved widespread support in relation to transboundary movements of hazardous wastes and, more recently, hazardous substances, and has been adopted in a range of instruments, including, *inter alia*, the 1985 FAO Pesticides Guidelines, the 1989 UNEP London Guidelines, the 1989 Basel Convention, the 1989 Lome´ Convention, the 1991 Bamako Convention and the 1996 Mediterranean Hazardous Wastes Protocol. It is also to be found in the EC Regulation on the Transfrontier Movement of Hazardous Substances and non-binding instruments adopted by the OECD and the IAEA, as well as in Agenda 21.

A second-generation formulation of the PIC procedures, developing the voluntary schemes of the FAO Pesticides Guidelines and the UNEP London Guidelines, is reflected in the 1998 Chemicals Convention. The 1998 Convention establishes a bifurcated PIC procedure. For chemicals listed under Annex III to the Convention, import countries must submit their approval, approval subject to limitations, or rejection of future imports to the Secretariat. For banned or severely restricted chemicals not listed under the Convention, export countries are required to ensure that proper notification is given to the import country before export of the chemicals. The 2000 Biosafety Protocol does not refer to a PIC procedure, as such, but rather an advance informed agreement (AIA) procedure prior to the 'first intentional transboundary movement of living modified organisms for intentional introduction into the environment of the Party of import'. The party of export is required to notify or ensure notification of an intent to export certain living modified organisms, which the party of import must acknowledge. The import may only proceed if the party of import has given written consent or, after not less than ninety days, where no such written consent is given. The Protocol also provides for a 'simplified procedure' specifying in advance cases in which intentional movements may take place simultaneously with notification and imports which are to be exempted from the advance informed agreement procedure.

NOTIFICATION OF EMERGENCY SITUATIONS

The early availability of information on the escape of hazardous substances following an accident or event likely to have a significant effect on the environment of another state or in areas beyond national jurisdiction is necessary to allow other states and members of the international community to take the necessary actions to minimise damage. Principle 18 of the Rio Declaration recognised this need, and declared that: states shall immediately notify other states of any natural disasters or other emergencies that are likely to produce sudden harmful effects on the environment of those states. Every effort shall be made by the international community to help states so afflicted.

As a result of developments following the Chernobyl accident (see below) and other emergency incidents, Principle 18 reflects broadly held views and crystallises developments in treaties, non-binding instruments and the practice of states. The 1982 Montreal ILA Rules and the 1987 Institut de Droit International Resolution refer to the existence of such a rule although evidence of state practice is hardly overwhelming; in the *Nicaragua* case, the ICJ affirmed that a substantive legal rule can be derived from principles of humanitarian law:

Although the facts leading up to this *dictum* differ from those relating to industrial or other accidents affecting the environment, particularly on the question of the intent of the acting state, underlying considerations of humanity could apply also to the danger to the security of citizens in foreign countries arising from a transboundary release of hazardous substances.

Numerous early treaties have required the provision of information, following the outbreak of 'especially dangerous' pests and diseases, or where there is 'evidence of serious danger to the environment and particularly to the water table', or in respect of oil pollution emergencies. More general requirements are set out in the 1982 UNCLOS, which requires a state to immediately notify other states it deems likely to be affected, and the competent international organisations, where the 'marine environment is in imminent danger of being damaged or has been damaged by pollution'. Specific obligations have been adopted for accidents occurring during the transboundary movement of hazardous or other wastes; under the 1992 Industrial Accidents Convention on transboundary accidents; and in treaties governing general environmental matters.

The 1992 Biodiversity Convention provides that each party shall, as far as possible and as appropriate, in the case of imminent or grave danger or damage, originating under its jurisdiction or control, to biological diversity within the area under jurisdiction of other states or areas beyond the limits of national jurisdiction, notify immediately the potentially affected states of such danger or damage, as well as initiate action to prevent or minimise such danger or damage;

Similarly, the 2000 Biosafety Protocol requires that parties shall take appropriate measures to notify affected or potentially affected States, the Biosafety Clearing-House and, where appropriate, relevant international organizations, when it knows of an occurrence under its jurisdiction resulting in a release that leads, or may lead, to an unintentional trans-boundary movement of a living modified organism that is likely to have significant adverse effects on the conservation and sustainable use of biological diversity, taking also into account risks to human health in such States.

Non-binding guidelines and recommendations also require the provision of such information. In 1974, the OECD recommended that '[c]ountries should promptly warn other potentially affected countries of any situation which may cause any sudden increase in the level of pollution in areas outside the country of origin of pollution'. In 1988, the OECD Council adopted a Decision on the exchange ofinformationin relationto accidents capable ofcausingtransfrontier damage. Principle 9 of the 1978 UNEP draft Principles of Conduct makes similar provision.

Nuclear accidents

Other treaties establish the duty to warn potentially affected states in case of nuclear and other emergencies, and several states have bilateral agreements requiring emergency information to be provided in the event of a nuclear accident. Thus, the 1983 Exchange of Notes Between the United Kingdom and France Concerning Exchanges of Information in the Event of Emergencies Occurring in One of the Two States Which Could Have Radiological Consequences for the Other State provides that 'Each state-party shall inform the other without delay of any emergency which occurs in its state as a result of civil activities which may have radiological consequences liable to affect the other state.The information is to be communicated through reciprocal warning centres capable of receiving and transmitting information twenty-four hours a day.

The question of whether a state must warn all other states which are or might be affected by a nuclear accident causing transboundary radioactive harm has been described as 'the main legal issue involved in the Chernobyl nuclear disaster'. In 1985, the IAEA drew up Guidelines on Reportable Events, Integrated Planning and Information Exchange in a Transboundary Release of Radioactive Materials (IAEA Information Guidelines). These recommend that in the event of a potential or actual release of radioactive material, which might cross or has crossed an international boundary and which could be of radiological safety significance, there should be a timely exchange of adequate information between the competent national authorities of the state in which the plant is situated and the authorities in neighbouring states. The information should relate to the site, the facility, the emergency response plan, and in the event of an off-site emergency should include the nature and time of the accident, the characteristics of the release and meteorological and hydrological conditions.

Following the Chernobyl accident, many states maintained that the obligation to provide emergency information was a rule of international law. Much of the criticism of the USSR's failure to provide information immediately after the accident was couched in legal terms. The IAEA Director General noted the failure of the Soviet system to inform its own citizens and neighbouring countries of a release which would affect them, the late implementation of the emergency measures and the apparent failure to warn immediately. During the negotiation of the 1986 Notification Convention, support for the view that there was a legal obligation to provide information under customary law was expressed on several occasions, and many writers have reached the same conclusion. Humanitarian principles also justify the provision of information to people who might be affected by a nuclear or other accident.

1986 Notification Convention

The failure of the USSR to provide immediate information led to the 1986 Notification Convention, which was opened for signature within six months of the Chernobyl accident. It incorporates many of the recommendations set out in the IAEA Information Guidelines, and applies in the event of any 'accident involving facilities or activities of a state party or of persons or legal entities under its jurisdiction or control'. In the event of such an accident, state parties must notify, directly or through the IAEA, those states which are or may be physically affected with details of the accident, its nature, the time of its occurrence and its exact location. They must also promptly provide the states and the IAEA with relevant available information so as to minimise the radiological of the Group of Seven: 'Each country . . . is responsib le for prompt provision of detailed and complete information on nuclear emergencies and accidents, in particular those with potential transboundary consequences. Each of our countries accepts that responsibility.' Group of Seven, Statement on the Implications of the Chernobyl Nuclear Accident, 5 May 1986, 25 ILM 1005 (1986).

The Convention is not, however, exhaustive or immune from criticism. First, theConventiondoesnotappearto applytoaccidentscausedbynuclearweapons and their testing. Secondly, certain of the recommendations contained in the IAEA Information Guidelines were not included. In particular, the recommendation in Chapter III that 'intervention levels for the introduction of protective measures such as sheltering and evacuation be set in advance by competent national authorities' was notincluded inthe Convention. Inaddition,the whole of Chapter V, on 'Integrated Planning', was excluded. Thirdly, the reference in Article 1(1) to an accident that 'could be of radiological safety significance for another state' leaves it to the discretion of the state in whose territory or under whose jurisdiction or control the accident has occurred to determine what is or is not of radiological safety significance and what are the chances that another state will be affected. Given the dangers of radioactivity, it would have been preferable that all radioactive releases be notified to the IAEA. Failing that, there should be an agreed level which would trigger the obligation to provide information. Fourthly, several states entered reservations restricting the application of the Convention. Most relate to the non-applicability of the dispute settlement provision, but some relate to the substantive provisions: the Government of the People's Republic of China stated that the Convention did not apply to cases caused by 'gross negligence'. Finally, the Convention does not require states giving or receiving information to make it available to members of the public. The IAEA Information Guidelines noted that:

Dissemination of information to the public is an important responsibility of the appropriate authorities in each state. Particular arrangements ensuring the necessary co-ordination across international borders should be established.

The importance of public access to information is recognised in other treaties, including at least one adopted prior to the 1986 Notification Convention, namely, the 1974 Nordic Convention. A final point concerning the provision of information in emergency situations relates to the responsibility of the mass media in the reporting of matters such as the Chernobyl accident. The reporting in the Western press was criticised by the USSR as being untruthful and creating mistrust, and the USSR subsequently proposed that the spreading of untrue information could entail liability for states. The IAEA Secretariat has noted the possibility of including in a new instrument 'an obligation to refrain from actions which might exacerbate the consequences of a nuclear accident'.

MONITORING AND OTHER INFORMATION GATHERING

Recent international environmental agreements have often required information relevant to specific or general environmental obligations to be collected. The term most frequently used to describe that requirement is 'monitoring', although other terms which have been used include 'systematic observation', 'surveillance', 'inspection', and 'verification', depending upon the precise activity which is envisaged. Monitoring can be carried out for a variety of purposes, of which the most usual include conducting research or identifying patterns and trends which reflect the state of the environment. Monitoring to ensure compliance with the objectives of an international treaty remains somewhat controversial because of the suggestion that a third party may become involved in the compliance process, and it is principally for that reason that, with only limited exceptions, inspection or verification by foreign states or international organisations remains relatively undeveloped in international environmental agreements. Monitoring has been defined as the 'repeated measurement' of three separate, but related, factors:

(a) the quality of the . . . environment and each of its compartments . . . ;

(b) activities or natural and anthropogenic inputs which may affect the quality of the . . . environment; [and]

(c) the effects of such activities.

Under international arrangements, monitoring and other forms of information gathering are carried out by states individually or jointly or by international organisations. Monitoring by international organisations for the purposes of research and the identification of trends and patterns is now a reasonably well-developed practice, with several international arrangements currently in operation. UNEP runs Earthwatch, a programme developed by the Stockholm Conference to provide a continuous assessment of the global environment. It comprises four parts: (1) review and evaluation of environmental conditions to identify gaps in knowledge and the need for action; (2) research on environmental problems; (3) monitoring of certain environmental variables; and (4) exchange of information among scientists and governments. The principal component of Earthwatch is the Global Environmental Monitoring System (GEMS), which is responsible for monitoring. UNEP also runs the International Environmental Information System (INFOTERRA), a global network of national information centres for the exchange of environmental information. The World Weather Watch system of the WMO, which compiles global data on basic meteorological parameters related to weather, has three main components: the Global Observing System; the Global Telecommunications System; and the Global Data Processing System. For the EU, the European Environment Agency is charged with monitoring the overall state of the environment and gathering information.

Treaty arrangements

Treaty arrangements require parties to carry out a range of monitoring and related activities. Treaty obligations are particularly developed for the Antarctic region, the marine environment, and freshwater resources. The 1959 Antarctic Treaty allows inspections by consultative parties of all areas of Antarctica, and rights of aerial observation. The 1972 London Convention requires each party to designate an appropriate authority to monitor the condition of the seas for the purposes of the Convention. Other treaties require the monitoring of concentrations of controlled substances and levels of marine pollution,and similar provision exists under UNEP Regional Seas Conventions. Under the 1982 UNCLOS, states should 'observe, measure, evaluate and analyse' the risks or effects of pollution of the marine environment, and 'keep under surveillance the effects of any activities which they permit or in which they engage in order to determine whether these activities are likely to pollute the marine en-vironment'. The 1992 OSPAR Convention requires the parties to undertake and publish joint assessments of the quality status of the marine environment, including an evaluation of the effectiveness of the measures taken and planned and an identification of priorities for action. Under the 1992 Watercourses Convention, riparian parties must implement joint programmes for monitoring the conditions of transboundary waters, as well as the assessment of the conditions and the effectiveness of implementing measures.

In relation to air quality, the 1979 LRTAP Convention established a 'cooperative programme for the monitoring and evaluation of the long-range transmission of air pollutants in Europe' (known as EMEP); the 1985 Vienna Convention requires partiesto undertake 'systematic observation' of the state of the ozone layer and other relevant parameters; and the 1992 Climate Change Convention commits all parties to develop and periodically update national inventories of anthropogenic emissions by sources and removals by sinks of all greenhouse gases not controlled by the Montreal Protocol and promote and cooperate in systematic observation. Participants in the 1997 Kyoto Protocol's Clean Development Mechanism are required to monitor levels of greenhouse gas emissions related to clean development projects in order to calculate the proper emissions reductions credits to be issued to the party.

Monitoring or its equivalent is also required for biological diversity. Examples include the 1946 International Whaling Convention, which provides for inspection of whaling ships and the measuring of whales, and the 1992 Biodiversity Convention, which requires all parties to identify and monitor the components of biological diversity and the processes and categories of activities which are likely to have significant adverse impacts on the conservation and sustainable use of biodiversity. Other environmental treaties provide for monitoring or inspection of record books in relation to the carriage of oil;certificationfor the carriage bysea of hazardous substances, importedspecies and goods; the health of workers; the air quality of the working environ-ment; the composition of waste to be dumped; the possible discharge by a ship of any harmful substances; and fisheries conservation levels. In certain circumstances, UNCLOS allows the physical inspection of foreign ves-sels, and the 1974 Nordic Environment Convention is probably unique in allowing for the supervisory authorities of one state to carry out on-site inspections to determine damage caused by their environmentally harmful activities in another state. Under the 1995 Straddling Stocks Agreement, states must ensure that fishing vessels flying their flag provide the information necessary to fulfil their obligations under the Agreement, and shall 'collect and exchange scientific, technical and statistical data with respect to fisheries for straddling fish stocks and highly migratory fish stocks', as well as ensuring that data are collected in sufficient detail to facilitate effective stock assessment and are provided in a timely manner to fulfil the requirements of subregional or regional fisheries management organisations or arrangements.

Few international organisations are granted independent monitoring or other information gathering powers by treaty. The European Environment Agency provides the EC and the member states with 'objective, reliable and comparable information at European level enabling them to take the requisite measures to protect the environment, to assess the results of such measures and to ensure that the public is properly informed about the state of the environ-ment'. To that end, it is required to 'record, collate and assess data on the state of the environment', although it has no powers of on-site inspection of industrial sites or facilities.

The Marrakech Accords to the 1997 Kyoto Protocol establish two separate independent monitoring bodies each with powers of oversight of the parties to the Protocol. The first body is an expert review team which will conduct reviews of each party's calculations of its assigned amount of greenhouse gas emissions and the party's various emissions credits, and also conduct in-country reviews and desk reviews of each party's national registry. The second body, the Enforcement Branch of the Compliance Committee, is responsible for determining whether each Annex I country is in compliance with its quantified emissions limitation or reduction commitment, as well as with certain methodological and eligibility requirements set up under the Protocol.

Some organisations may conduct factual investigations, while other treaties merely permit the relevant international organisation to be entrusted with surveillance functions or to prepare a document summarising the result of national monitoring efforts. Regulatory Committees established under the 1988 CRAMRA would be required to monitor the compliance of operators with Management Schemes.

UNCED

Despite the development and operation of these and other international arrangements, there is a widespread consensus on the need to improve data collection and use. Chapter 40 of Agenda 21, entitled 'Information for Decision-Making', establishes two programme areas. The first, called 'Bridging the Data Gap', aims: to promote more cost-effective and relevant data collection and assessment; to strengthen national and international capacity to use and collect data in decision-making; to ensure that planning for sustainable development is based on timely, reliable and usable information; and to make information accessible in form and time. The statistical office of the UN Secretariat and other UN organs and organisations are called upon to develop and use indicators of sustainable development and indicators related to areas outside of national jurisdiction, such as the high seas, the upper atmosphere and outer space, and to recommend the harmonised development of indicators at the national, regional and global levels for use at the international level 'subject to national sovereignty considerations'. Agenda 21 calls in particular for the development of inventories of environmental, resource and development data for the management of sustainable development and the strengthening of data collection activities, including Earthwatch and World Weather Watch, particularly for urban air, freshwater, land resources (including forests and rangelands), desertification, other habitats, soil degradation, biodiversity, the high seas and the upper atmosphere.

The second programme area ('Improving Availability of Information') calls for the strengthening of existing national and international mechanisms of information processing and exchange to ensure 'effective and equitable availability of information . . . subject to national sovereignty and relevant intellectual property rights'. It also supports the strengthening of electronic networking capabilities to facilitate implementation of Agenda 21 and intergovernmental negotiations, to monitor conventions, and to transmit environmental alerts. In 2002, the WSSD reaffirmed the commitments of Agenda 21, but set up no new substantial commitments or programmes. Instead, the WSSD Plan of Implementation calls for increased access to information or the gathering and dissemination of information on a wide variety of subject areas.

ACCESS TO ENVIRONMENTAL INFORMATION

D. Partan, 'The "Duty to Inform" in International Environmental Law', 6 *Boston University International Law Journal* 43 (1988); M. Pallemaerts (ed.), *The Right to Environmental Information* (1991); H. Smets, 'The Right of Information on the Risks Created by Hazardous Installations at the National and International Levels', in F. Francioni and T. Scovazzi (eds.), *International Responsibility for Environmental Harm* (1991); W. Birtles, 'Environmental Issues: The Right to Know', 137 *Solicitors Journal* 408 (1993); R. Hallo, *Access to Environmental Information in Europe, The Implementation and Implications of Directive 90/313/EEC* (1996).

The duty to provide – and the right to obtain – access to information on the environment, whether to the public at large or to specific categories of persons (such as workers), is a recent but now firmly entrenched development in international law. The right is closely connected to participation rights in environmental impact assessment procedures, and goes further than obligations to ensure public awareness, education or publicity (discussed in the following section). The 1990 EC Directive on Access to Environmental Information, the 1992 OSPAR Convention, and the Council of Europe's 1993 Civil Liability Convention were the first group of instruments to elaborate in detail the modalities for giving effect to the right of persons to access to information on the environment. More recently, the right has been extended – geographically and substantively – by the 1998 Aarhus Convention, which is also leading to revision of the EC Directive. It has also been recognised, in relation to activities which may affect the public, in Article 12 of the ILC's draft Articles on Prevention of Transboundary Harm.

In each instrument, the existence and exercise of such a right is subject to certain limitations, reflecting a reluctance on the part of states to allow an unlimited right of access to information, as previously illustrated by the two treaties adopted shortly after the

Chernobyl accident: the 1986 IAEA Notification Convention, which failed to provide citizens with any right of access to environmental information, and the 1986 IAEA Assistance Convention, which provided that an assisting party must make every effort to co-ordinate with the requesting state before releasing information to the public on the assistance provided in connection with a nuclear accident. Other treaties, such as the 1992 Industrial Accidents Convention, create a positive obligation on parties to provide information to the public rather than creating a citizen's right of access to information. The 1992 Climate Change Convention does not create a public right of access to information, although it requires information communicated by the parties to be made 'publicly available' at the time it is submitted to the conference of the parties once it has been made available to bodies involved in communication and review of information. The dissemination of this information will be subject to limitations on grounds of confidentiality in accordance with criteria to be established by the conference of the parties.

The Rio Declaration recognises the important role of public participation in environmental decision-making and provides in Principle 10 that:

Environmental issues are best handled with the participation of all concerned citizens, at the relevant level. At the national level, each individual shall have appropriate access to information concerning the environment that is held by public authorities, including information on hazardous materials and activities in their communities, and the opportunity to participate in decision-making processes.

The Rio Declaration is silent as to what information will be considered 'appropriate', although some guidance may be found in Agenda 21, which provides that 'individuals, groups and organisations should have access to information relevant to environment and development held by national authorities, including information on products and activities that have or are likely to have a significant impact on the environment, and information on environmental protection measures.

Some early treaties sought to ensure that information on hazardous substances was made available to workers. The 1985 Occupational Health Services Convention does not create a right of access in so many words, but does provide that 'all workers shall be informed of health hazards involved in their work'.The 1986 Asbestos Convention goes further by providing, without apparent qualification, that workers, their representatives and inspection services 'shall have access' to records of the monitoring of the working environment and of the exposure of workers to asbestos.

EC Directive on Access to Environmental Information

The EC Directive on Access to Environmental Information as the first international instrument to create a right of access to environmental information.It is intended to ensure free access to, and dissemination of, environmental information held by public authorities throughout the EC by setting out basic terms and conditions on which the information should be made available.The Directive is also intended to ensure greater environmental protection and remove disparities in member states' laws which create unequal conditions of competition. In 2000, the EC Commission proposed amendments to the 1990 Directive, to give effect to therequirements which wouldarise from Community ratification of the 1998 Aarhus Convention.

Under the 1990 Directive, any natural or legal person, anywhere in the EC, is entitled to access to information relating to the environment without having to show an interest, at a charge not exceeding a reasonable cost, upon re-quest. Under the Directive, a public authority must 'respond' to a request within two months. The right of access to environmental information is subject to certain limitations, including where a request affects: the confidentiality of proceedings of public authorities, international relations and national defence; public security; matters which are or have been *sub judice* or under enquiry or are the subject of preliminary investigation; commercial and industrial confidentiality, including intellectual property; confidentiality of personal files and data; material supplied by a third party without that party being under a legal obligation to do so; and requests which are 'manifestly unreasonable' or 'formulated in too general a manner'. Moreover, requests for information may be refused where they would involve the supply of 'unfinished documents or internal communications'. The Directive provides that a person who considers that his request has been unreasonably refused or ignored or inadequately answered may 'seek a judicial or administrative review of the decision in accordance with the relevant national legal system'. Member states were required to implement the Directive by 31 December 1992, and it has given rise to a discrete but significant case law in member states and in the ECJ. The leading ECJ case is *Wilhelm Mecklenburg* v. *Kreis Pinneberg*, which raised the question of whether a statement of views given to a countryside protection authority participating in development consent proceedings was environmental information within the meaning of Article 2(a) of the Directive. In answering that question in the affirmative, the ECJ ruled that the Community legislature intended the concept to be a broad one, embracing information and activities relating to the state of those aspects, and including all forms of administrative activity. The Court ruled:

In order to constitute information relating to the environment for the purposes of the directive, it is sufficient for the statement of views put forward by an authority, such as the statement concerned in the main proceedings, to be an act capable of adversely affecting or protecting the state of one of the sectors of the environment covered by the directive. That is the case, as the referring court mentioned, where the statement of views is capable of influencingthe outcome of thedevelopment consent proceedings as regards interests pertaining to the protection of the environment.

The ECJ also ruled that the exceptions set forth in Article 3 of the Directive should be interpreted restrictively, and should not be interpreted in such a way as to extend their effects 'beyond what is necessary to safeguard the interests which it seeks to secure', having regard to the aims pursued by the Directive.

1992 OSPAR Convention

The 1992 OSPAR Convention, which was the first international treaty to provide specific rules on the right of access to environmental information, draws significantly from the provisions of the 1990 EC Directive. Article 9 of the 1992 Convention requires the competent authorities of the parties to make available to any legal or natural person any available information in written, visual, aural or data-base form on the state of the maritime area, on activities or measures adversely affecting or likely to affect it and on activities or measures introduced in accordance with the Convention.

The information must be provided in response to any reasonable request, without the person seeking the information having to prove an interest, without unreasonable charges, and as soon as possible and at the latest within two months. As with the 1990 EC Directive, certain limitations apply: requests for information may be refused 'in accordance with their national legal systems and applicable international regulations' where the information affects, *inter alia*, the confidentiality of proceedings of public authorities, international relations and national defence, public security, matters which are *sub judice* or under enquiry, commercial and industrial confidentiality (including intellectual property), and the confidentiality of personal data or files.

In June 2001, Ireland instituted arbitration proceedings (under Article 32 of the OSPAR Convention) against the United Kingdom seeking access to information which had been redacted from two independent reports related to the authorisation of the MOX nuclear plant at Sellafield. The two reports had been commissioned by the UK Government to assess the 'economic justification' of the plant, as required by EURATOM law, but the government only put into the public domain versions which omitted large amounts of information relating to the operation and costs of the plant. Ireland requested access to the information under Article 9 of the OSPAR Convention. The United Kingdom refused to provide the information, on the grounds that it did not constitute information within the meaning of Article 9(1), or, alternatively, that if it was such information the United Kingdom was entitled to rely on the 'commercial confidentiality' exception to refuse disclosure. Further, in the course of its pleadings, the United Kingdom argued that Ireland was not entitled to rely on Article9ofthe Convention, which only required parties to put in place domestic arrangements to ensure access to information but did not entitle another party to bring an international claim premised on a right of access to information.

The arbitral tribunal gave its award in July 2002. The tribunal unanimously rejected the UK's arguments that the tribunal lacked jurisdiction and that Ireland's claims were inadmissible, and by a 2-1 majority (Mustill and Griffiths) rejected the UK's submission that the implementation of Article 9(1) was assigned exclusively to the competent authorities in the UK and not to a tribunal established under UNCLOS. But by a 2-1 majority (Reisman and

Mustill) the tribunal found that Ireland's claim did not fall within Article 9(2), on the ground that Ireland had not demonstrated that the categories of redacted information 'insofar as they may be taken to be activities or measures with respect to the commissioning and operation of a MOX Plant at Sellafield, are "information . . . on the state of the maritime area" or, even if they were, are likely adversely to affect the maritime area' (Award, para. 179). The dissenting opinion of Griffiths objected to the majority's approach on the grounds that: it failed to address 'the admitted environmental harm to the marine environment of the Irish Sea, as well as the fact that Article 9(2) only speaks of the likelihood of adverse effects'; the burden of proof lay with the UK, in accordance with the precautionary principle; the majority conclusion appeared to be unfounded since no evidence was presented in support of its finding; and the available material militated in favour of the conclusion that the probability of adverse effect might be demonstrated (Dissenting Opinion, para. 92). The majority's textual and 'acontextual' approach suggests that environmental considerations – including international legal developments which have occurred since the 1980s – have perhaps not yet fully permeated the reasoning processes of some classical international lawyers.

1993 Civil Liability Convention

Chapter III of the 1993 Civil Liability Convention, entitled 'Access to Information', includes provisions entitling persons to have access to environmental information held by public authorities on terms which are virtually identical to the 1990 EC Directive. However, the Convention additionally entitles persons to have access to environmental information held by 'bodies with public responsibilities for the environment and under the control of a public authority' on the same terms and conditions as information held by public authorities, and access to specific information held by operators. This latter entitlement introduces a novel approach which goes beyond the 1990 EC Directive and the 1992 OSPAR Convention. It would entitle a person who has suffered damage to request a court to order an operator to provide her with specific information necessary to establish the existence of a claim for compensation under the Convention, including the elements of information available to her and relating to the equipment and machinery used, the kind and concentration of the dangerous substances or waste, and the nature of genetically modified organisms.Operators may request a court to order another operator to provide specific information which may be necessary to establish the extent of her obligation or of her own right to compensation from the other operator, and may also rely on defences including the restrictions set out in Article 14(2), or where such information would incriminate her, or place a disproportionate burden on her, taking into account all the interests involved.

1998 Aarhus Convention

The 1998 Aarhus Convention is built on three pillars: access to information; public participation in environmental decision-making; and access to justice in environmental matters. On environmental information, the Convention introduces several innovations which clarify – or develop, depending upon one's perspective – the approaches reflected in the 1990 EC Directive and Article 9 of the 1992 OSPAR Convention, which it generally follows. The 1998 Aarhus Convention obliges parties to ensure that public authorities make available to the public 'environmental information' without any interest having to be stated, generally in the form requested, and without an unreasonable charge being made. The definition of environmental information is broader than earlier instruments, making express reference, for example, to factors of biodiversity such as genetically modified organisms, and a broad range of measures (such as environmental agreements, policies, plans and programmes and cost– benefit and other economic analyses and assumptions used in environmental decision-making). The time available for responding to requests is reduced to one month, and the exceptions are to be interpreted in a restrictive way and tightened (e.g. the commercial confidentiality exception may only be applied where 'legitimate economic interests' need to be protected, and a presumption is established in favour of disclosing information on emissions which is relevant for the protection of the environment). A refusal to disclose information is to be subject to the Convention provisions on access to review. The Convention also imposes a positive obligation on a public authority which does not hold the information to inform the applicant where it might be applied for, and makes provision for the separation of information which would be exempted from disclosure so that the remainder may be disclosed.

Article 5 of the Convention imposes a range of positive (and innovative) obligations on parties, beginning with the requirement that public authorities 'possess and update' environmental information relevant to their functions, and to establish mandatory systems to ensure an adequate flow of information to public authorities about activities which may significantly affect the environment. In the event of any imminent threat to human health or the environment (from any source), public authorities are also required to immediately disseminate all information which could enable the public to take measures to prevent or mitigate the harm arising from the threat. Parties are also requiredto ensurethat public authorities make environmental information available to the public in transparent and accessible ways, to ensure that such information progressively becomes available in electronic databases, to publish (at least every four years) a national report on the state of the environment, and to take measures to disseminate national and international legislation and measures, including treaties. The private sector is also targeted, although via the state: parties shall encourage operators whose activities have a significant impact on the environment to inform the public regularly of the environmental impact of their activities and products, where appropriate within the framework of voluntary eco-labelling or eco-auditing schemes or by other means.

Finally, each party must take steps to establish progressively a 'coherent, nationwide system of pollution inventories or registers on a structured, computerized and publicly accessible database'.

PUBLIC EDUCATION AND AWARENESS

A number of international environmental agreements include positive obligations requiring states to improve public education and awareness on environmental matters and give due publicity to matters of environmental importance. Principle 10 of the Rio Declaration synthesises commitments adopted in a number of international treaties. It recognises the importance of public education and provides that 'states shall facilitate and encourage public awareness and participation by making information widely available'. Chapter 36 of Agenda 21 (Promoting Education, Public Awareness and Training) elaborates upon Principle 10, and establishes three programme areas: reorienting education towards sustainable development; increasing public awareness; and promoting training. Article 5 of the 1998 Aarhus Convention – described above – goes far in this regard.

Several treaties include provisions on public awareness, education and publicity. One of the earliest was the 1987 Montreal Protocol, which calls on parties to co-operate in 'promoting public awareness of the environmental effects of the emissions of controlled substances and other substances that deplete the ozone layer'. Similar provisions are repeated in subsequent global instruments. Education and training are also addressed with increasing fre-quency, particularly in relation to instruments addressing the protection of workers. The 1989 Convention on the Rights of the Child specifies that education should include 'development of respect for the natural environment'.The 2000 Biosafety Protocol requires parties to promote public awareness, education and participation 'concerning the safe transfer, handling and use of living modified organisms in relation to the conservation and sustainable use of biological diversity'. Finally, certain treaties specifically require that publicity should be given to specially protected areas, or to maritime navigation dangers, or to particular requirements for the prevention, reduction and control of pollution of the marine environment.

ECO-LABELLING

P. Menell, 'The Uneasy Case for Ecolabelling', 4 RECIEL 304 (1995); E. Staffin, 'Trade Barrier or Trade Boon? A Critical Evaluation of Environmental Labelling and Its Role in "Greening" of World Trade', 21 *Columbia Journal of Environmental Law* 205 (1996); A. Appleton, *Environmental Labelling Programmes: International Trade Law Implications* (1997); E. Bartenhagen, 'The Intersection of Trade and the Environment: An Examination of the Impact of the TBT Agreementon Ecolabelling Programs', 17 *Virginia Environmental Law Journal* 1 (1997); S. Subedi, 'Balancing International Trade with Environmental Protection: International Legal Aspects of Eco-labels', 2 *Brooklyn Journal of International Law* 373 (1999).

The labelling of environmental aspects of goods and services (eco-labelling) emerged as an international issue in the trade context, following Mexico's complaint that the US 1990 Dolphin

Protection Consumer Information Act (allowing 'Dolphin Safe' labels to be placed on tuna products provided that dolphins had not been killed) was incompatible with the GATT. Although the GATT Panel upheld the legislation, it did so in terms which suggested that other eco-labelling rules might be incompatible with the GATT. Although there have been no subsequent GATT or WTO rulings regarding eco-labelling, debate continues in the WTO Committee on Trade and the Environment on the propriety of eco-labelling schemes under GATT/WTO rules, with particular focus on the compatibility with the WTO rules of mandatory labelling requirements for genetically modified organisms. For its parties, the matter will now be governed, in respect of living modified organisms, by the 2000 Biosafety Protocol, which requires living modified organisms intended for direct use as food, feed or for processing to be identified to show that they 'may contain' living modified organisms and are not intended for intentional introduction into the environment. More generally, the 1998 Aarhus Convention requires parties IMPLEMENTING INTERNATIONAL PRINCIPLES to develop mechanisms to ensure that product information is available to allow consumers to make informed environmental choices.

The European Community's 1992 Regulation on a Community eco-labelling scheme was the first international instrument to establish an eco-labelling scheme, functioning for several years until it was revised in 2000. The 2000 Regulation revises the Community eco-labelling scheme, the objective of which is to establish a voluntary scheme for the award of an EC eco-label for products and services that reduce negative environmental impacts and contribute to the efficient use of resources and a high level of environmental protection. The eco-label may be awarded to any product or service that possesses 'characteristics that enable it to contribute significantly to improvements in relation to key environmental aspects', on the basis that no substances or preparations which are classified as very toxic, toxic, dangerous to the environment, carcinogenic, toxic for reproduction, or mutagenic may be awarded the eco-label, and excluding certain products – food, drink and pharmaceuticals – from the scheme.The Regulation establishes a European Union Eco-labelling Board (EUEB), composed of the competent bodies of the member states and a Consultation Forum, which, in association with the EC

Commission and the Regulatory Committee, is responsible for establishing the product groupings and detailed criteria for awarding the eco-label in each grouping. The criteria for each product group are to be established according to specific environmental requirements set forth in an 'Indicative Environmental Matrix' in Annex I, and specific procedural requirements set out in Annex II. The Annex I Matrix requires account to be taken of pollution and contamination in eleven environmental fields, in five phases of the product's life cycle or three phases of the service's life cycle. The Regulation establishes a four-part procedure for establishing the detailed criteria. Applications for the eco-label are to be made to the competent body of the member states by manufacturers, importers, service providers, traders and retailers where the product originates or, where the product originates outside the EC, in any member state where the product is to be placed on the market in accordance with the established criteria for each product group. The label is to be awarded by contract limited to the remaining period of validity for the ecological criteria and covering the terms of the label's use, including withdrawal of authorisation, and will be subject to the payment of the costs of processing the application and the payment of an annual fee.

ECO-AUDITING AND ACCOUNTING

H. Gleckman, 'Proposed Requirements for Transnational Corporations to Disclose Information on Product and Process Hazards', 6 *Boston University International Law Journal* 89 (1988); L. Spedding, 'Environmental Auditing and International Standards', 3 RECIEL 14 (1994).

Environmental considerations are addressed in regulatory and voluntary schemes designed to identify the environmental effects of the activities of companies or industrial sites. These measures suggest that current accounting practices and statements need to be transformed to take into account the environmental costs of production and other activities, which are currently treated for the most part as 'zero-priced' resources. The primary purpose of environmental accounting is to ensure that environmental costs are accurately reflected in the individual accounts and balance sheets of companies, or the national accounts of states. An important secondary purpose is to ensure that information on the use of environmental resources is disclosed; information provided in accounts may relate to environmental policies and programmes, environmental improvements, or the financial impacts of environmental measures, as well as responsibilities for environmental clean-up or related measures. Environmental auditing, or 'eco-auditing', describes a technique for allowing a company or a state to assess the impact of its activities on the environment which includes procedures beyond the scope of a traditional financial audit which can be performed by an internal consultant or by an independent third person. The most important developments relating to environmental accounting and auditing have been taken at the national level. At the international level the most significant work on environmental accounting has been carried

predecessor) for, *inter alia,* light bulbs, copying and graphic paper, indoor paints and varnishes, textile products, hardfloor coverings, television, footwear, dishwashers, soil improvers, portable computers, dishwashing detergents, all-purpose cleaners, tissue paper products, and washing machines. out under the auspices of the former UN Centre on Transnational Corporations (UNCTC) and, subsequently, UNCTAD, while that relating to eco-auditing is reflected in the Regulation establishing a voluntary scheme, first adopted by the EC in April 1993 and revised in 2001. Additionally, the International Standards Organization (ISO) has developed its ISO 14000 series of standards for environmental management.

Environmental accounting

Although discussions regarding environmental accounting have taken place in the international community for over a decade, no international legal obligations, or soft law commitments, have been adopted by states or international organisationsin relationtoenvironmentalaccounting, andnone appears imminent. The best guide to possible future developments at the international level is reflected in the work of the Intergovernmental Working Group of Experts on International Standards of Accounting and Reporting (ISAR), established under the auspices of the former UNCTC, and now functioning under UNCTAD. The work of the former UNCTC in this area was submitted as a report to the UNCED Preparatory Committee, and was partly reflected in

Principle 16 of the Rio Declaration, which calls on national authorities to 'endeavour to promote the internalisation of environmental costs', and in Agenda 21. The 1991 UNCTC Report recognised that the main challenge for environmental accounting was to develop an acceptable valuation method for quantifying the costs of non-sustainable economic activity, and identifies some of the flaws in traditional accounting rules and practices in relation to environmental resources:

It does not account for the full costs of production, including the costs of consuming essential natural resources such as air, water and fertile land . . . In addition, accounting rules penalise, rather than encourage, the environmentally responsible corporation. The more a corporation spends on prevention and clean-up, the less per share it earns in the short run. Accounting lacks a vehicle for recording 'green assets' and monitoring their use, for distinguishing between the costs of renewable versus non-renewable resources and for providing accounting incentives to improve environmental protection.

The UNCTC recognised the need to ensure that accounts reflect environmental costs so that stakeholders have information to enable them to make the best uses of resources, taking account of 'the rights and obligations of shareholders, customers, and local communities affected by environmental degradation, as well as the implicit rights of other species and other habitats'. It also identified the need to improve traditional financial statements, principally to address the concerns of securities' regulators, insurance companies, banks and shareholders about unreported contingent liabilities which might have an adverse effect on the net worth of a corporation. This raises a major problem of access to, and dissemination of, information, described by the UNCTC report as 'unprecedented disclosure problems in how, and when, to account for the potential contingent liabilities'. The report identified three obstacles to the taking or reporting of environmental protection measures by companies. First, the lack of incentive to record liabilities which results from the rule in many countries that expenses are only deductible for tax purposes when paid; secondly, the impact of environmental costs on short-term earnings; and, thirdly, the difficulty of separating environmental costs from other costs. The report noted that accounting for environmental expenses is feasible, and raises reporting issues which are 'tractable and essentially of a definitional and classificatory nature'.Environmental liabilities raised more problems, in large part because of the difficulty in determining a 'reasonable estimate' of future obligations in the face of environmental liabilities which are dependent upon 'inherent uncertainties in future legislation, technological change and extent or nature of environmental clean-up required'.

Since 1990, ISAR has sought to address these and other accounting issues by proposing methods for integrating environmental costs and liabilities into traditional accounting methods, including incorporating environmental information into financial disclosures and annual reports. In 1998, it published a guidance document to provide assistance to enterprises, regulators and standard-setting bodies regarding best practice in accounting for environmental transactions and events in the financial statements and associated notes.The guidance document urges financial statements to recognise environmental costs, and to measure environmental liabilities, and recommends methods for recognising, measuring and disclosing environmental costs. In association with UNCTAD, ISAR is expected next to develop guidance on integrating 'environmental performance indicators' into traditional financial reports.

Environmental auditing

International legal developments on environmental auditing, which is a necessary component of environmental accounting, began with the adoption in April 1993 of the EC Regulation, revised in 2001. Multilateral development banks, led by the EBRD, have conducted environmental audits on certain projects as part of a screening process to determine their potential liability, as well as that of project sponsors, for environmental damage related to loans, and to enhance environmental management of the facility.

The EC's eco-management and audit scheme (EMAS) is intended to improve the environmental performance of companies' industrial activities. The scheme encourages companies to: implement environmental policies, programmes and management systems in relation to their sites; evaluate their environmental performance; provide information on environmental performance to the public; and encourage employee participation within the management system. The scheme, which is without prejudice to

EC or national environmental laws or standards, allows organisations to participate voluntarily by registering with the scheme. For an organisation to be registered, it must first conduct an environmental review of its activities, products and services, and, in light of that review, implement an environmental management system. The organisation must also: carry out an environmental audit in accordance with Annex II; prepare an environmental statement in accordance with Annex III; have the environmental review, management system, audit procedure, and environmental statement reviewed and validated by an environmental verifier to meet the requirements of Annex III; and submit the validated environmental statement to the competent body of a member state and, after registration, make the environmental statement publicly available.

An organisation will be registered by a national body after a validated environmental statement and a completed form including the minimum information required by Annex VIII have been received, a registration fee paid, and the competent body is satisfied that the organisation is in compliance with all environmental legislation and requirements of the Regulation. Under certain conditions, registration may be refused or suspended or deleted from the register. The environmental management system requirements chosen by the Regulation are those set forth in ISO 14001.

CONCLUSIONS

There now exists an extensive body of international rules aiming to improve the availability of environmental information, broadly recognised as a central technique for the implementation of environmental standards and procedures set by treaties and other international agreements. The original reporting, consultation and notification obligations which are well established in international law have been supplemented by a second generation of rules. These aim to increase the public availability of information by enhancing access, encouraging greater dissemination to consumers at various levels and, in a more limited fashion, imposing a positive obligation on certain states (in the ECE region) to collect, report on and publish environmental information. Existing arrangements remain incomplete, however, and there are significant gaps within and across regions. The overall objective remains an increase in the quantity and quality of information available, greater dissemination among all relevant members of the international community, and ensuring that it is used to inform decision-making at all national and international levels. To that end, a number of tasks appear particularly important.

First, international co-operation on the gathering of information on the state of the environment needs to be further enhanced. New arrangements such as those reflected in the clearing-house and information exchange mechanisms set up under the 2000 Biosafety Protocol and the 1997 Kyoto Protocol could be developed in other subject matter areas.

Secondly,compliance with basic reportingrequirementsunder environmental treaties remains inadequate and should be improved, including by establishing arrangements for compositereportsfulfilling obligationsundertwoor more conventions: if states are unable or unwilling to fulfil these primary obligations then it is unlikely that they will comply with the more onerous and important substantive standards established by the same treaties. Clearly, the collection of national information necessary to fulfil international reporting obligations can place heavy burdens on limited and already over-stretched human, institutional and financial resources. The availability of financial resources for reporting under agreements such as the Climate Change and Biodiversity Conventions have gone some way towards improving compliance with reporting requirements, but these need to be coupled with education and training, and an enhanced role for international organisations in assisting with reporting.

Thirdly, the general obligation in international law to consult and notify certain potentially harmful activities – now reflected in the ILC's 2001 draft Articles on Prevention of Transboundary Harm – has broad support, but is not always complied with. Incidents such as the Chernobyl accident and the cyanide spillage (Baia Mare) in the Tisa River basin involving Hungary and Romania reflect the need for constant vigilance where emergency situations occur.

Fourthly, the duty of states to provide – and the right of legal and natural persons to receive – environmental information is more broadly recognised but requires further development in practice, not least by making citizens aware of their rights. The 1998 Aarhus Convention is an important development beyond the EC, andcould providea model forother regions. EC experience suggests that the demand for environmental information increases as citizens become aware of their rights, and that the processing of requests places significant demands on public authorities which encourages them to find ways to avoid providing information. Accordingly, it will be necessary to ensure that the access to justice provisions of the Aarhus Convention are properly implemented and that other effective means of administrative or judicial redress are available at the national or international level to ensure that states fulfil their obligations.

3

Liability for Environmental Damage

INTRODUCTION

General principles of international law imposing liability on actors for their illegal acts, or for the adverse consequences of their lawful activities, are relatively well developed at a general level, and are now reflected in the Articles on State Responsibility adopted by the ILC in 2001. In relation to environmental damage, however, the liability rules are still evolving and in need of further development. Environmental damage refers here to damage to the environment, which has been defined in treaties and other international acts to include four possible elements: (1) fauna, flora, soil, water and climatic factors; (2) material assets (including archaeological and cultural heritage); (3) the landscape and environmental amenity; and (4) the interrelationship between the above fac-tors. Most legal definitions of environment do not, therefore, include people and their property.

Liability rules at the domestic or international level serve a variety of purposes. They may be a form of economic instrument which provides an incentive to encourage compliance with environmental obligations. They may also be used to impose sanctions for wrongful conduct, or to require corrective measures to restore a given environmental asset to its pre-damage condition. Finally, they may provide a technique for internalising environmental and other social costs into production processes and other activities in implementation of the polluter-pays principle. This chapter follows the distinction which has been drawn in practice between the liability of states and other international persons under public international law, and the liability of actors (which could include states) under rules of national law adopted pursuant to treaties which aim to harmonise national civil liability rules, or set minimum standards. State liability refers here to the liability of international persons under the operation of rules of international law of state responsibility. Civil liability refers to the liability of any legal or natural person under the rules of national law adopted pursuant to international treaty obligations establishing harmonised minimum standards. However, the distinction between state and civil liability is becoming increasingly difficult to draw, as treaties and other international acts have established an obligation for the state to provide public funds where an operator cannot meet certain costs of environmental damage.

States have long recognised the role of liability for environmental damage, as well as the gaps and inadequacies which exist. Principle 22 of the Stockholm Declaration recognised gaps and called on states to 'co-operate to develop further the international law regarding liability and compensation for victims of pollution and other environmental damage caused by activities within the jurisdiction or control of such states to areas beyond their jurisdiction'. The 1982 World Charter for Nature did not directly address liability, although it called for degraded areas to be rehabilitated and for individuals to have access to means of redress when 'their environment has suffered damage or degradation'. The Rio Declaration reflects the limited progress which has been made since 1972. It emphasises the development of national rules in addition to the further development of international rules for all adverse effects of environmental damage including, implicitly, liability for damage to the environment itself. Principle 13 of the Rio Declaration provides that: states shall develop national law regarding liability and compensation for the victims of pollution and other environmental damage. States shall also co-operate in an expeditious and more determined manner to develop further international law regarding liability and compensation for adverse effects of environmental damage caused by activities within their jurisdiction or control to areas beyond their jurisdiction.

The shift in emphasis in the Rio Declaration reflects an unwillingness to establish rules of international law which might impose excessive costs. This was also evident following the Chernobyl accident in 1986, following which no claims were made although it provided a relatively clear-cut case on which an international liability claim could be made. That episode illustrated the inertia which has limited developments since 1972 in the development of state liability rules for environmental damage, although a significant number of treaties have been, or are being, developed which establish international civil liability rules, as considered below. Other treaties commit their parties to develop rules on liability or responsibility, or support international efforts. For state and civil liability, international rules address certain substantive and procedural elements which determine the nature and extent of the liability. The common issues which emerge are:

- whether to designate environmental damage as a distinct head of damage (separate from personal injury and property damage);
- defining environmental damage;
- establishing the standard of care (absolute, strict or fault);
- establishing the measure of damages;
- identifying the person or persons against whom the claim should be brought;
- determining who may bring a claim;
- designating the forum or fora before which claims may be brought;
- determining the remedies which are available; and
- providing for the availability of certain defences.

Many similarities exist among the various instruments, although each of the civil liability regimes sets its own rules in relation to each of these and other issues. The same is true of state liability rules adopted by treaty. In respect of such rules as exist under customary or general international law it will be seen that, in the context of very limited state practice, defining the parameters of each aspect of state liability is not an easy task.

STATE LIABILITY

It is a well established principle of international law, recognised in Article 1 of the ILC Articles on the Responsibility of States for Internationally Wrongful Acts (2001), that every internationally wrongful act of a state entails the international responsibility of that state. The same principle applies to other international persons, including international organisations. A state responsible for an internationally wrongful act is under an obligation to cease that act, if it is continuing, and to offer appropriate assurances and guarantees of non-repetition if the circumstances so require, and to make full reparation for the injury caused by the internationally wrongful act. The obligation to make reparation – sometimes referred to as a liability – is well established. As the PCIJ stated as early as 1928 in the *Chorzow Factory* case, it is a principle of international law, and even a general conception of law, that any breach of an engagement involves an obligation to make reparation. In Judgment No. 8 (1927) (PCIJ, Ser. A, No. 9, 21) . . . the Court had already said that reparation was the indispensable complement of a failure to apply a convention, and there is no necessity for this to be stated in the convention itself.

The approach has been affirmed – in the environmental context – by the ICJ in the *Case Concerning the Gabcikovo-Nagymaros Project*. The operation of these principles refers to rules of state responsibility and liability, although the term 'state responsibility' is perhaps misleading as it emerged at a time when states alone were considered as subjects of international law. To the extent that international organisations and other legal and natural persons may also be subjects of international law, the concept of 'state responsibility' may also inform the principle of the liability of other international persons under the rules of public international law.

In the environmental field, no single instrument sets forth the generally applicable international rules governing responsibility and liability. The ILC's Articles on State Responsibility bring together the rules of general international law, and they are applicable (to the extent they reflect customary law) with environmental rules established by treaties and other internationally applicable rules.

A number of non-binding instruments adopted in the environmental field have sought also to restate general principles. Principle 12 of the 1978 UNEP draft Principles affirms that states are responsible for the fulfilment of their international environmental obligations relating to the utilisation of shared natural resources, and that they 'are subject to liability in accordance with applicable international law for environmental damage resulting from violations of these obligations caused to areas beyond their jurisdiction'. The WCED Legal Principles Group states that:

[i]f one or more activities create a significant risk of substantial harm as a result of a transboundary environmental interference, and if the overall technical and socio-economic cost or loss of benefits involved in preventing or reducing such risks far exceeds in the long run the advantage which such prevention or reduction would entail . . . the state which carried out or permitted the activities shall ensure that compensation is provided should substantial harm occur in an area under national jurisdiction of another state or in an area beyond the limits of national jurisdiction.

The Institut de Droit International (IDI) has made a singular contribution to this subject. Its 1987 resolution on transboundary air pollution recognised that 'states incur responsibility under international law for any breach of their international obligations with respect to transboundary air pollution', and calls on states to conclude international treaties and enact laws and regulations to ensure an effective system of prevention and compensation for victims of transboundary air pollution. In 1997, the IDI unanimously adopted a resolution on responsibility and liability under international law for environmental damage, which seeks to 'identify, harmonize and to the necessary extent develop the principles of international law applicable to responsibility and liability in the context of environmental damage'. The resolution affirms that 'the breach of an obligation of environmental protection established under international law engages responsibility of the State . . . entailing as a consequence the obligation to reestablish the original position or to pay compensation', the latter obligation also being capable of arising from a rule of international law providing for strict liability on the basis of harm or injury alone.

General international law

State liability for environmental damage is premised upon a breach of an international legal obligation established by treaty, or by a rule of customary international law, or possibly under general principles of international law. Article 2 of the ILC Articles on State Responsibility states: There is an internationally wrongful act of a State when conduct consisting of an act or omission:

(a) is attributable to the State under international law; and
(b) constitutes a breach of an international obligation of the State.

The ILC Articles on State Responsibility elaborate on the circumstances in which an act or omission will be attributable to a state, and indicate the circumstances in which a breach of an obligation will have occurred and that the state must be bound by the obligation in question 'at the time that act occurs'. They elaborate on the conditions which must be satisfied for one state to incur responsibility in connection with the acts of another state, for example where one state aids or assists another in the commission of an internationally wrongful act. And they indicate the circumstances in which wrongfulness may be precluded, including where a state invokes necessity to justify an action to safeguard an essential interest against a grave and imminent peril.

For present purposes, the most pertinent international obligation is that requiring a state to prevent particular environmental harm, or to refrain from carrying out or permitting activities which could lead to environmental damage. As discussed in chapter 6 above, the ICJ has affirmed that customary international law establishes an obligation to respect the environment of other states or of areas beyond national jurisdiction. To a large extent discussions of state liability are likely to be concerned with the consequences of a breach of this obligation, which encompasses the obligation not to cause significant harm. But responsibility and liability also arise in relation to other substantive obligations, as well as procedural requirements pertaining, for example, to access to information and the duty to carry out an environmental impact assessment. Additionally, some regimes (for example, the WTO system) establish their own rules and remedies governing the consequences of a failure to comply with the obligations there established.

With regard to the obligation to prevent environmental damage, general international law requires at least four related issues to be addressed: is the obligation aiming to prevent any transboundary environmental damage, or only transboundary environmental damage which has serious, or significant, or appreciable consequences? Is the obligation based upon the need to prove fault or is it imposed by operation of absolute or strict liability? What reparation should be made for environmental damage? And what is the extent of liability and the measure of damages? Other legal requirements would need to be satisfied to bring an international claim, including (as appropriate) the exhaustion of local remedies rule, the nationality of claims rule, any rules governing limitation on the time within which a claim can be brought, and the rules governing attribution of state responsibility for the acts of public bodies and private persons. In respect of these and other questions, state practice, case law, treaties and the writings of jurists do not provide conclusive answers. Each case must be judged on its own merits.

DEFINING ENVIRONMENTAL DAMAGE

Defining environmental damage remains a complex issue. Two related issues need to be distinguished: what constitutes environmental damage? And what level of environmental damage might give rise to liability?

In defining environmental damage, treaties and state practice reflect various approaches. A narrow definition of environmental damage is limited to damage to natural resources alone (air, water, soil, fauna and flora, and their interaction); a more extensive approach includes damage to natural resources *and* property which forms part of the cultural heritage; the most extensive definition includes landscape and environmental amenity. On each approach, environmental damage does not include damage to persons or damage to property, although such damage can be consequential to environmental damage. Loss of environmental amenity, which may be included under the provisions of the 1993 Council of Europe Convention on Liability for Environmental Damage (1993 Lugano Convention) referring to the 'characteristic aspects of the landscape', could be treated as environmental damage or damage to property, depending on the definition of the latter. Environmental damage has been defined in instruments establishing civil liability, particularly in relation to oil pollution. In respect of state liability the only treaty definition is provided by the 1988 CRAMRA, which defines damage to the Antarctic environment or ecosystem very broadly, to include: any impact on the living or non-living components of that environment or those ecosystems, including harm to atmospheric, marine or terrestrial life, beyond that which is negligible or which has been assessed and judged to be acceptable pursuant to [the] Convention.

The concept of 'pollution', which is defined in the 1979 LRTAP Convention, the 1982 UNCLOS and elsewhere, provides some assistance but cannot be used interchangeably with 'environmental damage'. 'Air pollution' in the 1979 LRTAP Convention is defined by reference to deleterious effects (which are themselves undefined) on living resources and ecosystems, human health and material property, as well as interference with amenities and other legitimate uses of the environment. The distinction between environmental damage (and compensable environmental damage) and pollution is illustrated by the 1993 Lugano Convention which provides that an operator of a dangerous activity will not be liable for damage (impairment of the environment) caused by pollution at 'tolerable' levels under local relevant circumstances. Other treaties require 'adverse effects', rather than pollution, to define the consequences of activities which are to be avoided. Like pollution, the term 'adverse effects' provides some assistance in establishing a basis for, but cannot be used interchangeably with, a general definition of environmental damage. The 1985 Vienna Convention defines 'adverse effects' in relation to ozone depletion as, *inter alia*, 'changes in the physical environment or biota, including changes in climate, which have significant deleterious effects on human health or on the composition, resilience and productivity of natural and managed ecosystems, or on materials useful to mankind'. The 1992 Climate Change Convention introduces a similar definition, although it reverses the order by placing deleterious effects on the environment before effects on human health, and extends the definition to include effects on socio-economic systems and human welfare.Thus, 'pollution' and 'adverse effects' help in determining the threshold beyond which environmental damage might trigger liability, but they do not actually define it.

Other state practice is limited. Environmental damage in the pure sense was not considered by the arbitral tribunal in the *Trail Smelter* case, although the *Lac Lanoux Arbitration* implicitly recognised the possibility of pure environmental damage when it referred to changes in the composition, temperature or other characteristics of the waters of the River Carol which injured Spanish inter-ests. Treating environmental damage as a separate head was recognised in the claims by Australia and New Zealand in the *Nuclear Tests* cases, and by Nauru in the *Case Concerning Certain Phosphate Lands in Nauru*. It has been recognised – implicitly– by the ICJ in the *Case Concerning the Gabcikovo-Nagymaros*

Project. Clear support for the provision of compensation for environmental damage under rules of state liability was provided by the UN Security Council in 1991 when it reaffirmed that Iraq was 'liable under international law for any direct loss, damage, including environmental damage and the depletion of natural resources, or injury to foreign Governments, nationals and corporations' occurring as a result of its unlawful invasion and occupation of Kuwait. UN Security Council Resolution 687, which is binding on the world, unequivocally determines that a state can be liable for the environmental damage and depletion of natural resources which result from unlawful use of force. Resolution 687 does not, however, define environmental damage or depletion of natural resources, or provide guidance to the Compensation Commission on their assessment, or the measure, of reparation or compensation. The practice of the Claims Commission in defining environmental damage could provide assistance to other international bodies, including courts and tribunals, which may be required to deal with this issue in the future.

THRESHOLD AT WHICH ENVIRONMENTAL DAMAGE ENTAILS LIABILITY

Whilst all pollution or human activity having adverse effects might give rise to environmental damage, it is unlikely that all environmental damage results in state liability. There are no agreed international standards which establish a threshold for environmental damage which triggers liability and allows claims to be brought. State practice, decisions of international tribunals and the writings of jurists suggest that environmental damage must be 'significant' or 'substantial' (or possibly 'appreciable', which suggests a marginally less onerous threshold) for liability to be triggered.

A 1993 EC Commission Green Paper on Environmental Liability identified several possibilities for determining the level of environmental damage triggering liability. These include defining environmental damage by reference to 'critical loads', which describe the point at which a pollutant becomes concentrated in the environment at a level which cannot be diluted or broken down by natural processes; or by reference to environmental indicators and environmental accounting to measure environmental performance, pressures and conditions; or by reference to existing international legislation which establishes quality standards for flora and fauna, water and air quality and which might be considered to establish a threshold for environmental damage above which a person responsible for the increase would be considered liable for the consequences. International instruments which set environmental quality standards, or product, emissions or process standards, may also provide some guidance as to the level of environmental damage considered to be tolerable or acceptable by the international community.

Someguidance may also be found inthe exchange between the thenPresident of the ICJ, Sir Humphrey Waldock, and the Government of Australia in the *Nuclear Tests* case, reflecting a view that not every transmission of chemical or other matter into another state's territory, or into the global commons, will create a legal cause of action in international law. The tribunal in the *Trail Smelter* case held that the injury must have a 'serious consequence' to justify a claim. In its claim against Australia, Nauru argued for general principle based upon an obligation not to bring about changes in the condition of territory which will cause 'irreparable damage to, or substantially prejudice' the legal interest of another state. A similar approach underlies Hungary's Original Application in the *Case Concerning the Gabcikovo-Nagymaros Project*. The Canadian claim following the crash of Cosmos 954 was brought in the context of damage to land which made it 'unfit for use', a level of damage which supports the view that the impact on the environment must be more than nominal to establish a claim. A number of the civil liability instruments discussed below establish thresholds for environmental damage or adverse effects which are 'significant', or 'serious', or above 'tolerable levels', and the ILA Montreal Rules call on states to prevent 'substantial injury'.

Establishing the appropriate threshold turns on the facts of each case, and may vary according to local or regional circumstances. The limited state practice supports the view that the threshold to be crossed may still be established at a relatively high level of environmental damage. The difficulty of agreeing a threshold isillustrated by the Chernoby laccident, which raised numerous issues over what constituted harmful levels of radioactivity in the absence of legally binding international standards. Several international guidelines establish radiation dose limits for the whole human body or for specific organs or tissues. The EC Commission had published recommendations on dose levels as guidelines for national authorities in setting specific levels at which products might be deemed unsafe (intervention levels), and similar guidelines had also been prepared by the International Commission on Radiological Protection (ICRP),the WHO, the IAEA, and UNSCEAR. At the time of the Chernobyl accident, little consideration had been given to the control of foodstuffs contaminated by an accidental release of radioactivity, and national authorities set their own intervention levels according to a range of different standards, which led to disputes on the permissibility of intervention measures which affected international trade. The EC Commission initially suspended the import of certain agricultural products from central and eastern Europe, and then laid down the maximum permitted level of radioactivity for products originating from these countries. Individual EC member states adopted their own intervention levels which were used as the basis for undertaking national compensation to affected farmers and other businesses.

The absence of generally accepted standards on safe levels of radioactivity made it difficult to assess whether these measures were justified, and resulted in confusion, concern and public suspicion, as well as constraints on international food trade. The FAO subsequently proposed 'Interim International Radionuclide Action Levels for Food' (IRALFs) to cover food being traded internationally, which, while non-binding and *ex post facto*, provided a useful standard for assessing whether the increases in radioactivity caused by the Chernobyl accident were harmful to foodstuffs and whether intervention levels were justified under international law.

Liability can be closely related to the adoption of regulatory standards. As the international community adopts such standards, the task of identifying the level of compensable environmental damage will become easier. In the absence of international standards concerning the quality of the environment, including conservation of flora and fauna, states will set their own standards, resulting in divergences with resulting economic and environmental consequences.

STANDARD OF CARE

If there is an obligation to prevent significant, substantial or serious environmental damage, what is the standard of care applicable to that obligation? Options include fault (based upon intention or negligence), strict liability ('essentially a *prima facie* responsibility, and various qualifications or defences may be available') and absolute liability ('for which there can be no mode of ex-culpation'). Although this question has received considerable attention from writers, it is reasonable to conclude that there 'is probably no single basis of international responsibility, applicable in all circumstances, but rather several, the nature of which depends on the particular obligation in question'. The obligation in question may distinguish between ultra-hazardous activities and other activities. This approach can be justified on policy grounds: dangerous activities are more likely to cause serious environmental damage, and a strict or absolute obligation is more likely to provide an incentive to states to adopt special precautions when engaging in or permitting such activities.

International law remains inconclusive on general rules governing the standard of care to be shown in fulfilling international environmental obligations. Principle 21 of the Stockholm Declaration and Principles 2 and 13 of the Rio Declaration do not provide guidance either way, and the decisions of international tribunals in the *Trail Smelter* case, the *Corfu Channel* case, the *Lac Lanoux* case and the *Nuclear Tests* cases can be interpreted to support conclusions of absolute/strict liability or fault-based liability. In respect of ultra-hazardous activities, certain treaties do support a standard of absolute or strict, liability. The 1972 Space Liability Convention supports absolute liability, and, in reliance on this provision and general principles of international law, following the Cosmos 954 accident Canada claimed that 'the principle of absolute liability applies to fields of activity having in common a high degree of risk . . . [and] has been accepted as a general principle of international law'. The 1988 CRAMRA also supports liability without the need to prove fault.

Strict liability for ultra-hazardous activities might also be considered a general principle of law as it is to be found in the national law of many states in relation to ultra-hazardous activities. Under English law, 'a person who for his own purposes brings on his land and collects and keeps there anything likely to do mischief if it escapes, must keep it in at his peril, and, if he does not do so, is *prima facie* answerable for all the damage which is the natural consequence of its escape'. Many civil liability treaties also adopt the principle of strict liability for hazardous activities, including nuclear activities and the carriage of oil by sea, as well as dangerous activities generally. Strict liability is also supported by Jenks, who considered that in relation to nuclear damage the principle of absolute liability 'is generally accepted, but the expression is somewhat misleading in that it does not exclude the possibility of exceptions'.The ILC draft Articles on International Liability for Injurious Consequences Arising Out of Acts Not Prohibited by International Law proposed that a state of origin would be strictly liable for harm to the environment and the resulting harm to property and persons.

For general industrial and other activities which are not ultra-hazardous or dangerous, it is less easy to argue for a standard of care based upon strict or absolute liability. In considering this matter the OECD's Environment Committee has observed that there is a 'custom based rule of *due diligence* imposed on all states in order that activities carried out within their jurisdiction do not cause damage to the environment of other states', which includes establishing and applying an effective system of environmental law and regulations, and principles of consultation and notification.

REPARATION

The principle is well established that the perpetrator of an internationally wrongful act is under an obligation to make reparation for the consequences of the violation. As expressed in the judgment of the *Chorzow Factory* case, the PCIJ stated that:

The essential principle contained in the actual notion of an illegal act – a principle which seems to be established by international practice and in particular by the decisions of arbitral tribunals – is that reparation must, as far as possible, wipe out all the consequences of the illegal act and reestablish the situation which would, in all probability, have existed if that act had not been committed. Restitution in kind, or, if this is not possible, payment of a sum corresponding to the value which a restitution in kind would bear; the award, if need be, of damages for loss sustained which would not be covered by restitution in kind or payment in place of it – such are the principles which should serve to determine the amount of compensation due for an act contrary to international law.

The approach is now reflected in the ILC Articles on State Responsibility (2001), which envisage that the reparation for the injury caused by an internationally wrongful act shall take the form of restitution, compensation and satisfaction, either singly or in combination. Restitution is aimed at re-establishing the situation which existed before the wrongful act was committed, provided and to the extent that it is not materially impossible and does 'not involve a burden out of all proportion to the benefit deriving from restitution instead of com-pensation'. Compensation is to be provided for damage which is not made good by restitution, and should cover 'any financially assessable damage including loss of profits insofar as it is established'. Satisfaction is to be provided if the injury cannot be made good by restitution or compensation, for example by an acknowledgment of the breach, an expression of regret or a formal apology.

In most environmental cases, the victim will be seeking an end to the harmful act, or restitution, or financial compensation to cover the costs associated with material damage to environmental resources (pure environmental damage) and consequential damage to people and property (consequential environmental damage), including restoration or reinstatement. In relation to restitution, it will be necessary to identify the baseline conditions prior to which the damage occurred, which may be difficult. Compensation raises the problem of assessing the measure of environmental damage: should it be by reference to the costs of measures of reinstatement, or on the basis of an abstract quantification calculated in accordance with a theoretical model, or on some other basis? The problem arises because environmental damage does not fit easily with the traditional approaches of civil and state liability which are designed to compensate an injured person by requiring the responsible person to pay the economic costs of resulting damage, which is frequently calculated by reference to a depreciation of the economic value of the damaged item, or the cost of repairing the damage. Pure damage to the environment may be incapable of calculation in economic terms, although it may have a non-economic value requiring restoration to the state prior to the damage occurring. Even here difficulties of law and policy will continue to exist, as the EC Commission's 1993 Green Paper on Environmental Liability recognised:

> An identical reconstruction may not be possible, of course. An extinct species cannot be replaced. Pollutants emitted into the air or water are difficult to retrieve. From an environmental point of view, however, there should be a goal to clean-up and restore the environment to the state which, if not identical to that which existed before the damage occurred, at least maintains its necessary permanent functions... Even if restoration or clean-up is physically possible, it may not be economically feasible. It is unreasonable to expect the restoration to a virgin state if humans have interacted with that environment for generations. Moreover, restoring an environment to the state it was in before the damage occurred could involve expenditure disproportionate to the desired results. In such a case it might be argued that restoration should only be carried out to the point where it is still 'cost-effective'. Such determinations involve difficult balancing of economic and environmental values.

The rules of international law relating to reparation for environmental damage remain undeveloped, as evidenced by the lack of legal precedents. Similar limitations exist at the national level. In the United States, restoration of damaged environments has been described as a 'fledgling activity shot through with uncertainty and controversy'. Alternatives to valuing the environment for the purpose of assessing claims include the price that the environmental resource commands in the market, the economic value attached to the use of environmental resources (such as methods of costing travel relying on expenditures made by an individual to visit and enjoy a resource, or a hedonic pricing method which takes the extra market value enjoyed by private property with certain environmental amenities and assumes that public resources with comparable amenities have similar economic values), or contingent valuation methods to measure the willingness of individuals to pay for environmental goods such as clean air or water or the preservation of endangered species (usually taken from public opinion surveys).

The efforts of the UN Compensation Commission in applying Security Council Resolution 687 (see below) are likely to go some way in developing this aspect of international law, building on the precedents established by the *Tr a i l Smelter* case and limited state practice, including the submission of claims. The approach taken by some of the civil liability precedents may also provide useful analogies in relation to state liability.

TrailSmelterCase(1941) The tribunal in the *Trail Smelter* case found that the smelter at Trail in Canada had caused damage in the United States. The tribunal was called upon to decide what indemnity should be paid for the damage.In applying the 'law and practice followed in dealing with cognate questions in the United States of America as well as international law and practice', the tribunal considered the indemnity claimed by the United States for damage occurring after January 1932 in respect of: (a) cleared land and improvements thereon; (b) uncleared land and improvements thereon; (c) livestock; (d) property; (e) the wrong done to the United States in violation of sovereignty; (f) interest on the US$350,000 awarded by the ICJ on 1 January 1932 but not paid until 2 November 1935; and (g) business enterprises. The United States did not put forward a pure environmental damage claim, although this could be read into the claim in respect of 'uncleared land'. In its 1938 award, the tribunal found that damage to cleared land used for crops had occurred in varying degrees from 1932 to 1936 but not in 1937, and adopted the measure of damages applied by the US courts for nuisance or trespass, namely, 'the amount of reduction in the value of use or rental value of the land caused by fumigations'. The tribunal also recognised some evidence of 'special damage' (rust and destruction of metalwork) which entitled owners to a nominal amount.

As to damage for cleared land not used for crops and to all uncleared land other than that used for timber, the tribunal adopted the same measure of damages, and rejected the US claim to the value of uncleared land at a ratio of loss measured by the reduced crop yield on cleared land. No damages were awarded for pasture lands, and as to cleared land used for merchantable timber the measure of damages was also that applied by US courts, namely, 'the reduction in the value of the land due to such destruction of timber'. For growing timber, the measure of damages was 'the reduction in the value of the land itself due to such destruction and impairment', but the tribunal rejected the claim for damages due to lack of reproduction. On the basis of these considerations, the tribunal awarded US$62,000 for damage to cleared and uncleared land (other than land used for timber), and US$16,000 for damage to uncleared land used for timber.

The tribunal rejected the claim for damage to livestock (due to the failure to prove injury from fumes from the smelter), damage to property in the town of Northport (lack of proof) and damage to business enterprises ('too indirect, remote and uncertain to be appraised and not such for which an indemnity can be awarded'). The tribunal also rejected the US claim for damages from the 'injurious effects' to the Columbia River caused by the disposal of waste slag. The tribunal held that it was 'unnecessary to decide whether the facts proven did or did not constitute an infringement or violation of the sovereignty of the United States under international law independent of the Convention establishing the tribunal, since the Convention only submitted to the tribunal the question of damages caused by the Trail Smelter in the state of Washington, and it interpreted the intention of the parties as evidenced in the Convention not to include moneys spent by the US in investigating the problems, since the Convention used the words 'damages caused by the Trail Smelter'. For the same reason, the tribunal rejected the claim for interest on the earlier payment of US$350,000.

In its 1941 award, the tribunal held that the United States had failed to prove that any fumigation between 1 October 1937 and 1 October 1940 had caused injury to crops, trees or otherwise and that no indemnity was due. As to any damage occurring after 1 October 1940, irrespective of compliance with the regime it had established, the tribunal held that an indemnity should be paid for such damage when and if the two governments arranged for the settlement of claims under Article XI of the Convention, as well as up to US$7,500 per year to be paid to the United States as compensation in order to ascertain whether damage had occurred, provided that the two governments had determined under Article XI of the Convention that damage had occurred in the year in question.

The two awards of the tribunal did not deal with pure environmental damage *per se,* and rejected the opportunity to assess damages in respect of injurious consequences to the Columbia River. The tribunal basically took a market value approach which did not take account of loss of environmental amenity. In so doing, the tribunal took the measure of damage used by US courts, an approach which would most likely produce a different result today because of changes in US law which reflect loss of environmental amenity or resources as a separate measure of damage.

Other developments In January 1955, the US Government paid US$2 million to Japan for the 'purposes of compensation for the injuries or damage sustained' by Japanese nationals as a result of thermonuclear tests carried out by the US near the Marshall Islands in March 1954. The payments were made *ex gratia* and 'without reference to legal liability', and it is unclear whether the compensation included an amount for damage to the marine environment or loss of environmental amenity. In its argument in the *Nuclear Tests* case, Australia argued that, if the existence of harm or damage was essential to liability, it could point to, *inter alia*, the 'harm, all the more real for being incapable of precise evaluation, to which its population, both present and future, and environment have been subjected for no benefit to them'. In April 1981, the USSR agreed to pay, and Canada agreed to accept, C$3 million in final settlement of the Canadian claim, under the 1972 Space Liability Convention and general principles of international law, for damage incurred by way of expense in locating, recovering, removing and testing radioactive debris and for cleaning up affected areas following the crash of Cosmos 954 in January 1978. And Nauru claimed 'appropriate reparation' in respect of the losses it had suffered as a result of Australia's alleged breaches of legal obligations relating to, *inter alia*, changes in the condition of Nauru's territory causing irreparable damage.

Following the Chernobyl accident, no state made a formal claim against the USSR for damage resulting from radioactive fallout, although several reserved their right to do so, including the Federal Republic of Germany, as they subsequently paid large sums of compensation to persons within their jurisdictions affected by the fallout. Their reasons for not bringing claims reflect political and legal uncertainties. According to the Swedish Government:

In terms of treaties there is no international agreement existing, whether bilateral or multilateral, on the basis of which a Swedish claim for damages against the USSR could be conceived. Insofar as customary international law is concerned, principles exist which might be invoked to support a claim against the USSR. The issues involved, however, are complex from the legal as well as the technical point of view and warrant careful consideration. In present circumstances, the Government has felt that priority should be given, in the wake of the Chernobyl accident, to endeavours of another nature.

The position of the United Kingdom Government was complicated by outstanding disputes relating to the problem of acid rain in Scandinavia, contamination of the Irish Sea by nuclear waste from the Windscale/Sellafield nuclear plant, and alleged damage to Australian territory, from the nuclear tests carried out by the United Kingdom in the 1950s. On 21 July 1986, the Secretary of State for Foreign and Commonwealth Affairs in a written answer in the House of Commons said:

> On 10 July we formally reserved our right with the Soviet government to claim compensation on our own behalf on behalf of our citizens for any losses suffered as a consequence of the accident at Chernobyl. The presentation of a formal claim, should we decide to make one, would not take place until the nature and full extent of any damage suffered had been assessed.

Three months later, the Minister of State for Agriculture, Fisheries and Food stated that:

> We have reserved our position on whether the USSR will be required – as it should be if the case is proved – to pay compensation.

More recently, the position has been put thus by the Parliamentary UnderSecretary of State for Scotland:

> The USSR is not a party to any of the international conventions relating to third party liability in nuclear energy, and is therefore not subject to any specific treaty obligation to compensate for damage caused outside its national boundaries.

Following the accident, the IAEA convened various meetings on liability for nuclear damage, which ultimately led to the establishment of the Standing Committee on Nuclear Liability. The IAEA Board of Governors requested the Director General to invite comments from member states on the question of international liability, which elicited responses from thirty-two states representing a broad range of views on the current rules of international law.

Responses of states can be categorised into four types: five states considered that principles or rules of international law existed upon which state liability for nuclear damage could be established; one state saw lacunae; twenty-four states expressed no view either way; and two states considered or suggested that norms of liability could only be based upon treaty. It is therefore difficult to discern firm principles arising from the Chernobyl experience.

In the *Case Concerning the Gabcikovo-Nagymaros Project*, the ICJ confirmed that Hungary was entitled to 'compensation for the damage sustained as a result of the diversion of the Danube', but did not specifically indicate that Hungary was entitled to reparation for purely environmental damages.

As regards the measure of compensation, the Court merely observed that 'the issue of compensation could satisfactorily be resolved in the framework of an overall settlement if each of the Parties were to renounce or cancel all financial claims and counter-claims'. The judgment therefore provides no practical guidance on how to calculate the measure of such environmental damage as the Court appeared willing to take into account in proposing the settlement. The reluctance is consistent with the limited international practice concerning reparation for environmental damage at the inter-state level. The work of the UN Compensation Commission may, however, provide some guidance on the future development of this area.

In April 2002, the Marshall Islands Nuclear Claims Tribunal made an award of US$324,949,311 to the People of Enewatak, as 'just and adequate' settlement for claims of Marshall Islanders in respect of damages to land arising out of the nuclear testing programme carried out by the United States between 1946 and 1958. The award included payments in respect of past and future loss of use (US$199,154,811), restoration to a 'safe and productive state' (US$91,710,000), and hardship as a result of relocation (US$34,084,500). The Tribunal applied standards agreed by the parties, in particular standards applicable under US law. In relation to restoration, the Tribunal accepted the position adopted by the IAEA to the effect that 'policies and criteria for radiation protection of populations outside national borders from releases of radioactive substances should be at least as stringent as those for the population within the country of release', and accordingly applied the current standards applied by the US Environmental Protection Agency.

UN COMPENSATION COMMISSION

The UN Compensation Commission was established in 1991 to provide reparation for the consequences of Iraq's unlawful invasion of Kuwait. The Commission has established criteria for claims in respect of environmental damage and the depletion of natural resources. The language was drawn from a Working Paper submitted by the United States, which drew upon its domestic legislation, including provisions of the Oil Pollution Act of 1990 adopted following the *Exxon Valdez* oil spill in 1989. In paragraph 35 of Decision 7, the Commission's Governing Council decided that payments would be available for direct environmental damage and the depletion of natural resources, including losses or expenses resulting from:

(a) abatement and prevention of environmental damage, including expenses directly relating to fighting oil fires and stemming the flow of oil in coastal and international waters;

(b) reasonable measures already taken to clean and restore the environment or future measures which can be documented as reasonably necessary to clean and restore the environment;

(c) reasonable monitoring and assessment of the environmental damage for the purposes of evaluating and abating the harm and restoring the environment;

(d) reasonable monitoring of public health and performing medical screenings for the purposes of investigation and combating increased health risks as a result of the environmental damage; and

(e) depletion of or damage to natural resources.

In addressing these claims, the Commission is directed to apply Security Council Resolution 687 (1991) and the above criteria and, where necessary, 'other relevant rules of international law'. Claims relating to the environment are referred to as category 'F4' claims, and may only be made by states and international organisations. A first group comprises claims for environmental damage and the depletion of natural resources in the Persian Gulf region, including those resulting from oil-well fires and the discharge of oil into the sea. The Commission has received about thirty such claims, requesting some US$40 billion in compensation. A second group comprises claims for costs incurred by states outside the region in providing assistance to states that were directly affected by the environmental damage, including the alleviation of damage caused by oil-well fires and the prevention and clean-up of pollution. The Commission has received seventeen such claims seeking some US$23 million in compensation. To date, the Panel of Commissioners charged with processing F4 claims has addressed two instalments of claims relating to preliminary matters, namely, compensation of assessment and monitoring activities undertaken or to be undertaken to identify and evaluate damage, relating to air pollution, depletion of water resources, groundwater, cultural heritage, oil pollution, fisheries, wetlands and rangelands and public health. In relation to the first instalment, the claims related to investigations of whether environmental damage or depletion of natural resources had occurred, studies to quantify the loss, and assessment of methodologies to abate or mitigate the damage. All the remaining claims are, in principle, to be addressed by the end of 2003, although this may be an ambitious timetable. The Panel's initial work indicates the basis upon which they may proceed on the outstanding larger claims. It has indicated that conclusive proof of environmental damage was not a prerequisite for monitoring and assessment claims, but has excluded claims which were 'theoretical or speculative' or which had only a tenuous link with damage resulting from Iraq's invasion. In assessing the link, the Panel has had regard to the particular circumstances of each case and four considerations:

1. whether there was a possibility that damage or depletion could have been caused as a result of the invasion;
2. whether the areas or resources in respect of the activity claimed for could have been affected by pollutant released as a result of the invasion;
3. whether there was evidence of environmental damage or risk of such damage as a result of the invasion; and
4. whether there was a reasonable prospect that the activity could produce results that would assist the panel in reviewing claims.

ThePanel has identifiedthedifficulty of ascertaining whether and to whatextent damage which was identified was attributable to Iraq's invasion, and the inadequacy of documented baseline information on the state of the environment or of conditions and trends regarding natural resources prior to the invasion.It has also confirmed that loss or damage occurring outside Kuwait and Iraq was compensable. In respect of the first instalment, the Panel recommended compensation payments of US$243 million (out of US$1,007 million claimed) to Iran, Jordan, Kuwait, Saudi Arabia, Syria and Turkey.

The second 'F4' instalment related to claims incurred for measures to abate and prevent environmental damage, to clean and restore the environment, to monitor and assess environmental damage, and to monitor public health risks alleged to have resulted from the invasion. Iran, Kuwait and Saudi Arabia claimed US$829 million compensation for measures to respond to environmental damage and health risks from mines and other remnants of war. oil lakes, oil spills and pollutants released from oil-well fires. From outside the region, Australia, Canada, Germany, the Netherlands, the UK and the US claimed compensation of US$43 million for expenses incurred in providing assistance to states in the Persian Gulf region to respond to environmental damage or the threat of damage to the environment or health. The Panel has determined that 'environmental damage' is not limited to losses or expenses resulting from the activities and events which are identified in paragraph 35 of Decision 7 (above), but could also cover other direct losses or expenses, such as measures undertaken to prevent or abate harmful impacts of airborne contaminants, provided that they were a direct result of the invasion. The Panel has also decided that Iraq cannot be exonerated from liability because other factors may have contributed to the loss or damage, and that expenses resulting from activities undertaken by military personnel will be compensable if there is evidence to show that the predominant purpose of the activity engaged in was to respond to environmental damage or threats of damage to the environment or health.The Panel has further recommended that compensation should be payable to cover expenses resulting from assistance rendered to countries in the region to respond to damage or threats, provided it does not duplicate compensation paid to any country in the region. In reviewing the second instalment of claims, the Panel was assisted by a multidisciplinary team of independent experts retained by the Commission, having regard to the complexity of the issues and the need to consider scientific, legal, social, commercial and accounting issues. The Panel recommended compensation payments of US$711 million, out of US$872 million claimed.

The claims yet to be processed – relating to paragraphs 35(b) and (e) of Decision 7 – are complex, requiring consideration, among other issues, of the 'reasonableness' of the claim, causality, and the methodology for assessing and valuing environmental damage. To the extent that the Panel applies 'other relevant rules of international law', as directed, the Panel may contribute to the elucidation of the international rules in this emergent – but important – area. Paragraph 35(b) recognises a liability in respect of 'reasonable measures . . . to clean and restore the environment', whereas paragraph 35(e) recognises what appears to be an additional liability in respect of loss relating to 'depletion of or damage to natural resources'. No guidance is provided as to the meaning of the distinction which is drawn between claims in respect of 'environmental damage' and those in respect of 'depletion of natural resources'. In 1995, a UNEP Working Group suggested that the distinction may relate to the idea that a 'natural resource' has, primarily, a commercial value, whereas 'environmental damage' relates to injury caused to components of the environment to which typicallynocommercialvalueattaches. TheUNEPWorkingGroupsuggested that environmental damage could relate to 'impairment of the environment', which may be defined as:

A change which has a measurable adverse impact on the quality of a particular environment of any of its components including its use and non-use values and its ability to support and sustain an acceptable quality of life and a viable ecological balance.

On the definition of 'depletion of natural resources, the UNEP Working Group suggested that it could be desirable to treat depletion of natural resources as referring to the destruction of natural resource assets which occur in their natural state . . . and which have a primarily commercial use or commercial value rather than a noncommercial use or value.

As regards methodology, the Commission will have to decide

whether it will allow claims in accordance with methods of assessment which rely upon the abstract quantification of damage, or whether it will only allow claims in respect of clean-up costs of environmental damage which have been *actually* incurred, or are reasonably likely to be incurred. This was the issue faced by the International Oil Pollution Convention Fund, which decided in 1980 that the assessment of compensation would not be made on the basis of 'an abstract quantification of damage calculated in accordance with theoretical models', an approach which does not allow claims for loss of environmental amenity. The approach of the International Oil Pollution Convention Fund has been reflected in certain other civil liability treaties: the 1993 Lugano Convention allows compensation for impairment of the environment damage, other than loss of profit from such impairment, limited to 'the costs of measures of reinstatement actually undertaken or to be undertaken'.

INTERNATIONAL CRIMES

G. Gilbert, 'The Criminal Responsibility of States', 39 ICLQ 345 (1990); A. Vercher, 'The Use of Criminal Law for the Protection of the Environment in Europe: Council of Europe Resolution 77(28)', 10 *Northwestern Journal of International Law and Business* 442 (1990); R. Pre´vost, 'International Criminal Environmental Law', in G. Goodwin-Gill and S. Talmon (eds.), *The Reality of International Law: Essays in Honour of Ian Brownlie* (1999).

International responsibility may also trigger liability of a criminal nature. The ILC has proposed that certain environmental damage may be so serious in the eyes of the international community that it should be categorised as criminal, or delictual. In Article 19 of its 1980 draft Articles on State Responsibility, the ILC had proposed classifying as an international crime or delict 'a serious breach of an international obligation of essential importance for the safeguarding and preservation of the human environment, such as those prohibiting massive pollution of the atmosphere or of the seas'. However, the Articles on State Responsibility adopted in 2001 eliminated Article 19, having regard to the fact that the responsibility with which it was concerned was that of a state, and not of individuals. The provisions which were adopted – Articles 40 and 41 on serious breaches – identify the legal consequences for violations of peremptory norms of general international law, but do not state exhaustively what those norms are. Massive pollution and other environmental catastrophes are not referred to as examples of serious breaches in the Articles or in the commentary on the Articles, although the commentary does not purport to be exhaustive.It is plain also that Articles 40 and 41 were intended to be open-ended, so as not to preclude the development of rules detailing the consequences of serious breaches.

Other ILC work has maintained a reference to environmental crimes, although in the context of individual (as opposed to statal) criminality. The ILC's Draft Code of Crimes Against the Peace and Security of Mankind, adopted on second reading in 1996, identifies widespread environmental damage as a crime against the peace and security of mankind. By draft Article 20(g) (formerly Article 22), an individual who employs methods or means of warfare 'which are intended or may be expected to cause widespread, long-term and severe damage to the natural environment' would be liable to be guilty of an exceptionally serious war crime. The standard applicable to the level of environmental damage is taken from the 1977 ENMOD Convention and Protocol I Additional to the 1949 Geneva Conventions. The draft Articles as adopted exclude draft Article 26 (from the first draft), which was stated to apply in times of peace as well as during armed conflict, and which provided that an individual who 'wilfully causes or orders the causing of widespread, long-term and severe damage to the natural environment' would also be guilty of a crime.

The ILC's work informed the drafting of the Statute of the International Criminal Court (ICC Statute), which defines as a war crime an intentional attack with the knowledge that it will cause 'widespread, long-term and severe damage to the natural environment which would be clearly excessive in relation to the concrete and direct overall military advantage anticipated'. It remains to be seen whether the ICC Statute will be interpreted to include environmental crimes in relation to acts of genocide or crimes against humanity, as has been suggested.

It should also be noted that in 1998 the Council of Europe adopted a Convention on the Protection of the Environment Through Criminal Law, requiring parties to criminalise under their domestic law intentional (Article 2) or grossly negligent (Article 3) acts falling within certain categories which cause substantial environmental damage. The Convention identifies certain categories of environmentally damaging acts as being especially serious, and other acts in respect of which sanctions or other measures may be appropri-ate. The Convention identifies as sanctions imprisonment, fines and reinstatement of the environment, and allows parties to establish criminal liability for corporations.

Treaties

The liability of states for environmental damage in relation to particular activities or regions is addressed by a small number of treaties. These establish rules of state liability, or provide a basis for the development of such rules on state liability, or deny that the treaty contains any such rule on liability.

SPACE LIABILITY CONVENTION

R. E. Alexander, 'Measuring Damages under the Convention on International Liability for Damage Caused by Space Objects', 6 *Journal of Space Law* 151 (1978); C. Q.

Christol, 'International Liability for Damage Caused by Space Objects', 74 AJIL 346 (1980); B. Schwartz and N. L. Berlin, 'After the Fall: An Analysis of Canadian Legal Claims for Damage Caused by Cosmos 954', 27 *McGill Law Journal* 676 (1982).

The Convention onInternational Liability forDamage Caused by Space Objects (1972 Space Liability Convention) is one of the few treaties to establish a clear rule of state liability. Subject to the exceptions set out in Articles VI and VII, a state which launches a space object is 'absolutely liable to pay compensation for damage caused by its space object on the surface of the earth or to aircraft in flight'. 'Damage' is defined as 'loss of life, personal injury or other impairment of health; or loss of or damage to property of states or of persons, natural or judicial, or property of international intergovernmental organisations'.Although the definition does not refer to 'environmental' harm, it can be interpreted to allow compensation claims for the 'property of states' which are environmental assets or other natural resources:

Compensation is to be determined in accordance with international law and the principles of justice and equity, in order to provide such reparation in respect of the damage as will restore the person, natural or judicial, state or international organisation on whose behalf the claim is presented to the condition which would have existed if the damage had not occurred.

A party will be liable for damage other than on the surface of the earth to another space object or persons or property on board only if the damage is due to fault. In some situations, states may be jointly and severally liable, notably where damage is caused on the surface of a third state as a result of damage by one space object to another.

The only claim under the 1972 Convention was presented by Canada in 1979 to the former USSR for damage caused by the crash of Cosmos 954, a nuclear-powered satellite which disintegrated over Canada. Canadian authorities took steps to locate, recover, remove and test the radioactive debris and to clean up the affected areas of the Northwest Territories and the Provinces of Alberta and Saskatchewan, claiming some C$6 million from the USSR. The Canadian claim was based on relevant international agreements (the 1972 Convention and Article VII of the 1967 Outer Space Treaty) and general principles of international law. Canada claimed that the deposit and presence of hazardous radioactive debris over large areas of Canadian territory rendering part of it unfit for use constituted damage to property within the meaning of the 1972 Convention.

Canada also claimed the USSR had failed to minimise the effects by providing timely and complete answers to its questions, and under general principles of international law the USSR was bound to prevent and reduce harmful consequences and mitigate damage. The claim covered the costs of restoring Canadian territory, to the extent possible, to the condition which would have existed if the intrusion had not occurred. In calculating the costs, Canada applied 'the relevant criteria established by general principles of international law and has limited the costs included in the claim to those costs that are reasonable, proximately caused by the intrusion of the satellite and deposit of debris and capable of being calculated with a reasonable degree of certainty'.

Canada also claimed under Article VII of the 1967 Outer Space Treaty that the USSR must compensate in accordance with international law for the consequences of the intrusion of the satellite into Canadian air space and the deposit on Canadian territory of hazardous radioactive debris. Finally, Canada claimed under general principles of international law that the violation of its sovereignty was established by 'the mere fact of the trespass of the satellite, the harmful consequences of this intrusion, being the damage caused by the presence of hazardous radioactive debris and the interference with the sovereign right of Canada to determine the acts that will be performed on its territory'.This violation gave rise to an obligation to pay compensation and was based on a standard of absolute liability for space activities, which applied to activities in common having a high degree of risk and had been accepted as a general principle of international law.

The measure of compensation under this head was the same as that applied under the 1972 Convention. Canada additionally reserved its rights to present additional claims for compensation for damage not yet identified, for the costs incurred in establishing a Compensation Commission under the 1972 Convention, and for interest.

The matter was settled in 1981 when the USSR agreed to pay C$3 million in full and final compensation, and Canada agreed to accept such payment in full and final settlement of its claim. Although the settlement agreement was silent as to the basis of the settlement, the reference in Article II of the agreement to Canada's claim allows a conclusion that the settlement was agreed on the basis of all the legal arguments proposed by Canada.

LRTAP CONVENTION

The 1979 LRTAP Convention is of interest mainly because of a footnote entered inrelationtoArticle 8,which commits partiesto exchangeavailableinformation on, *inter alia*, the extent of the damage which physico-chemical and biological data indicate can be attributed to long-range transboundary air pollution. The footnote provides that the Convention 'does not contain a rule on state liability as to damage', and reflects concern over inadvertently entering into an international agreement which may subsequently be used to establish their liability for damage. The footnote is neutral in its effect and does not prevent the application of general rules of international law concerning state liability for damage resulting from the breach of the terms of the 1979 LRTAP Convention itself.

UNCLOS

B. Kwiatkowska-Czechowksa, 'States' Responsibility for Pollution Damage Resulting from the Exploration for and Exploitation of Sea-Bed Mineral Resources', 10 *Polish Yearbook of International Law* 157 (1980); B. D. Smith, *State Responsibility and the Marine Environment* (1988); G. Kasoulides, 'State Responsibility and Assessment of Liability for Damage Resulting from Dumping Operations', 26 *San Diego Law Review* 497 (1989).

UNCLOS contains two rules on state liability for damage. Under Article 139, which applies to the 'Area' (i.e. the seabed and ocean floor and subsoil beyond the limits of national jurisdiction), states parties and international organisations have the responsibility to ensure that activities in the Area carried out by them, or by their nationals or by those effectively controlled by them or their nationals, comply with the UNCLOS rules on the Area. Moreover:

Without prejudice to the rules of international law and Annex III, Article 22, damage caused by the failure of a State Party or international organization to carry out its responsibilities under this Part shall entail liability; State Parties or international organizations acting together shall bear joint and several liability.

A state party may argue, as a defence, that it has taken all necessary and appropriate measures to secure effective compliance under the relevant provisions of UNCLOS. State parties are also required to take appropriate measures to ensure that international organisations of which they are members implement their responsibilities under Article 139.

The second provision is Article 235, according to which states are themselves responsible for the fulfilment of their international obligations concerning the protection and preservation of the marine environment. They shall be liable in accordance with international law.

Article 235 incorporates existing rules of state liability into the Convention and does not create a new rule of liability for damage to the marine environment. UNCLOS does not define 'damage' to the marine environment and, with the exception of the provision for the measure of damage in relation to the liability of contractors or the enterprise, does not establish a measure of compensation. Thedefinitionof marine 'pollution' in Article 1(4) provides someguidance as to the standard of damage which might be applied: 'deleterious effects' envisaged include harm to living resources and marine life, hazards to human health, hindrance to marine activities, impairment of water quality, and reduction of amenities.

CRAMRA

H. C. Burmester, 'Liability for Damage from Antarctic Mineral Resource Activities', 29 *Virginia Journal of International Law* 621 (1989); M. Poole, 'Liability for Environmental Damage in Antarctica', 10 *Journal of Environmental and Natural Resources Law* 246 (1992).

Under the 1988 CRAMRA, a sponsoring state will be liable, in accordance with international law, if damage under Article 8(2) of the Convention would not have occurred or continued if it had 'carried out its obligations under [the] Convention' with respect to the operator. Although liability will be limited to that not satisfied by the operator or otherwise, this provision establishes potentially unlimited state liability for environmental damage.

CLIMATE CHANGE CONVENTION

The 1992 Climate Change Convention does not contain a rule on the consequences of activities by states which harm the environment, although during the negotiations some states wanted to include a provision that the Convention did not prejudice the rules of international law concerning state responsibility and liability. The Climate Change Convention defines 'adverse effects of climate change', and under Article 4(4) requires developed country parties listed in Annex II and the EC to 'assist the developing countries parties that are particularly vulnerable to the adverse effects of climate change in meeting costs of adaptation to those adverse effects'. While this novel provision is not a formal expression of liability under the principles of state responsibility, it reflects an admission of responsibility with financial consequences.

The work of the ILC

R. Quentin Baxter, ' "Schematic Outline" on International Liability for Injurious Consequences Arising out of Acts Not Prohibited by International Law, *Yearbook of the International Law*

Commission (1982), II/1, 51–64; J. Barboza, 'Preliminary Report on International Liability for Injurious Consequences Arising out of Acts Not Prohibited by International Law', UN Doc. A/CN.4/394 (1985); D. B. Magraw, 'Transboundary Harm: The International Law Commission's Study of International Liability', 80 AJIL 305 (1986); S. C. McCaffrey, 'The Work of the International Law Commission Relating to Transfrontier Environmental Harm', 20 NYUJILP 608 (1988); A.Boyle, 'State Responsibility and International Liability for Injurious Consequences of Acts Not Prohibited by International Law: A Necessary Distinction?', 39 ICLQ 1 (1990); C. Tomuschat, 'International Liability for Injurious Consequences Arising Out of Acts Not Prohibited by International Law: The Work of the ILC', in F. Francioni and T. Scovazzi (eds.), *International Responsibility for Environmental Harm* (1991); J. Barboza, 'International Liability for the Injurious Consequences of Acts Not Prohibited by International Law and Protection of the Environment', 247 RdC 295 (1994-III).

Apart from its now completed work on state responsibility, the ILC began working in the late 1970s on the issue of the liability of states for acts not prohibited by international law, and in 1990 prepared a first set of draft Articles.The draft Articles remain incomplete, and somewhat controversial. They were intended to supplement the rules on state responsibility and to establish principles governing state and civil liability in respect of transboundary harm which arises from activities which are not unlawful *per se*. In 1992, the ILC divided the topic of international liability into prevention and remedial measures and decided to focus initially on developing draft Articles on prevention. In 2001, the Drafting Committee of the ILC adopted, upon second reading, final draft Articles on the Prevention of Transboundary Harm from Hazardous Activities, completing its work on that part of the topic. This part does not address liability and reparation, as earlier drafts had done, although some states expressed the view that liability and reparation were closely related to prevention and should be considered jointly. The ILC has decided, nevertheless, to develop the topics separately. In 2002, the ILC returned to its work on the related topic of liability. Initial consideration of the topic addressed its scope and the roles of the operator and the state in the allocation of loss. Other topics identified for future consideration include: inter-state or intra-state mechanisms for the consolidation of claims; issues arising out of the international representation of the operator; the processes for assessment, quantification and settlement of claims; access to the relevant forums; and the nature of available remedies.

The direction to be taken by the ILC remains unclear, so its earlier 1990 draft Articles may well turn out to be of historic interest only. Nevertheless, they repay consideration since they indicate an authoritative basis upon which to reflect upon some of the issues addressed in this chapter. The draft Articles were intended to establish basic principles applicable to the activities carried out in the territory of a state, or in other places under its jurisdiction, or under its control, the physical consequences of which cause, or create a risk of causing, transboundary harm throughout the process. They envisaged five principles to govern such activities. The first principle, reflecting elements of Principle 21 of the Stockholm Declaration, proposed that the sovereign freedom of states to carry out or permit human activities 'must be compatible with the protection of the rights emanating from the sovereignty of other states'. The second principle required states to co-operate in good faith and to 'take appropriate measures to prevent or minimise the risk of transboundary harm or, where necessary, to contain or minimise the harmful transboundary effects of such activities' by the 'best practicable, available means'. The third principle related to reparation, requiring a state of origin to make reparation for appreciable harm caused by activities following negotiation between states and guided by the criteria set out in the draft Articles. Such reparation should restore the balance of interests affected by the harm. Finally, a principle of non-discrimination would require state parties to 'treat the effects of an activity that arise in the territory or under the jurisdiction or control of another state in the same way as effects arising in their own territory'.

Chapter III of the ILC's 1990 draft Articles proposes procedural rules for the prevention of transboundary harm, including provisions on assessment, notification and information (including provision for industrial and other confidentiality) and consultations. To assist in achieving an equitable balance of interests, draft Article 17 identified factors to be taken into account in negotiations or consultations. Although not binding, they reflect one considered approach to the identification and application of principles of equity in environmental matters, and provide a point of reference for courts or tribunals faced with a balancing exercise. That said, they remained in draft form only.

Chapter IV of the ILC's 1990 draft Articles addresses the issue of liability if transboundary harm arises. Bearing in mind that the harm must, in principle, be fully compensated, concerned states would be required to negotiate to determine the legal consequences of the harm. The draft Articles proposed that an affected state may agree a reduction in payments for which the state of origin is liable if it appears equitable for certain costs to be shared. Under draft Article 24, a distinction was to be drawn between different harms. With regard to environmental harm, the state of origin would be required to 'bear the costs of any reasonable operation to restore, as far as possible, the conditions that existed prior to the occurrence of the harm' or, if that proved impossible, to reach agreement on monetary or other compensation for the deterioration suffered. Harm to persons or property as a consequence of environmental harm would also be compensated. The draft Articles do not settle on the consequences if there was more than one state of origin: two options considered were joint and several liability, or liability in proportion to the harm caused by each state. The draft Articles also envisage certain exceptions to liability, a limitation period for the bringing of claims, and the exclusion of the exhaustion of local remedies rule.

Chapter Vof theILC's1990draftArticles envisagescivil claims being brought in the national courts of the state of origin as an alternative to inter-state claims for the same harm, and to provide access to affected states, individuals or legal entities. Individuals or states would be able to institute proceedings in the courts of the affected state or the state of origin. The draft Articles propose the non-discriminatory application of national law, the recognition of judgments, and a limitation on state immunity, except in respect of enforcement measures. It remains to be seen whether, and if so to what extent, the ILC will return to these approaches as it reconsiders the subject in 2003 and beyond.

CIVIL LIABILITY FOR ENVIRONMENTAL DAMAGE UNDER INTERNATIONAL LAW

S. C. McCaffrey, 'Private Remedies for Transfrontier Pollution Damage in Canada and the United States: A Comparative Survey',

15 *University of Western Ontario Law Review* 35 (1981); S. E. Gaines, 'International Principles for Transnational Environmental Liability: Can Developments in Municipal Law Help Break the Impasse?', 30 *Harvard International Law Journal* 311 (1989); Hague Conference on Private International Law, *Note on the Law Applicable to Civil Liability for Environmental Damage* (1992); G. Betlem, *Civil Liability for Transfrontier Pollution* (1993); C. Von Bar, 'Environmental Damage in Private International Law', 268 RdC 291 (1997); E. Reid, 'Liability for Dangerous Activities: A Comparative Analysis', 48 ICLQ 731 (1999).

A growing number of treaties establish rules on civil liability for environmental or related damage, although several are not yet in force, and some will probably never enter into force. This suggests that the willingness of states to establish and apply principles of civil liability turns on the nature of the activity to be regulated, and the content of the rules agreed upon. In broad terms, there appears to be an inverse relationship between the scope of application of the rules – in terms of the activity targeted and the potential financial consequences proposed – and the prospects that they will enter into force. Generally, the civil liability regimes have been developed in relation to specific activities which are considered to be ultra-hazardous, and rules have been in force for some time for damage caused by nuclear activities and as a result of oil spills. International rules have also been adopted for damage caused by waste (including its international trade) and for environmental damage resulting from certain dangerous activities. The current trend – not altogether successful – has been towards general rules of civil liability for damage arising from unspecified activities: the Council of Europe has recently adopted a convention which takes this approach, and rules which would be of relatively generalised application to hazardous activities are being considered by the EC and the ECE.

Typically, the civil liability regimes follow a similar approach, establishing rules which:

1. define the activities or substances covered;
2. define the damage (to persons, property and the environment);
3. channel liability;
4. establish a standard of care (usually strict liability);

5. provide for liability amounts;
6. allow exonerations;
7. require the maintenance of adequate insurance or other financial security;
8. identify a court or tribunal to receive the claims; and
9. provide for the recognition and enforcement of judgments.

Nuclear installations

M. J. L. Hardy, 'Nuclear Liability: The General Principlesof Law and Further Proposals', 36 BYIL 223 (1960); W. Berman and L. M. Hyderman, 'A Convention on Third Party Liability for Damage from Nuclear Incidents', 55 AJIL 966 (1969); OECD, *Nuclear Third Party Liability: Nuclear Legislation* (1976); L. A. Malone, 'The Chernobyl Accident: A Case Study in International Law Regulating State Responsibility for Transboundary Nuclear Pollution', 12 *Columbia Journal of Environmental Law* 203 (1987); P. Sands, *International Law of Liability for Nuclear Damage* (1990); O. Von Busekist, 'A Bridge Between Two Conventions on Civil Liability for Nuclear Damage: The Joint Protocol Relating to the Application of the Vienna Convention and the Paris Convention', 43 *Nuclear Law Bulletin* 10 (1990); L. de La Fayette, 'Nuclear Liability Revisited', 1 RECIEL 443 (1992).

Two conventions specifically regulate civil liability for risks from the peaceful use of nuclear energy: the 1960 Paris OECD Convention on Third Party Liability in the Field of Nuclear Energy (1960 Paris Convention); and the 1963 IAEA Vienna Convention on Civil Liability for Nuclear Damage (1963 Vienna

Convention). Other agreements have been concluded in respect of damage caused by nuclear ships. The Paris and Vienna Conventions generally follow the same approach, although the latter is potentially of global application.

Both agreements are now obsolete, and in 1997 a Protocol amending the 1963 Vienna Convention was adopted, together with a new Convention on Supplementary Compensation (1997 Supplementary Compensation Convention). Compared to oil spill regimes, the recent 'improvements' are somewhat marginal, and it is likely that these instruments would be overwhelmed and inadequate in the event of a major nuclear accident.

1960 PARIS CONVENTION

The purpose of the Paris Convention is to harmonise national legislation with regard to third party liability and insurance against nuclear risks and establish a regime of minimum standards for liability and compensation in the event of a nuclear incident, as defined in Article 1(a)(i). The Paris Convention generally applies only to nuclear incidents occurring, and damage suffered, in the territory of contracting parties. A party in whose territory the nuclear installation of the operator liable is situated is free to provide otherwise in its national legislation, but the Convention is silentasto damage in areas beyond national jurisdiction.

The operator of the nuclear installation, whether a private entity or the state, is strictly liable for injury to or loss of life of any person and damage to or loss of property; no provision is made for liability in respect of environmental damage. Liability generally extends to damage caused by incidents outside the installation during carriage to another installation or to other persons.This applies also to incidents involving nuclear substances in the course of carriage to or from that installation.

The operator's liability may be established by proving a causal connection between the damage and the nuclear incident; proof of fault on the part of the operator is not required, although the rule does not establish 'absolute' liability since exceptions to the operator's liability are provided by Articles 4 and 9. Unless a longer period is provided by national legislation, claims must be brought within ten years from the date of the nuclear incident. Jurisdiction over actions will generally lie with the courts of the party in whose territory the nuclear incident occurred, and a state may not, except in respect of measures of execution, invoke any jurisdictional immunities. Judgments are enforceable in the territory of any party, and the Convention is to be applied without discrimination as to nationality, domicile or residence.

The operator's maximum liability for damage caused by a nuclear incident is fifteen million European Monetary Agreement units of account (approximately US$15 million), although any party may establish a greater or lesser amount, but not less than five million units of account. Operators are required to maintain insurance or other financial security.

Recognising that in many cases the damage suffered might

exceed the operator's liability, most parties have ratified the Brussels Supplementary Convention of 1963, which increases the total amount of compensation available to 120 million units of account per incident. Under the 1963 Supplementary Convention, the operator's liability is unchanged, but the party in whose territory the installation is situated is required to provide additional compensation of up to seventy million units of account. Should the damage exceed this amount, further compensation up to 120 million units of account is to be paid jointly by the parties to the 1963 Supplementary Convention according to a formula reflecting each party's gross national product and the thermal power of reactors situated in its territory. In 1982, further Protocols to the Paris Convention and the Brussels Supplementary Convention were adopted, which changed the unit of compensation to the 'special drawing rights' (SDR) of the IMF and increased the compensation payable by a party and by parties jointly to 175 million SDR and 300 million SDR respectively.

1963 VIENNA CONVENTION

The provisions of the 1963 Vienna Convention, which are not to be construed as 'affecting the rights, if any, of a contracting party under the general rules of public international law in respect of nuclear damage', are generally to the same effect as those of the Paris Convention. The operator is liable for 'nuclear damage', which is defined as loss of life, personal injury or damage to property, upon proof that such damage was caused by a nuclear incident in the installation or, with certain limitations, in the course of carriage to or from the installation. The Vienna Convention does not specifically provide for liability for environmental damage, although it allows the law of the competent court to provide for other damage. Liability is stated to be absolute, although provision is made for certain defences and exceptions. Generally, actions must be brought within ten years from the date of the nuclear incident, and jurisdiction over actions lies only with the courts of the party within whose territory the nuclear incident occurred. If an action is brought against a state it may not, except in respect of measures of execution, invoke anyjurisdictional immunities. Final judgments which are recognised are enforceable in the territory of any party. The Vienna Convention allows the installation state to limit the operator's liability, but in no event may it be limited to less than US$5 million for any nuclear incident. Operators must maintain insurance or other financial security; however, if the security is inadequate to satisfy claims, Article VII provides that the installation state is required to meet any deficiencies up to the limit, if any, of the operator's liability as established under Article V In contrast to the position under the 1963 Supplementary Convention, no provision is made for further compensation beyond this limit by either the installation state or the parties jointly.

The Chernobyl accident highlighted the inadequacies of the liability regime established by the Paris and Vienna Conventions. The accident on 26 April 1986 released large amounts of radioactivity and led to increased levels of radiation over an extensive area. In the former USSR, more than 100,000 people were evacuated from a radius of twenty miles around the plant within thirty-six hours, and thirty-one people died as a direct result within a few weeks. Within six months of the accident, the IAEA had sponsored two new international conventions on emergency notification and assistance, and the issue of nuclear liability returned to the international agenda. The Board of Governors of the IAEA, having considered a background paper by the IAEA secretariat on the question of international liability for nuclear damage, asked the secretariat to 'consider whether it was necessary to devise a new instrument on state liability for nuclear damage . . . full account being taken of the work of the [ILC]'. The secretariat concluded that 'there seems to be no doctrinal obstacle to the elaboration of special rules intended to regulate international liability for nuclear damage', the rules of which might result from the work of the ILC, and suggested that a new instrument could complement the existing civil law conventions on nuclear liability . . . in those areas where their regimes are incomplete because of legal lacunae (claimsbetween states, damageto the environment) andit couldprovide the necessary framework for possibly combining international liability aspects and the issues already covered by the Vienna and Paris Conventions into a comprehensive nuclear liability regime, giving the parties to either of these instruments the option of providing remedies in accordance with appropriate procedures to be embodied within the framework.

In 1989, the IAEA established a Standing Committee on

Nuclear Liability to revise the 1963 Vienna Convention, which resulted in the adoption of the 1997 Protocol to the 1963 Vienna Convention, and the 1997 Convention on Supplementary Compensation. The slow progress of the Standing Committee's work reflected political and economic sensitivities, and illustrated the difficulties in developing liability rules in other areas. A number of important nuclear power states, including France, the United Kingdom and the United States, strongly opposed rules of state liability in the amendments.

Controversial issues in the negotiations included the extension of the 1963 Vienna Convention to military installations, its application to damage in areas outside the territory of parties (including areas beyond national jurisdiction), and liability for environmental damage. Two other difficult issues concerned the extent to which the limits on the operator's liability should be increased, and the differences between states supporting full compensation for the victim and restoration of the environment, and states wishing to limit liability to protect nuclear industries from insurance and other costs. Underlying the debate was concern that increases in the operator's maximum liability to adequately cover a Chernobyl-type accident would make the insurance of nuclear plants difficult (if not impossible) in many countries and could limit the further development of nuclear power. On the other hand, it was clear that any limitation on liability amounted to an interference with the application of the polluter-pays principle and a *de facto* subsidy to the nuclear industry.

Another issue which caused difficulty at the IAEA Standing Committee was the question of whether to establish an international claims tribunal to handle claims which might follow a major nuclear incident. Supporters of the original 1963 system, which requires all claims to be channelled to the courts (or a court) of the state in which the accident occurred, argued that this was the only way to achieve a uniform interpretation of the rules and an equitable disbursement of the funds in the context of the limited sums available. Opponents pointed out that it was unrealistic to expect individuals to file claims in a court located several thousand miles away and that no national court could cope with the deluge of claims which would follow a major accident. They also pointed out that the original system provided no incentive for countries such as Ireland and Luxembourg to join the conventions when their citizens could benefit from rights provided under the conventional rules of private international law, allowing them to choose their jurisdiction. In the end, the proponents of the original arrangements prevailed.

When it enters into force, the 1997 Protocol will introduce several amendments for its parties. As to the definition of 'nuclear damage', the Protocol specifies with greater particularity the types of damage which the laws of the competent court may treat as giving rise to liability, including economic loss, the costs of measures of reinstatement of impaired environment (unless insignificant), the costs of preventive measures, and loss of income deriving from an economic interest in any use or enjoyment of the environment (as a result of a significant impairment of that environment). It is important to note, however, that the amended Convention will not require environmental damage to be compensated: only loss of life or personal injury or damage to property must be compensated. Among the other clarifications is provision to the effect that nuclear installations used for 'non-peaceful purposes' are excluded from the Convention, and that the Convention applies 'to nuclear damage suffered anywhere', subject to the right of a party to exclude damage suffered in the territory of a non-party or in any maritime zones established by a non-party in accordance with international law (provided these non-parties also possess nuclear installations within their territory and maritime zones but do not provide reciprocal benefits). The ability of a party to limit the liability of an operator is amended to establish a floor of not less than 300 million SDRs, with consequential changes to the provisions on financial security.Prescription periods are amended to a minor extent. The exclusive jurisdiction of the courts of the party in whose territory the nuclear incident occurred remains, but is extended to encompass damage occurring in the exclusive economic zone. States will be able to bring an action (in the party's courts having jurisdiction) on behalf of persons who have suffered damage, and the Protocol introduces a dispute settlement clause into the Convention.These are modest amendments which do not modify the basic approach of the 1963 Convention or address the fundamental criticisms which have been levelled towards it.

Together with the 1997 Protocol there has also been adopted the new 1997 Convention on Supplementary Compensation. This is intended to supplement the system of compensation which is provided under national law pursuant to the 1960 and 1963 Conventions (and any amendments to them) or which complies with the standards established in the Annex to the 1997 Convention.

Parties are to ensure the availability of 300 million SDRs or other amount as permitted and notified and, beyond that amount, additional public funds as required pursuant to a formula established under Article IV of the Convention.The Convention provides detailed rules on the organisation of supplementary funding once it appears that damage caused by an incident exceeds the amount available under Article III(1)(a), as well as rules on jurisdiction and applicable law, generally following the approach in the 1960 and 1963 Conventions.

1988 JOINT PROTOCOL

In 1988, a Joint Protocol Relating to the Application of the Vienna Convention and the Paris Convention linked the operative parts of the Paris and Vienna Conventions by providing that the operator of a nuclear installation in the territory of a party to either the Paris or Vienna Convention will be liable under that Convention for nuclear damage suffered in the territory of a state which is a party to the other Convention and the Protocol. The Joint Protocol provides for the exclusive application of each Convention and sets forth choice-of-law rules.

Civil liability for damage caused by oil pollution is principally governed by two well-developed and well-applied international instruments adopted under the auspices of the IMO: the Brussels International Convention on Civil Liability for Oil Pollution Damage (1992 CLC) and the Brussels International Convention on the Establishment of an International Fund for Compensation of Oil Pollution Damage (1992 Oil Fund Convention), together with a Convention on Civil Liability for Bunker Oil Pollution Damage, adopted in 2001. In the 1970s, three private arrangements were set up to increase the amounts of funding available, but two – TOVALOP and CRISTAL – were wound up in 1997, after the entry into force of the 1992 IMO Protocols.

1992 CIVIL LIABILITY CONVENTION

The original 1969 CLC was adopted following the accident involving the Liberian-registered *Torrey Canyon*, which ran aground in the Atlantic off the south-west coast of Britain on 18 March 1967 while carrying nearly 120,000 tons of crude oil. The escape of oil caused widespread damage to the British coastline and to marine life, and eventually polluted the coast of France.

The accident led to the Brussels Conference of 1969 and the adoption of two new conventions: the 1969 Intervention Convention and the 1969 CLC. The latter has been the subject of three amending Protocols, most recently by the 1992 Liability Protocol. With the entry into force of the 1992 Protocol, the 1969 CLC is now known as the International Convention on Civil Liability for Oil Pollution Damage 1992 (1992 CLC).

The 1992 CLC establishes the liability of the owner of a ship for pollution damage caused by oil escaping from the ship as a result of an incident on the territory of a party (including its territorial sea), and covers preventive measures to minimise such damage. Under the 1969 CLC, 'pollution damage' was defined as: loss or damage caused outside the ship carrying oil by contamination resulting from the escape or discharge of oil from the ship, wherever such escape or discharge may occur, and includes the cost of preventive measures and further loss or damage caused by preventive measures.

The view that this includes environmental damage is supported by the amended text of the 1992 CLC, which defines pollution damage as:

(a) loss or damage caused outside the ship by contamination, resulting from the escape or discharge of oil from the ship, wherever such escape or discharge may occur, provided that compensation for impairment of the environment other than loss of profit from such impairment shall be limited to costs of reasonable measures of reinstatement actually undertaken or to be undertaken;

(b) the costs of preventative measures and further loss or damage caused by preventative measures.

This current definition, which develops the 1969 definition, implies that the latter is intended to include compensation for impairment of the environment. However, in order for a claim for environmental damage to be brought, the 1992 definition requires measures taken to be 'reasonable' and to have actually been undertaken or to be undertaken. The 1992 CLC establishes joint and several liability for damage which is not 'reasonably separable', and allows a limited number of exceptions, including war and hostilities, intentional acts, governmental negligence and contributory negligence, and it extinguishes all other claims for compensation. Under the original 1969 CLC, the owner could limit liability to 2,000 francs for each ton of the ship's net tonnage with an overall limit on liability of 210 million francs, but may not avail itself of the limit if the incident is the result of the owner's 'actual fault or privity'. The permitted limits were increased by the 1992 Protocol to 3 million SDRs for ships not exceeding 5,000 units of tonnage, and 420 SDRs for each additional unit of tonnage to a maximum of 59.7 million SDRs. The owner must maintain insurance or other financial security to cover its liability and, to limit its liability, establish a fund for the total sum of liability with the court in which action is brought. Under the 1992 CLC, claims may be brought before the courts of any party or parties in which the pollution damage has occurred or the preventive measures have been taken, and judgments are generally recognisable and enforceable in the courts of all parties. The court in which a fund is established is exclusively competent to apportion and distribute the fund.

The 1992 Protocol makes a number of consequential changes to the 1992 CLC, and establishes a hierarchical relationship between the 1992 Liability Convention and the 1992 Fund Convention by providing for the prior application of the latter.

THE 1992 FUND CONVENTION

The 1992 (originally 1971) Fund Convention was adopted under the auspices of an International Legal Conference on Marine Pollution Damage to provide additional compensation for victims of oil pollution and to transfer some of the economic consequences to the owners of the oil cargo, as well as the shipowner subject to the original 1969 CLC. The original 1971 Convention was amended by three Protocols, most recently by the 1992 Fund Protocol. With the entry into force of the 1992 Protocol, the 1971 Fund Convention is known as the International Convention on the Establishment of an International Fund for Oil Pollution Damage, 1992 (1992 Fund Convention). By May 2002, the 1971 Fund had been involved in the settlement of claims arising out of 107 incidents, and the total compensation paid amounted to

£283 million, and the 1992 Fund had been involved in fifteen incidents and made compensation payments of £61 million.

In general, the 1992 Fund Convention adopts the same definitions as the 1992 CLC. The 1992 Fund Convention, which establishes an International Oil Pollution Compensation Fund (IOPC Fund), has as its objective to provide compensation for pollution damage which is inadequately compensated by the 1992 CLC. The 1971 Convention represented the first time that linkage in an international legal instrument was explicitly made between the extent of a person's liability and compliance with obligations found in other treaties.

To fulfil its objective, the Fund pays compensation to any person suffering pollution damage if that person has been unable to obtain 'full and adequate' compensation under the 1992 CLC because no liability arises under that Convention, or the owner cannot meet obligations under that Convention, or the liability exceeds the limit established by that Convention. The 1992 Fund Convention limits the obligation of the Fund in certain situations, including war, lack of evidence that the damage resulted from an incident involving one or more ships, damage by warships or state operated non-commercial ships, and contributory negligence. Originally, compensation payable under the Fund was limited to 450 million francs per incident, and an aggregate of 450 million francs for pollution damage 'resulting from a natural phenomenon of an exceptional, inevitable and irresistible character'. At its ninth session, the Fund Assembly increased the aggregate amount of compensation payable by the Fund for any one incident to 900 million francs (60 million SDRs) for incidents occurring after 30 November 1987.

The 1976 Protocol amended the ceilings to 30 million SDRs or 450 million monetary units and 60 million SDRs or 900 million monetary units respectively. The 1992 Protocol replaced the entire text of Art. 4(4) of the 1971 Fund Convention with a new provision increasing the maximum liability to 135 million SDRs per incident or for certain natural damage, and to 200 million SDRs for any period when there are three parties to the Convention where the combined relevant quantities of contributing oil received by persons in the territories of those parties equalled or exceeded 600 million tons in the preceding year.

The 1992 Fund Convention limits periods for the bringing of claims, and requires any action against the Fund for compensation to be brought only before a court competent under Article IX of the 1992 CLC. Where an action has been brought before a court against an owner under the 1992 CLC, that court has exclusive competence over any action against the Fund under Article 4 of the 1992 Fund Convention in respect of the same damage. Where that court is in a state which is not a party to the 1992 Fund Convention, the claimant may bring the case before the court where the Fund is headquartered (London) or any court of a party to the 1992 Fund Convention competent under Article IX of the 1992 CLC. The 1992 Fund Convention also sets forth rules concerning the effect of judgments on the Fund, the recognition and enforcement of judgments, and rights of recourse and subrogation.

Annual contributions to the Fund are made, in respect of each party, by any person (including associated persons) who has received a total of more than 150,000 tons of contributing oil in the ports or terminals in the territory of that party contributing oil carried by sea, and contributing oil first received in any installations situated in the territory of that party which has first been carried by sea and discharged in a port or terminal of a non-party. The assessment of each person's annual contribution which may be needed to balance the budget comprises a proportion of the total amount of contributions required by the Fund to fulfil its estimated annual expenditure. The 1992 Protocol's transitional provisions govern contributions and place a limit, for up to five years, on the contribution of any one party to a maximum of 27.5 per cent of the total contributions to the Fund.

The IOPC Fund, which has legal personality under the laws of each party,comprises an Assembly, a Secretariat and an Executive Committee. The Assembly, in which all parties to the Convention are members, has overall responsibility for the administration of the Fund and for the proper execution of the Convention, and its functions include approving the settlement of claims, taking decisions in respect of distributions under Article 4(5) and provisional payments, and electing the Executive Committee. There are fifteen members of the Executive Committee, elected on the basis of equitable geographic distribution, including parties particularly exposed to the risks of oil pollution and having large tanker fleets, and approximately one-half from those parties in whose territory the largest quantities of oil were received. The functions of the Executive Committee include approving the settlement of claims and giving instructions to the Director.

IOPC Fund Resolution No. 3 The IOPC Fund has received numerous claims forenvironmentaldamage, and itspracticemay prove instructiveto the international community as it seeks to define environmental damage in other contexts. It will be recalled that the Fund pays compensation for pollution damage, which means 'loss or damage outside the ship carrying oil by contamination'. The first claim to the Fund, arising out of the grounding of the USSR-registered *Antonio Gramsci* off Ventspils, in the former USSR, on 27 February 1979, raised the question of whether this definition included environmental damage or damage to natural resources, as claimed by the USSR and others. The response of the Fund Assembly is to be found in Resolution No. 3, adopted in 1980, which determined that 'the assessment of compensation to be paid by the IOPC Fund is not to be made on the basis of an abstract quantification of damage calculated in accordance with theoretical models'.

The Patmos claim In 1985, on the basis of Resolution No. 3, the IOPC Fund addressed a £9.2 million claim (later reduced to £2.3 million) by the Italian Government for damage to the marine environment arising out of a spillage from the *Patmos*, a Greek-registered tanker, off the coast of Calabria on 21 March 1985. In the absence of any documentation from the Italian Government indicating the nature of the damage which had been caused or the basis on which the amount claimed had been calculated, the IOPC Fund rejected the claim. The Italian Government took the case to the Italian courts, and in 1986 the Court of First Instance rejected the government's claim for compensation for ecological damage to marine flora and fauna on the grounds that the territorial sea was not crown or patrimonial property of the state but a *res communis omnium* which could not be violated by private parties, and that even if it was the state had not incurred any direct or indirect loss as a result of the oil spill since no disbursements for the cleaning of the coastline had been incurred nor had any loss of profit occurred. In 1989, the Court of Appeal overruled the decision, interpreting the Convention to include as environmental damage 'everything which alters, causes deterioration in or destroys the environment in whole or in part'. The Court of Appeal interpreted the terms of the 1969 CLC by reference to the 1969 Intervention Convention, which defines the threat to 'related interests' justifying intervention as including 'the conservation of living marine resources and of wildlife'. The Court of Appeal went on to hold that: the environment must be considered as a unitary asset, separate from those of which the environment is composed (territory, territorial waters, beaches, fish etc.) and it includes natural resources, health and landscape. The right to the environment belongs to the state, in its capacity as representative of the collectivities. The damage to the environment prejudices immaterial values, which cannot be assessed in monetary terms according to market prices, and consists of the reduced possibility of using the envi-ronment. The damage can be compensated on anequitable basis, which may be established by the Court on the grounds of an opinion of experts . . . The definition of 'pollution damage' as laid down in Article 1(6) is wide enough to include damage to the environment of the kind described above.

The Court of Appeal held that the traditional view of property damage was no longer valid, and that the owner of the *Patmos*, the UK Club(an insurers' group) and the IOPC Fund were liable for the environmental damage claimed by the Italian Government. It appointed three experts to ascertain the existence, if any, of damage to the marine resources resulting from the oil spillage. In their March 1990 report, the experts found that, with the exception of damage to fishing activities which they valued at approximately £465,000, there was a lack of data to evaluate the economic impact on other activities and that a precise assessment of damage to such activities was impossible. The experts also determined that the court was the appropriate body to carry out the evaluation.In December 1993, the Court of Appeal awarded a final judgment of £827,000 for environmental damage. The court decided that the lack of data and inability of the experts to determine a precise damage award for environmental harms were not reasons to refuse compensation. It found that the experts were wrong to calculate damages based only on market prices for fish. Because the environment and its natural resources were worth more to the community, the Court of Appeal determined damages according to principles of equity. The decision itself does not make clear exactly how the judge assessed and calculated the environmental damages beyond the £465,000 previously indicated by the panel of experts.

The Haven case Another case before the Fund indicated the differences of interpretation which may be applied to the concept of 'environmental damage'. On 11 April 1991, the *Haven*, a Cypriot-registered tanker, caught fire and broke apart seven miles from Genoa in Italy and released over 10,000 tonnes of oil, causing damage to the Italian and French coasts and necessitating extensive clean-up operations. The Italian Government submitted a claim for damage to the marine environment, this time in the provisional amount of 100,000 million Italian lire (£47 million), a figure which the Region of Liguria requested should be doubled. One thousand two hundred Italian claimants, the French Government, twenty-two French municipalities and two other public bodies also submitted claims. In the subsequent court proceedings at the Court of First Instance in Genoa, the question arose as to whether claims for damage to the marine environment could be pursued against the shipowners outside the Conventions under the relevant Italian law if such damage was not admissible under the 1969 CLC and the 1971 Fund Convention.

In his report on this matter, the Director of the Fund concluded that the 1969 and 1971 Conventions were designed to provide compensation to victims of pollution damage, that claims which did not relate to such compensation fell outside the scope of the Conventions, and that claims relating to non-quantifiable elements of damage to the environment were of a punitive nature and beyond the scope of the Convention. The Director took the view that the drafters of the 1971 Fund Convention could not have intended that the Fund should pay damages of a punitive character calculated on the basis of the seriousness of the fault of the wrongdoer or the profit earned by the wrongdoer, and that the result of including such damage would be unacceptable. On this basis, the Director concluded that such claims could be pursued outside the Conventions on the basis of national law. In rejecting the Director's analysis during a session of the Executive Committee, the Italian delegation maintained its view that the 1969 and 1971 Conventions did not exclude compensation for environmental damage which was non-quantifiable, that the state had a legal right to compensation for damage to the environment which had irreversible consequences or where the environment could not be reinstated, and that Italian law envisaged the possibility of compensation for damage to the marine environment for quantifiable and non-quantifiable elements. The Director's point of view was supported by France, the United Kingdom, Japan and the observer delegation of the International Group of P&I Clubs (shipping, insurance and freight companies).

On 5 April 1996, the Court of First Instance in Genoa ruled that 'pollution damage' in the 1969CLC and 1971 Fund Convention had awide enough meaning to include natural resource and environmental damage. Because these could not be calculated according to commercial or economic valuations, the court awarded £13 million (40,000 million lire), about one-third of the cleanup cost, on the basis that the clean-up did not repair all the damage caused; the award essentially compensated the unremedied residual damage.

The IOPC Fund appealed, and in response Italy requested that the environmental damages be increased to £284 million (883,435 million lire). On 4 March 1999, the parties (Italy, the shipowner, the UK Mutual Steam Ship Assurance Association and the IOPC Fund) withdrew all legal action from Italian courts and signed an agreement. The shipowner and the UK clubmade an *ex gratia* payment of £9.1 million (25,000 million lire), in addition paying the amount indicated by the Court of First Instance to Italy, without admitting liability beyond the shipowner's limits under the 1969 CLC.

2001 BUNKER OIL CONVENTION

In 2001, the IMO adopted the International Convention on Civil Liability for Bunker Oil Pollution Damage, filling a lacuna left by previous oil pollution conventions, which did not cover liability for fuel spills from ships' bunkers, except for tankers. The 2001 Convention is largely based on the 1992 CLC, which makes shipowners strictly liable for fuel spills, but also allows states to limit liability in accord with national or international regimes, such as the amended 1976 Convention on Limitation of Liability for Maritime Claims.Article 7 of the 2001 Convention requires owners of ships registered in state parties to maintain insurance or other financial security equal to the limitation provided in Article 6. The 2001 Convention relies on the same approach to environmental damage as the 1992 CLC, limiting compensation for environmental damage to 'reasonable measures of reinstatement'.

TOVALOP, CRISTAL AND OPOL

In addition to these international treaty arrangements, shipowners and oil companies have entered into private agreements establishing compensation schemes. These are the 1969 Tanker Owners Voluntary Agreement Concerning Liability for Oil Pollution (TOVALOP), the 1971 Contract Regarding a Supplement to Tanker Liability for Oil Pollution (CRISTAL) and the 1974 Oil Companies Offshore Pollution Liability Agreement (OPOL). TOVALOP and CRISTAL were wound up in 1997, as a result of greater acceptance by states of the IMO civil liability regimes. OPOL is a voluntary agreement that came into effect on 1 May 1975, and originally applied only to offshore oil pollution incidents within the jurisdiction of the UK. All offshore oil operators working on the UK continental shelf are a party to OPOL. However, OPOL has been extended to European Community states, Norway and the Isle of Man. The Agreement provides for a voluntary regime of strict liability, with limitations to liability, for pollution caused by offshore facilities engaging in oil exploration or production from the seabed and its subsoil. In 1996, OPOL was amended to require its operators to accept strict liability for up to US$120 million per pollution incident and US$240 million in aggregate.

Marine environment

Apart from the various marine environment conventions which encourage the development of liability and compensation rules, two civil liability conventions have been adopted. The 1977 Convention on Civil Liability for Oil Pollution Damage Resulting from Exploration for and Exploitation of Seabed Mineral Resources, which has not entered into force, provides for the liability of the operator of an installation under the jurisdiction of a party for pollution damage resulting from an incident occurring beyond the coastal low-water line. Only states with coastlines on the North Sea, the Baltic Sea or northern parts of the Atlantic may become parties. The pollution damage must be suffered in the territory of a party, including the internal waters and territorial sea, or in areas in which the party has sovereign rights over natural resources under international law, as well as in respect of preventive measures wherever taken. The definition of 'pollution damage' as 'loss or damage outside the installation caused by contamination resulting from the escape or discharge of oil from the installation' is sufficiently broad to include environmental damage. The Convention provides for strict liability, joint and several liability, the extinction of other claims against the operator for pollution damage, an entitlement to limit liability, an insurance requirement, and recognition and enforcement of judgments. Liability may not be limited if it is proved that the damage occurred 'as a result of an act or omission by the operator himself, done deliberately with actual knowledge that pollution damage would result', and there will be no liability in respect of abandoned wells where the damage occurred more than five years after abandonment 'under the authority and in accordance with the requirements' of the controlling party. Actions under the Convention are subject to an overall limitation period of four years. By limiting actions to the courts of any party where the damage was suffered or in respect of an area in which 'in accordance with international law, a state has sovereign rights over natural resources', or the courts of the controlling party, the Convention appears to exclude the possibility of environmental claims concerning damage in areas beyond national jurisdiction.

The 1992 Black Sea Convention requires each party to adopt rules and regulations on liability for damage caused by natural or juridical persons to the marine environment of the Black Sea, and to ensure that recourse is available for 'prompt and adequate' compensation or other relief for damage caused by pollution of the marine environment. The object of the rules is to ensure the 'highest degree of deterrence and protection for the Black Sea as a whole', and to that end the parties are committed to co-operating on the development and harmonisation of their laws and procedures relating to liability, assessment and compensation for damage.

Waste General

Liability for damage caused by waste has been an international legal issue since Article X of the 1972 London Convention committed parties to 'develop procedures for the assessment of liability' regarding dumping, in accordance with the principles of international law regarding state responsibility for environmental damage. The 1991 Bamako Convention requires each party to impose strict and unlimited liability, as well as joint and several liability, on hazardous waste generators, as well as committing the parties to develop a Protocol on liability and compensation.

In 1999, pursuant to Article 12 of the 1989 Basel Convention, parties adopted the Protocol on Liability and Compensation for Damage Resulting from Trans-boundary Movements of Hazardous Wastes and Their Disposal. The Protocol includes numerous innovative provisions, and compares favourably with other recently adopted instruments. It is intended to provide a comprehensive regime for liability and for adequate and prompt compensation for damage, defined to include damage to persons and property and loss of income deriving from an economic interest in the environment, costs of measures reinstating the impaired environment, and preventive measures. The Protocol expressly requires any person who is in operational control of the waste to take all reasonable measures to mitigate damage arising from an incident.

The Protocol applies to damage due to an incident occurring during a trans-boundary movement, including illegal traffic and in respect of re-import, 'from the point where the wastes are loaded on the means of transport in an area under the national jurisdiction of the state of export'. Its application is subject to certain other exclusions. It covers all damage suffered in an area under the national jurisdiction of a party, but only damage to persons and property and preventive measures in areas beyond national jurisdiction, and provides particular rules where the state of import, but not the state of export, is a party to the Protocol.

The Protocol provides generally for strict liability, with fault liability where there is a failure to comply with the Convention or damage occurs because of intentional, reckless or negligent acts or omissions. The Protocol does not affect the rights and obligations of parties under general international law.Under a regime of strict liability, the notifying entity is generally liable for damage until the disposer takes possession of the waste, at which point liability shifts to the disposer, with a special rule governing hazardous waste within the meaning of Article 1(1)(b) of the Convention (wastes determined to be hazardous by a party but not included in Annex I to the Convention).Liability is excluded upon proof of damage arising as a result of certain acts, including armed conflict and insurrection, certain natural phenomena, and the wrongful conduct of a third party.

Liability is limited for non-fault-based incidents to amounts determined by domestic law, but there are no liability limits for damage from fault-based incidents. The Protocol sets minimum liability for damage, and liable persons must also have insurance or financial guarantees covering these amounts. Claims may be brought in the courts of the party where the damage was suffered, or where the incident occurred, or where the defendant has his habitual residence or principal place of business, and provision is made for the mutual recognition and enforcement of judgments. Matters not regulated by Protocol are governed by the law of the competent court. Claims under the Protocol are inadmissible unless brought within ten years of the incident and within five years from the date when the claimant knew or ought reasonably to have known of the damage.

EUROPEAN COMMUNITY

The EC has been deliberating the adoption of rules on civil liability for damage caused by waste since 1984. In 1989, the EC Commission first proposed a Directive on civil liability for damage caused by waste, which was amended in 1991, and in 1993 published a first Green Paper on liability for environmental damage. The EC's Fifth Environmental Action Programme committed the EC 'as soon as practicable' to establish a mechanism whereby damage to the environment is restored by the person or body responsible for the damage incurred. On 23 January 2002, the European Commission published a new proposed Directive on environmental liability with the objective of preventing and remedying environmental damage. The proposal was based on principles set out in the Commission's White Paper on environmental liability, published in February 2000, taking into account comments received from member states, and aims to apply an approach of strict liability without financial limits.

The draft Directive is notable, however, for its focused approach, and is distinguishable from existing arrangements in a number of significant respects. First, it is only intended to cover 'environmental damage', meaning damage to biodiversity, water and land, and does not extend to damage to persons and property (which would continue to be governed by national law). Secondly, the Directive would apply only to environmental damage caused by the operation of any of the activities expressly identified in an Annex to the Directive (and to imminent threats of such damage), although biodiversity damage would be covered irrespective of whether the activity causing it was listed in the Annex.Thirdly, the scheme it proposes to establish is centred on the requirement that the member state must, in respect of prevention and remediation, either require the operator to take the necessary measures or itself take such measures.

The proposed Directive includes other distinguishing features. For example, it includes detailed rules on the extent of remediation, with the objective of restoring 'the environment as a whole to its baseline condition'; it encourages – but does not require – operators to have insurance or other forms of financial security to pay for environmental damage; and it provides that persons adversely affected or likely to be adversely affected by environmental damage will be entitled to request the member state to take action under the Directive, with a right of access to a court (or other independent and impartial public body) to review the procedural and substantive legality of the decisions, acts or failures to act of the member state. The draft Directive also contains rules on the allocation of certain costs and limitation periods, and permits member states to maintain or adopt more stringent provisions. It is also notable for the broad range of exceptions proposed: it would not apply to damage regulated by various international agreements, or to damage caused by certain nuclear activity regulated by certain agreements, and would exclude the personal liability of an operator acting in his capacity as an insolvency practitioner. And it would not apply to damage caused by pollution of a widespread, diffuse character, where it is impossible to establish a causal link between the damage and the activities of certain individual operators, or to activities the sole purpose of which is to serve national defence, or to damage caused by:

1. an act of armed conflict, hostilities, civil war or insurrection;
2. a natural phenomenon of exceptional, inevitable and irresistible character;
3. an emission or event allowed in applicable laws and regulations, or in the permit or authorisation issued to the operator;

4. emissions or activities which were not considered harmful according to the state of scientific and technical knowledge at the time when the emission was released or the activity took place.

It remains to be seen whether the approach set forth in this new draft of the Directive will find favour with the member states. In the meantime, in 1991, the European Court of Justice adopted a ruling which may have blurred the distinction between civil and state liability and may have informed the potential development of the EC rules of environmental liability. In *Francovich* v. *Italian Republic*, the ECJ had to decide whether the failure by a member state to implement a Directive which protected the rights of employees in the case of insolvency of their employer gave rise to the liability of the state. Although the case did not relate to the environment, it established principles pertinent to violations of environmental obligations. The Court held that 'it is a principle of Community law that the member states are obliged to pay compensation for harm caused to individuals by breaches of Community law for which they can be held responsible'. The Court considered that the full effectiveness of Community law, and the protection of rights thereunder, would be affected if individuals could not recover compensation when their rights were infringed, and that compensation by a member state was 'particularly indispensable' where 'the full effectiveness of Community rules is subject to prior action on the part of the state and consequently individuals cannot, in the absence of such action, enforce the rights granted to them by Community law before the national courts'. The Court set forth three conditions which had to be satisfied before a violation of EC law by a member state gave rise to liability: first, the result prescribed by the Directive in question should entail the grant of rights to individuals; secondly, it should be possible to identify the content of those rights on the basis of the provisions of the Directive; and, thirdly, there should be a causal link between the breach of the obligation by the state and the damage suffered by the persons affected. These conditions could clearly be fulfilled in the case of a violation of an EC environmental obligation.

The Court went on to hold that in the absence of EC rules it was for the internal legal order of each member state to determine the competent courts and to lay down the procedural rules for legal proceedings intended to safeguard rights which individuals derive from law. However, the Court did rule that national substantive and procedural conditions on compensation could not be 'less favourable than those relating to similar internal claims and may not be so framed as to make it virtually impossible or excessively difficult to obtain compensation'.

The judgment establishes a basis for member states to be liable for damages resulting from their failure to implement environmental Directives which create individual rights, including obligations setting water or air quality standards, or creating participatory rights in environmental impact assessments, or granting rights of access to environmental information. Provided that environmental Directives confer rights for the benefit of individuals, the conditions established by the Court seem capable of opening up a new type of 'state liability' being applied in the civil or administrative courts of the EC or EFTA states. Finally, it should be noted that, since the amendments introduced by the Amsterdam Treaty came into force, in 1999, the ECJ has been empowered to levy fines on member states which do not comply with earlier judgments of the Court. In July 2000, the ECJ applied this provision, Article 228(2), for the first time, ordering Greece to pay a penalty of 20,000 euros for each day of delay in implementing the measures necessary to comply with a 1992 judgment concerning violations of Directive 75/442/EEC (on waste) and 78/319/EEC (on toxic and dangerous waste) which endangered human health and harmed the environment. In setting the amount of the penalty, the Court noted that the failure to comply with 'the obligation resulting from Article 4 of Directive 75/442 could, by the very nature of that obligation, endanger human health directly and harm the environment and must, in the sight of the other obligations, be regarded as particularly serious'.

Transport

Transport issues are addressed by two instruments: the Geneva Convention on Civil Liability for Damage Caused during Carriage of Dangerous Goods by Road, Rail and Inland Navigation Vessels (1989 CRTD); and the 1996 International Convention on Liability and Compensation for Damage in Connection with the Carriage of Hazardous and Noxious Substances by Sea (1996 HNS

Convention). Neither instrument is in force. The 1989 CRTD was adopted under the auspices of the ECE, and provides for the liability of the carrier (the registered owner or person controlling the road vehicle or inland navigation vessel or operator of a railway line) for damage caused during the transport of dangerous goods.

Compensable damage includes loss of life or personal injury, loss of or damage to property, and: loss or damage by contamination to the environment caused by dangerous goods, provided that compensation for impairment of the environment other than for loss of profit caused from such impairment shall be limited to costs of reasonable measures of reinstatement actually undertaken or to be undertaken.

The carrier may limit its liability in case of rail or road transport to 18 million SDRs for claims covering loss of life or personal injury and to 12 million SDRs for other claims, and in the case of inland navigation vessels to 8 million SDRs and 7 million SDRs respectively. Under the CRTD, a victim has a choice of courts in which to bring actions: the courts of the party in which the accident occurred, or the damage or loss occurred, or where preventive measures were taken, or where the carrier has its habitual residence.

The 1996 HNS Convention, adopted under the auspices of the IMO, provides a two-tiered system of liability and compensation similar to the 1992 CLC and 1992 Fund Convention, and uses the same definitions as the 1989 CRTD to determine compensable damage, including environmental damage. The approach of the HNS Convention follows the 1992 CLC. Chapter II establishes a regime of strict liability for shipowners and a list of defences to liability, rules for joint and several liability for damage that is not reasonably separable by shipowner, and compulsory shipowner's insurance. Article 9(1) limits the shipowner's liability to specified amounts; Article 9(2), however, imposes no limit to liability if the shipowner intended to cause damage or acted recklessly with knowledge that damage would result. Chapter III establishes the HNS Fund which, like the 1992 Fund Convention for oil pollution, will compensate any person who suffers damage under Chapter II but is unable to obtain compensation because the shipowner is not liable, the shipowner is incapable of meeting all its financial obligations, or the damages exceed the shipowner's liability under Chapter II.

Antarctic

CRAMRA

The 1988 CRAMRA was the first Antarctic treaty to address liability, although it is now unlikely to enter into force. Of particular note are the provisions concerning liability for environmental damage, and the relationship between the liability of the operator and the operator's sponsoring state. Under Article 8, the operator is under an obligation to take necessary and timely response action if its activities result in, or threaten, damage to the Antarctic environment or its dependent or associated ecosystems. Such action includes prevention, containment, clean-up and removal measures. The operator will be strictly liable for damage to the Antarctic environment or dependent or associated ecosystems (including: payment in the event that there has been no restoration to the *status quo ante*); loss of or impairment to established use; loss of or damage to people and property; and reimbursement of reasonable costs relating to necessary response action to restore the *status quo ante* (including prevention, containment, clean-up and removal). Environmental liability is widely defined.

Where the damage would not have occurred if the sponsoring state had carried out its obligation under the Convention, that state will be liable for the part which remains unsatisfied by the operator. This innovative approach links civil and state liability in a unique way. CRAMRA would allow limited defences to liability, and provides for the elaboration of further rules and procedures on liability in a supplementary Protocol. Guidance is provided on the content of those rules and procedures, which are to be designed to enhance the protection of the Antarctic and discourage commercial activity. The rules and procedures could include provisions for appropriate limits on liability where they can be justified, means and mechanisms to assess and adjudicate claims, and means to provide immediate assistance for response action including where the operator is financially incapable of meeting its obligation in full or there is a defence to liability.

ANTARCTIC ENVIRONMENT PROTOCOL

The 1991 Antarctic Environment Protocol dispensed with CRAMRA's substantive liability rules, and commits the parties to elaborate rules and procedures relating to liability for damage arising from activities taking place in the Antarctic and covered by the Protocol. The rules will have to be consistent with the objectives of the Protocol for the comprehensive protection of the Antarctic environment and dependent and associated ecosystems. In 1998, the group of legal experts, convened under Article 16 of the 1991 Protocol, presented their Final Report to the twenty-second Antarctic Treaty Consultative Meeting (ATCM). Members of the ATCM were unable to reach a consensus on the key issues contained in the group's report, including whether to adopt a comprehensive liability annex or a set of specific liability annexes, whether to compensate irreparable environmental damage, whether to establish an environmental protection fund, and whether to exclude environmental damages resulting from activities found to be acceptable by national authorities after environmental impact assessments. The ATCM member states decided to dissolve the group of legal experts and shift the responsibility for developing an Antarctic liability regime to its Working Group I. By the twenty-fourth ATCM in 2001, the group seemed to be no closer to forming a consensus on the key issues of liability.

General instruments relating to dangerous goods or activities

Council of Europe

The 1993Councilof EuropeConvention on Civil Liability forDamageResulting from Activities Dangerous to the Environment (1993 Lugano Convention)aims to provide adequate compensation for damage resulting from activities dangerous to theenvironment, and to provide for preventionand restitution.Its far-reaching provisions have not commended themselves to many states, and it is unlikely to enter into force. Nevertheless, it is of interest in suggesting a different approach. In establishing rules of application beyond a particular industrial sector or activity or source of harm, the 1993 Lugano Convention moves beyond the earlier efforts described above, and is noteworthy as the first civil liability instrument to include provisions on access to information.The Convention will not be construed as limiting or derogating from rights of persons who suffer damage, oraslimitingprovisionsconcerningenvironmental protection or reinstatement provided under the laws of any party or under any other treaty to which it is a party, and expressly provides that in their relations parties which are members of the EC are to apply EC rules and not the rules of the Convention except where there is no EC rule governing the subject concerned.

The Convention is a regional instrument, which is open to signature by the members of the Council of Europe, non-member states which have participated in its elaboration, and the EC, although it is possible for any other state to become a party after its entry into force, and is potentially applicable regardless of where the damage is suffered when the incident occurs in the territory of a party. Article 4 sets out exceptions to which the Convention will not apply, including damage arising from carriage or to the extent that it is incompatible with the rules of applicable law relating to workmen's compensation or social security schemes. The Convention will not apply to damage caused by a nuclear substance which arises from a nuclear incident 'the liability of which is regulated either by' the 1960 Paris Convention (and its 1963 Additional Protocol) or by the 1963 Vienna Convention, or if liability for such damage is regulated by a specific internal law which is as favourable as these instruments. The drafting of the nuclear exception leaves a certain ambiguity which arises through the use of the word 'regulated'. Article 4(2)(a) would appear to permit an interpretation allowing for the application of the 1993 Lugano Convention to the consequences of a nuclear incident in France which had effects in Luxembourg, or in the United Kingdom which had effects in Ireland (assuming all were parties to the 1993 Convention), since Luxembourg and Ireland are not parties to the 1960 Paris Convention or the 1963 Vienna

Convention, and the liability in respect of damage in or to their territory would not appear to be 'regulated' by those treaties. Similarly, to the extent that a state is a party to the 1993 Lugano Convention and the 1960 Paris Convention or the 1963 Vienna Convention, the 1993 Convention may apply to damage caused by the disposal or permanent deposit (as opposed to storage) of nuclear waste, or in respect of environmental damage, not regulated by the 1960 or 1963 Conventions. However, Article 4(2)(b) creates further difficulty by excluding the application of the 1993 Convention if liability for damage caused by a nuclear substance 'is regulated by a specific internal law, provided that such law is as favourable' as the 1960 or 1963 Conventions: the issue is whether that specific internal law is that of the state in which the accident occurred, or that of the state in which the damage was suffered, or both. The text does not provide clear guidance.

The 1993 Convention channels liability to the operator in respect of incidents causing damage from a dangerous activity, and departs from earlier instruments by not including a provision allowing parties to limit liability.The Convention does not require operators to be covered by mandatory insurance or other financial security, only requiring each party to ensure that operators are covered by a financial security scheme up to a certain limit where appropriate and taking due account of the risks of the activity. An incident includes any 'sudden occurrence or continuous occurrence or any series of occurrences having the same origin, which causes damage or creates a grave and imminent threat of causing damage', leaving open the possibility that preventive measures taken by a potential victim, such as evacuation or prohibitive measures taken to prevent an activity from being carried out, could give rise to the liability of the operator.

The operator is the 'person who exercises control of a dangerous activity'; no guidance is provided by the Convention on what constitutes control. The Convention applies only to incidents occurring after its entry into force, and transitional provisions apply in respect of damage occurring before and after entry into force. The Convention distinguishes between two sources of harm, and for both sources of harm the operator's right of recourse against third persons is not prejudiced.

For dangerous substances, genetically modified organisms and micro-organisms, and for certain waste installations or sites, the operator will be liable for damage caused by the activity as a result of any incident when he was exercising control of the activity. Rules of joint and several liability apply for damage caused by continuous occurrences, or a series of occurrences having the same origin, although if the operator can prove that the occurrence during the period when he was exercising control of the dangerous activity caused only a part of the damage he will be liable only for that part of the damage. Where the damage becomes known after dangerous activity has ceased, the last operator of the activity will be liable, unless he or the person who suffered damage can prove that all or part of the damage occurred before he became the operator, in which case the provisions of Article 6(1) to (3) apply.

The operator of a site for the permanent deposit of waste will be liable for damage caused by waste deposited at the site, and the last operator will be liable for damage caused by waste deposited before the closure of a site, which damage only becomes known after the site has closed. Liability under this provision will generally preclude liability under Article 6.

Damage Damage includes loss of life or personal injury, loss of or damage to property, and the costs of preventive measures and any loss or damage caused by preventive measures. The Convention also applies to environmental damage, which is: loss or damage by impairment of the environment in so far as this is not considered to be damage within the meaning of [Article 2(7)(a) or (b)] . . . provided that compensation for impairment of the environment, other than for loss of profit from such impairment, shall be limited to the costs of reasonable measures of reinstatement actually undertaken or to be undertaken . . .

The environment includes natural resources, property forming part of the cultural heritage, and the characteristic aspects of the landscape. Measures of reinstatement means: any reasonable measures aiming to reinstate or restore damaged or destroyed components of the environment, or to introduce, where reasonable, the equivalent of these components into the environment. Internal law may indicate who will be entitled to take such measures.

This definition must be read in the context of the Article 8 exceptions, which provides, *inter alia,* that the operator will not be liable for damage which he proves 'was caused by pollution at tolerable levels under local relevant circumstances'.

This approach calls for comment. It indicates clearly the distinction to be drawn between pollution and liability for environmental damage; defined by reference to, *inter alia,* EEC Council Directives 67/548/EEC and 88/379/EEC, providing evidence of the growing international reach of EC environmental law. Annex II lists different types of waste installation or site. while all environmental damage is likely to be included in the definition of pollution, not all pollution will give rise to liability.

Moreover, it does not define a 'tolerable level' of pollution, which is problematic in the absence of agreed international standards. Finally, it recognises that tolerable levels are not absolute and may vary between localities or regions, and implements a shift in the burden of proof requiring the operator to prove that the pollution is at a tolerable level, and not for the victim to prove that the level of pollution is intolerable.

Exemptions and other rules The operator may benefit from exemptions if it is able to prove that damage was caused by, *inter alia*, war or a natural phenomenon of an 'exceptional, inevitable and irresistible character', or by the intent of a third party, or as a result of compliance with an order or compulsory measure of a public authority, or by a dangerous activity lawfully undertaken in the interests of the person who suffered the damage. Contributory fault of the person suffering damage can result in a reduction or disallowance of compensation. The Convention also includes a basic rule on proving causality, requiring the court to take due account of the increased danger of causing damage which is inherent in the dangerous activity.

Actions for compensation and other claims Under the Convention, claims may be brought to the court of the place where the damage was suffered, or where the dangerous activity was conducted, or where the defendant has his habitual residence. The Convention envisages claims by environmental organisations. Under Article 18, any association or foundation whose statute aims at the protection of the environment and which complies with the requirements of the internal law of the party where the request is submitted may request the prohibition of a dangerous activity which is unlawful and poses a grave threat of damage to the environment, or that the operator be ordered to take measures to prevent an incident or damage (including after an incident), or that the operator be ordered to take measures of reinstatement.

Internal law may determine the admissibility of such requests, and the administrative or judicial body before which such a request should be made, and the Convention sets out rules governing requests by environmental organisations registered under the law of another party.

Requests by organisations for the prohibition of a dangerous activity may only be brought within a court or administrative authority of the place where the dangerous activity is or will be conducted, and other requests may be taken to such a court or to the court of the place where the measures are to be taken. Provision is made for limitation periods, notification of proceedings, *lis pendens*, related actions, and the recognition and enforcement of judgments.

The Convention establishes a Standing Committee to review problems related to the Convention and provides for amendment. Of note is the procedure envisaged for amendment of the definition of dangerous substances set out in Annex I which is necessitated because of the definition by reference to EC Directives which are frequently amended by the EC member states.

Reservations The sensitive and legally complex nature of the 1993 Lugano Convention required the permissibility of reservations in relation to three matters. Reservations are permitted to allow a party: to apply the Convention to damage suffered in the territory of non-parties only on the basis of reciprocity; to provide in internal law that the operator will not be liable for damage caused by substances or genetically modified organisms or micro-organisms if he proves that the state of scientific and technical knowledge at the time of the incident was not such as to enable the existence of the dangerous properties of the substance or the significant risk involved in the operation dealing with the organism to be determined; and to refrain from applying Article 18 (requests by organisations).

UNECE

In 2001, the governing bodies of and parties to the UNECE's 1992 Watercourses Convention and 1991 Industrial Accidents Convention established a working group to develop a Draft Legally Binding Instrument on Civil Liability for Transboundary Damage Caused by Hazardous Activities, Within the Scope of Both Conventions. The working group's mandate is to develop draft Articles to be adopted by a joint special session of the parties to both the Watercourses and Industrial Accidents Conventions in 2003. The proposal follows the work of an earlier UNECE Task Force, which considered rules on responsibility and liability for transboundary water resources.

CONCLUSIONS

With the exception of the oil pollution regime, the rules of international law governing liability for environmental damage remain in their early phases of development, particularly in relation to rules of state liability. States remain reluctant to put in place rules which have the potential to impose significant constraints on the conduct of potentially hazardous activities, as well as being aware of significant costs to the public sector. This is particularly reflected in the amendments to the 1963 Vienna Convention on civil liability for nuclear damage, and in the remote prospects for the entry into force of the 1993 Lugano Convention. States also appear unwilling to bring claims against other states for environmental and other damage even where there might be good legal grounds for doing so, as the practice following the Chernobyl accident indicated.

In relation to civil liability, Principle 13 of the Rio Declaration recognised the importance of national laws on liability and compensation. The failure of states to put such laws in place, or to enforce them, will increasingly be a matter of legitimate international concern for environmental and economic reasons. This applies equally at the regional level, as reflected in the continuing (and longstanding) efforts by the EC Commission to adopt minimum standards for all EC member states.

The body of international civil liability instruments in force is now impressive, and the case law under some, such as the oil pollution rules, has established useful precedents on the basis of which further developments and innovations can be based. Significant developments in the past five years include the adoption of liability protocols to the 1989 Basel Convention and regimes on hazardous and noxious substances, as well as the entry into force of the IMO's two 1992 Protocols.

Efforts are underway to establish new regimes, in particular in relation to the 1991 Antarctic Environment Protocol and the 2000 Biosafety Protocol, which poses particular challenges in respect of defining what constitutes damage. Gaps still need to be filled for activities which are not covered by liability rules, and the geographical coverage of existing instruments needs to be enhanced by bringing on board the large number of states who remain outside the liability regimes. A 'second generation' of civil liability rules will face new issues, including: the possibility of conflicting approaches to the definition of environmental damage; ensuring that such limitations on liability as are permitted do not serve to subsidise potentially harmful activities; establishing effective procedures before courts and tribunals for dealing with mass claims in the event of catastrophic accidents or events; and developing

Customary Principles of Law Revisited', 13 *Canadian Yearbook of International Law* 156 (1975); J. G. Polakiewicz, 'La Responsabilite´ de l'e´tat en matie`re de pollution des eaux flu-viales ou souterraines internationales', *Journal de Droit International* 283 (1991); A. Rest, 'New Tendencies in Environmental Responsibility/ Liability Law: The Work of the UNECE Task Force on Responsibility and Liability Regarding Transboundary Water Pollution', 21 *Environmental Policy and Law* 135 (1991). schemes to provide for supplementary funding in the event that a liable person runs out of funds, or cannot be located, or the damage exceeds a permitted financial limit of liability.

It is in regard to state liability that the 'expeditious and more determined' co-operation called for by Principle 13 of the Rio Declaration remains to be addressed. Since the 1972 Stockholm Conference, developments have been limited. Although the ILC's 2001 draft Articles on State Responsibility introduce a codified framework, the Commission's progress in its efforts to develop principles of state liability for environmental damage which are of general application remains limited.

In view of the unwillingness of anystate to bring aclaim against the USSR following the Chernobyl accident in 1986 for environmental or other damage, the principal developments have been: the adoption and recent entry into force of Article 235 of the 1982 UNCLOS; the innovative approach of the 1988 CRAMRA towards the linkage of civil and state liability; and the affirmation in 1991 by Security Council Resolution 687 that Iraq was liable for the environmental damage caused by its unlawful invasion of Kuwait. Indeed, the UN Compensation Commission may well have the responsibility of defining an approach which may be applied more broadly.

Few state claims have been made since 1972, notable exceptions being the successful Canadian claim against the USSR following the crash of Cosmos 954 in 1978 and the Hungarian claim against Slovakia in relation to the consequences of the operation of the Gab-cikovo barrage (although the ICJ did not take up the opportunity to address the particularities of that claim). The legal issues which will need to be addressed in relation to state liability are broadly similar to those concerning civil liability, although the range of activities for which a state might be liable is extensive.

Specific issues of particular concern include liability for damage to the environment in areas beyond national jurisdiction, the question of financial limits (if any) of a state's liability, and the distinction between liability for damage to the environment of a state and liability for damage to its property interests. In coming years, the fora for addressing these and other issues will include the ILC and those bodies dealing with civil liability which are coming under increasing pressure to further define the relationship between civil and state liability. Other bodies, such as the conference of the parties of the 1992 Climate Change Convention and – increasingly – international courts and tribunals, are likely to emerge as fora for addressing the responsibilities of states for new environmental challenges.

4

International Trade and Competition

INTRODUCTION

UNCED marked a further stage towards the integration of economic and environmental aspects of international law, prompted in part by considerations of the relationship between differing environmental standards and economic competitiveness. Principle 4 of the Rio Declaration reflects this

interdependence, providing that 'in order to achieve sustainable development environmental protection shall constitute an integral part of the development process and cannot be considered in isolation from it'. The theme of integration was central to the preparations for UNCED. Agenda 21 recognised that the international economy should provide a 'supportive international climate for achieving environment and development goals', and identified the following as objectives for the international community:

- making trade and the environment mutually supportive;
- encouraging macroeconomic policies conducive to environment and development; and
- providing adequate financial resources to developing countries and dealing with international debt.

This chapter considers the international legal aspects of the first two of these issues: the relationship between international trade and environmental protection, and the application of international rules of competition law to environmental issues. In chapter 20, other aspects of the relationship between international economic law and environmental protection are addressed, including financial resources, transfer of technology, and intellectual property rights. Chapter 21 addresses the relationship between rules of international law for the promotion of foreign investments and the protection of the environment.

One of the consequences of an emphasis on greater integration of economics and the environment has been to bring together two very different groups of international legal practitioners who have traditionally had very little to do with one another. International trade law in the past had been seen as a separate, self-contained field, dominated by the principles and ideology of free trade. More recently, environmentalists and others have challenged the dominance of free trade ideals and particularly their utility to achieve other international goals such as environmental protection.

Greater integration between economics and the environment has manifested itself in many other ways than simply as a clash of intellectual cultures. A number of international legal issues relating to trade, competition and the environment have been controversial in recent years. Three principal issues concern the use in environmental treaties of international trade measures, the circumstances in which one or more states may lawfully adopt 'unilateral' environmental protection measures (measures taken outside the context of an international agreement) which limit international trade and may conflict with obligations under global and regional free trade agreements, such as the GATT, the EC Treaty, the United States–Canada Free Trade Agreement, the NAFTA and the African Economic Community Treaty, and the requirements for states to adopt trade measures in furtherance of national goals of human, animal or plant health and safety protection. The chapter also addresses the emerging relationship between competition law and environmental protection.

TRADE MEASURES IN INTERNATIONAL ENVIRONMENTAL AGREEMENTS

J. Cameron and J. Robinson, 'The Use of Trade Provisions in International Environmental Agreements and Their Compatibility with GATT', 2 *Yearbook of International Environmental Law* 3 (1991); J. Cameron and J. Robinson, *The Use of Trade Provisions in International Environmental Agreements: A Report for the OECD* (1991); I. Cheyne, 'Environmental Treaties and the GATT', 1 RECIEL 14

(1992); T. Swanson, 'The Evolving Trade Mechanism inCITES', 1 RECIEL52(1992); J. Werks-man, 'Trade Sanctions under the Montreal Protocol', 1 RECIEL 69 (1992); J. Dunoff, 'Reconciling International Trade with Preservation of the Global Commons: Can We Prosper and Protect?', 49 *Washington and Lee Law Review* 1407 (1992); R. Tara-sofsky, 'Ensuring Compatibility Between Multilateral Environmental Agreements and GATT/WTO', 7 *Yearbook of International Environmental Law* 52 (1996); A. Qureshi, 'The Cartagena Protocol on Biosafety and the WTO – Coexistence or Incoherence?', 49 ICLQ 835 (2000); A. Bianchi, 'The Impact of International Trade Law on Environmental Law and Process', in F. Francioni (ed.), *Environment, Human Rights and International Trade* 105 (2001).

The use of trade measures in international environmental agreements has a long history. The 1933 London Convention controlled and regulated the import, export and traffic in certain trophies. Other agreements establish quantitative restrictions on international trade to achieve environmental protection objectives. Three types of environmental objectives have been addressed by trade regulations: agreements to protect wildlife, agreements to protect the environment of the importing state from harmful organisms and products, and agreements to protect the global commons.

Agreements for the protection of wildlife usually make use of restrictions on export or import between parties, often based on a permit system, as well as on transit through the territory of parties, and restrictions on trade with non-parties. Agreements to protect the environment of the importing state from harmful organisms or products, which have generally been concerned with plant pests, hazardous waste and pesticides, but which have more recently been extended to include genetically modified organisms, rely primarily on import restrictions, although restrictions on transit through the territory of parties and on trade with non-parties are also used. Agreements to restrict exports and imports either establish a complete ban, or make imports conditional upon the grant of a permit or the prior informed consent of the relevant authorities of the importing state, or a combination of techniques. The 2000 Biosafety Protocol combines a prior informed consent procedure and risk assessment, while also allowing importing parties to restrict imports where there is a '[l]ack of scientific certainty due to insufficient relevant scientific information and knowledge regarding the extent of the potential adverse effects of a living modified organism on the conservation and sustainable use of biological diversity in the Party of import, taking also into account risks to human health'. For hazardous waste, export restrictions supplement the import restrictions.

To date, the only international agreement which has used trade measures to protect the global commons is the 1987 Montreal Protocol. Article 4 controls the import and export of certain ozone-depleting substances from and to non-parties, whereas Article 4B requires parties which are unable to phase out production of controlled substances by the required phase-out dates to ban the export of used, recycled and reclaimed quantities of the substances, other than for the purpose of destruction. The 1992 Climate Change Convention and the 1992 Biodiversity Convention do not use trade provisions as an international enforcement measure, although, when it comes into force, the 1997 Kyoto Protocol will make use of such measures under its compliance mechanism.As discussed below, both the climate change and biodiversity regimes address the permissibility of unilateral measures adopted by parties.

The use oftrade sanctions to implement international environmental obligations raises possible conflicts between obligations under environmental agreements and those under free trade agreements. Such conflicts would be subject to the general rules of international law, as reflected in the 1969 Vienna Convention on the Law of Treaties. Applying these rules, it follows that the trade restrictions established under post-1994 agreements, such as the 2000 Biosafety Protocol and the 2001 POPs Convention, will prevail over inconsistent obligations established under the 1994 GATT (to the extent that they are inconsistent) as between parties to both, but that the free trade obligations of the GATT might prevail where a state was not a party to the relevant multilateral agreement (to the extent that GATT obligations were inconsistent). The situation is slightly more complex in the case of pre-1994 multilateral environmental agreements, such as the 1987 Montreal Protocol and the 1989 Basel Convention. With GATT 1947 being re-adopted as GATT 1994 at the Uruguay Round of trade negotiations, the trade agreement is (at least technically) the *lex posterior*.However, the ruling of the WTO Appellate Body in the *Shrimp/Turtle* dispute (discussed below) suggests that trade restrictions in multilateral environmental agreements like the 1987 Montreal Protocol and the 1989 Basel Convention are unlikely to fall foul of GATT 1994 requirements.

Even for international environmental agreements concluded after 1994, the relationship between the trade measures used in environmental agreements and the requirements of trade treaties is sometimes unclear. Despite the prominence of the issue of the relationship between trade and environmental commitments during the negotiations for the 2000 Biosafety Protocol, the only clue as to the appropriate relationship is given by opaque language in the Protocol's Preamble. Further clarification may be forthcoming if new negotiations on the relationship between trade rules and environmental agreements, being conducted under the auspices of the WTO's Committee on Trade and Environment, are successful (see below).

The GATT envisages certain exceptions to the prohibition on import restrictions, and support has been expressed for the view that import restrictions could be justified under the Article XX exceptions when they are based on measures adopted pursuant to a multilateral environmental agreement, such as the 1987 Montreal Protocol. In 1992, the EC suggested that, for an exception to be so justified, the multilateral environmental agreement should fulfil certain conditions, including:

1. the agreement should have been negotiated under the aegis of the UN and the procedures for negotiation should have been open to the participation of all GATT members; and
2. the agreement should be open for accession by any GATT members on terms which are equitable in relation to those which apply to original members.

The EC also recognised that the same criteria should apply to regional agree-ments,butthat inno circumstances could suchagreements providejustification for applying extra-jurisdictional trade measures *vis-a'-vis* countries outside the region. The requirement for multilaterality in order to justify trade action for environmental purposes was stressed by the WTO Appellate Body in the *Shrimp/Turtle* dispute.

The 1987 Montreal Protocol raises further legal issues by

requiring parties to ban the import and export of controlled substances from non-parties and, following amendments adopted in 1991, 1992 and 1995, to ban the import from non-parties of certain products which contain controlled substances.Here the question arises as to whether these bans can be enforced, under international law, against states which are not parties to the Montreal Protocol but which are parties to the GATT. The dispute settlement bodies of the WTO have not yet been called upon to consider the question; at first sight such a restriction might appear to be incompatible with Article XI of the GATT (elimination of quantitative restrictions) but might be brought within the exceptions established under Article XX. A WTO Panel or the Appellate Body might find it difficult to hold that an import ban imposed pursuant to an international treaty (to which more than 180 states are party) was not 'necessary to protect human, animal or plant life or health' although the result would not be certain. Under the NAFTA, Mexico, Canada and the United States have adopted a different approach, expressly providing that trade sanctions in the 1973 CITES, the 1987 Montreal Protocol (and the 1990 amendments thereto) and the 1989 Basel Convention will prevail over the NAFTA.

UNILATERAL ENVIRONMENTAL MEASURES AND INTERNATIONAL TRADE

Unilateral environmental measures are national environmental protection measures adopted by states which include an international trade limitation or prohibition and which are adopted in the absence of agreed international standards or rules, or go beyond agreed international standards. Examples of such measures include national laws establishing product-labelling requirements, import bans or quotas, and other environmentally related measures which can have the effect, directly or indirectly, of limiting international trade. The main international trade agreements of relevance to the adoption of environmental measures of this type are the 1994 GATT, the 1957 EC Treaty (as amended), the 1988 Free Trade Agreement between Canada and the United States and the 1992 North American Free Trade Agreement (NAFTA) between Mexico, Canada and the United States. The 1991 Treaty establishing the African Economic Community is also likely to be important.

The rapid development of national environmental legislation

limiting imports and trade in the past few years, usually adopted outside the context of agreed international standards, has led to more trade-related disputes between states. This trend is likely to continue in the face of increased disparities between countries' environmental protection standards and the failure to adopt binding international standards. As a result, international courts, tribunals and other bodies find themselves increasingly called upon to determine the compatibility of national environmental protection measures with international legal obligations which prohibit restrictions or barriers to international trade.

WTO/GATT

K. W. Dam, *The GATT Law and International Economic Organisations* (1970); F. Kirgis, 'Effective Pollution Control in Industrialised Countries: International Economic Disincentives, Policy Responses and the GATT', 70 *Michigan Law Review* 860 (1972); O. Long, *Law and its Limitations in the GATT Multilateral Trade System* (1985); E.-U. Petersmann, 'Trade Policy, Environmental Policy and the GATT: Why

Trade Rules and Environmental Rules Should be Mutually Consistent', 46 *Aussen-wirtschaft* 197 (1991); S. Charnovitz, 'Exploring the Environmental Exceptions in GATT Article XX', 25 *Journal of World Trade* 37 (1991); P. Sorsa, 'Environment – A New Challenge to GATT?' (World Bank, 1991); E.-U. Petersmann, 'International Trade Law and International Environmental Law – Prevention and Settlement of International Disputes in GATT', 27 *Journal of World Trade* 43 (1993); J. Cameron, 'The GATT and the Environment', in P. Sands (ed.), *Greening International Law* (1993), 100; D. Esty, *Greening the GAT T: Trade, Environment, and the Future* (1994); S. Charnovitz, 'The World Trade Organization and the Environment', 8 *Ye a r b o o k of International Environmental Law* 98 (1997); D. McRae, 'Trade and Environment: The Development of WTO Law', 9 *Otago Law Review* 221 (1998); WTO Secretariat, *Guide to the Uruguay Round Agreements* (1999); M. Blakeney and F. MacMillan, *The WTO and the Environment* (2001).

The GATT was originally adopted in 1947 as the main international arrange-menttoencouragetradebetween states. InDecember1993,aftersevenyearsof negotiation, the Trade Negotiations Committee of the Uruguay Round adopted by consensus the Final Act. The Final Act includes the Agreement

Establishing the World Trade Organization (WTO) and annexed agreements on, *inter alia*: the General Agreement on Tariffs and Trade 1994 (GATT 1994), the General Agreement on Trade in Services (GATS), the Agreement on Trade-Related Aspects of Intellectual Property Rights (TRIPs) and the Understanding on Rules and Procedures Governing the Settlement of Disputes (DSU). These and related agreements were opened for signature at Marrakesh on 15 April 1994 and entered into force on 1 January 1995.

The entire package established a permanent organisation, the WTO, which, with a current membership of 144 states and the EC, has become an important forum for the development of international law on matters relating to trade and the environment. The WTO replaces the former GATT Council as 'the common institutional framework for the conduct of trade relations among its Members in matters related to the agreements and associated legal instruments included in the Annexes [to the WTO Agreement]'. As a permanent multilateral institution, the WTO takes its place alongside the World Bank and the IMF. Although it does not have express environmental objectives, the Preamble recognises that the WTO must allow 'the optimal use of the world's resources in accordance with the objective of sustainable development' and seek 'both to protect and preserve the environment and enhance the means for doing so in a manner consistent with' the respective needs and concerns of the parties at different levels of economic development. The WTO's tasks are: to implement the WTO Agreement and the multilateral trade agreements; to provide the framework for the implementation of the plurilateral trade agreements; to administer the DSU and the Trade Policy Review Mechanism; to provide a forum for the negotiations among members; and to co-operate with the World Bank and the IMF. Despite the new institutional overlay, the GATT 1994 remains the central substantive agreement under the WTO umbrella, which is designed to encourage trade between WTO members by reducing tariffs and preventing trade barriers.

Article III(1) of the GATT 1994 prohibits the application to imported or domestic products of internal taxes and other internal charges, laws, regulations and requirements so as to afford protection to domestic products. Article III(2) prohibits the application, directly or indirectly, of internal taxes or other internal charges of any kind in excess of those applied, directly or indirectly, to like domestic products or in a manner contrary to Article III(1). Under Article XI, prohibitions or restrictions, including quotas, import or export licences or other measures, on the import or export of any product from or to another contracting party are prohibited. Article XX permits exceptions to these limitations. It provides, *inter alia*:

Subject to the requirement that such measures are not applied in a manner which would constitute a means of arbitrary or unjustifiable discrimination between countries where the same conditions prevail, or a disguised restriction on international trade, nothing in this Agreement shall be construed to prevent the adoption or enforcement by any contracting party of measures:

... (b) necessary to protect human, animal or plant life or health;

... (g) relating to the conservation of exhaustible natural resources if such measures are made effective in conjunction with restrictions on domestic production or consumption.

The GATT 1994 does not include a reference to environmental protection.Efforts during the Uruguay Round to strengthen provisions on environmental protection, in particular by amending Articles XX(b) and (g), failed, although pursuant to Article 2.2 of the Agreement on Technical Barriers to Trade (discussed below) the contracting parties did identify 'environmental protection' as a 'legitimate objective' to be considered in evaluating the GATT compatibility of environmental regulations.

TECHNICAL BARRIERS TO TRADE

During the 1973–9 Tokyo Round, an Agreement on Technical Barriers to Trade (1979 TBT Agreement) was negotiated and adopted to deal with the growing problem of trade barriers resulting from disparate national regulations. It established basic guidelines which governed, among other matters, the acceptability of national environmental regulations. The 1979 TBT Agreement did not attract widespread ratification by GATT contracting parties and during the Uruguay Round it was renegotiated. The result of the Uruguay Round negotiations was two new agreements dealing with national regulatory standards: the Agreement on the Application of Sanitary and Phytosanitary Measures (SPS

Agreement), which deals with measures designed to protect human, animal and plant life or health, and the Agreement on Technical Barriers to Trade (TBT Agreement), which covers other technical standards not regulated by the SPS Agreement. The main objective of the new TBT Agreement is to ensure that technical regulations and standards, including packaging, labelling and marking requirements and methods of certifyingconformity with technical regulations and standards, are not adopted or applied so as to create unnecessary obstacles to trade. Environmental regulations may be technical barriers to trade. The TBT Agreement adopts the principles of national treatment and non-discrimination by stating that, in relation to such technical regulations or standards, imported products are not to receive less favourable treatment 'than thataccorded to like products of national origin and to like products originating in any other country'. WTO members must also ensure that technical regulations 'are not prepared, adopted or applied with a view to or with the effect of creating unnecessary obstacles to international trade'. Accordingly, technical regulations must not be 'more trade-restrictive than necessary to fulfil a legitimate objective, taking account of the risks non-fulfilment would create'. The list of 'legitimate objectives' in Article 2.2 includes 'the protection of human health or safety, animal or plant life or health, or the environment'. In assessing the risks to health or the environment, the relevant factors for consideration include 'available scientific and technical information, related processing technology or intended end-uses of products'. This formulation suggests that both characteristics of the product itself, and the process by which it is produced, are relevant in assessing the health or environmental risks posed by a product.

The main distinction between technical regulations and standards, which lay down technical specifications relating to the characteristics of a product, is that in the case of the former compliance is mandatory while in the case of the latter it is not. All products are subject to the provisions of the TBT Agreement, which recognises that technical regulations and standards would not pose problems to international trade if the parties used international standards as the basis for their adoption. The TBT Agreement obliges parties, where 'relevant international standards exist or their completion is imminent', to use them as a basis for their technical regulations, except when they are an inappropriate means for the fulfilment of the legitimate objective pursued, for example 'because of fundamental climatic or geographical factors or fundamental technological problems'. The TBT Agreement thus explicitly recognises that environmental protection could allow deviation from international standards. Such a deviation would, however, be subject to the basic obligation of the TBT Agreement to ensure that technical regulations should not create unnecessary obstacles to international trade. The TBT Agreement also imposes certain procedural requirements. The members must publish technical regulations in draft form where they are not based on international standards, or where such standards do not exist, and where the technical regulation or standard that is being adopted is likely to have a significant effect on trade. To ensure that exporting countries, particularly developing countries, have time to adapt their products or methods of production to the requirements of the importing country, the Agreement requires that there should be a reasonable interval between the publication of technical regulations and their entry into force. However, where 'urgent problems of safety, health, environmental protection or national security arise or threaten to arise for a Member', the member may fast-track the introduction of a technical regulation, provided that other members are notified immediately through the WTO Secretariat and given an opportunity to present their comments in writing, discuss these comments upon request, and have their written comments and the results of discussions taken into account. The TBT Agreement requires each party to set up enquiry points from which relevant information about technical regulations, standards and conformity assessment procedures can be obtained.

The TBT Agreement also recognises that developing countries are entitled to special treatment and that technical assistance should be made available to them. Such special treatment could include, *inter alia,* taking into account their trade and financial needs in the preparation of technical regulations, standards, test methods and certification systems, and ensuring that the adoption of technical regulations does not create unnecessary obstacles to exports from developing countries. Additionally, the technical regulations and standards adopted should be based on scientific considerations and, to that end, in the event of a dispute arising, a WTO panel may establish a technical expert group to assist it with questions of a technical nature. This assists the panel by advising whether the measure is necessary for the protection of human, animal or plant life or health and whether it was based on a legitimate scientific judgment.

COMMITTEE ON TRADE AND THE ENVIRONMENT

At Marrakesh, in April 1994, ministers adopted a Decision on Trade and the Environment to co-ordinate policies in the fields of trade and the environment within the competence of the multilateral trading system. The Decision called for the establishment of a Committee on Trade and the Environment (CTE) to take over the role of the previous GATT Group on Environmental Measures and International Trade, which, despite being established in 1971, was not activated until October 1991, in preparation for UNCED. The terms of reference of the CTE are to identify the relationship between trade and environmental measures to promote sustainable development, and to recommend whether there is a need for modifications to the multilateral trading system to (a) enhance positive interaction between trade and environment, (b) avoid protectionist trade measures while ensuring responsiveness to the environmental objectives of Agenda 21 and the Rio Declaration, and (c) provide for surveillance of trade measures for environmental purposes, of trade-related aspects of environmental measures, and of effective implementation of 'multilateral disciplines' governing such measures. The Decision identified seven matters to be initially addressed by the CTE. To date, intergovernmental deliberations

have produced little progress on substantive issues. However, the role of the CTE may potentially be revitalised by new negotiations taking place under its auspices dealing with the relationship between existing WTO rules and trade obligations in multilateral environmental agreements, as agreed in the Doha Ministerial Declaration in November 2001. Following Doha, the first meeting of the CTE's Trade Negotiations Committee was held in February 2002.

WTO/GATT DISPUTE SETTLEMENT

R. E. Hudec, 'The New WTO Dispute Settlement Procedure: An Overview of the First Three Years', 9 *Minnesota Journal of Global Trade* 1 (1999); J. Jackson, *The Jurisprudence of GATT and the WTO*

(2000); P. K. Rao, *World Trade Organization and the Environment* (2000).

In the event of a dispute between WTO members concerning environmental measures and agreements and trade obligations, the matter may be referred to dispute settlement in accordance with the procedures of the DSU. The DSU introduced significant changes to the dispute settlement procedures formerly employed under the GATT. The Dispute Settlement Body (DSB) established under the WTO is responsible for administering the rules and procedures governing dispute settlement. The traditional approaches used under GATT 1947 (consultation, good offices, conciliation and mediation) remain in place, with amended rules for the Dispute Settlement Panels and new provisions on appellate review and arbitration. Panels assist the DSB in making recommendations or in giving the rulings provided for in the relevant agreements. Third parties having a substantial interest in a matter before a Panel are entitled to participate in Panel proceedings. Most significantly, Panel reports become binding unless one of the parties to the dispute decides to appeal or the DSB decides by consensus not to adopt the report. Appeal is permitted only on points of law related to a panel ruling. The appeal is made to a standing Appellate Body, which is composed of seven independent persons, three of whom serve on any one case. Appellate Body reports must be adopted by the DSB and unconditionally accepted by the parties to the dispute unless the DSB decides by consensus not to adopt the report within thirty days of its issuance. The DSU also provides for rules on surveillance of implementation of recommendations and rulings of the DSB, compensation and suspension of concessions, and binding arbitration by mutual agreement of the parties as an alternative means of dispute settlement.

Prior to the entry into force of the DSU in January 1995, six GATT panels had been established for disputes relating – directly or indirectly – to international environmental issues, and many other panel decisions provided guidance on interpretation of relevant provisions of the GATT. The most important of these decisions were two panel reports issued in 1991 and 1994 concerning the dispute between Mexico and the United States over the latter's ban of imports of yellow-fin tuna from Mexico and 'intermediary nations' which had been caught in a manner which harmed dolphins. The dispute was controversial and, unlike previous GATT panel decisions, subject to intense public scrutiny.

TUNA/DOLPHIN CASES (1991 AND 1994)

M. Hurlock, 'The GATT, US Law and the Environment: A Proposal to Amend the GATTin Light of theTuna/Dolphin Decision', 92 *ColumbiaLaw Review* 2098(1992); B. Kingsbury, 'The Tuna-Dolphin Controversy, the World Trade Organization and the Liberal Project to Reconceptualize International Law', 5 *Yearbook of International Environmental Law* 1 (1994); A. Ferrante, 'The Dolphin-Tuna Controversy and Environmental Issues', 5 *Journal of Transnational Law and Policy* 279 (1996).

The *Tuna/Dolphin* dispute arose over regulations adopted under the US 1972 Marine Mammal Protection Act (MMPA), as amended. The MMPA regulates, *inter alia,* the harvesting of tuna by US fishermen and others who are subject to the jurisdiction of the US. Under the MMPA, US authorities granted licences for the fishing of yellow-fin tuna by United States vessels in the Eastern Tropical Pacific Ocean (ETPO), on condition that the domestic fleet did not exceed an incidental taking of a total of 20,500 dolphins per year in the ETPO. The MMPA also required the US Secretary of State to ban the importation of commercial fish or products from fish which have been caught with commercial fishing technology which results in the incidental kill or incidental serious injury of ocean mammals in excess of United States standards.

The MMPA amounted to a requirement that US environmental standards should be applied to all countries in respect of their fishing activities. Under US law, fish caught by a vessel registered in a country is deemed to originate in that country. As a condition of access to the US market for the yellow-fin tuna or yellow-fin tuna products caught by its fleet, each country of registry of vessels fishing yellow-fin tuna in the ETPO was required to prove to the satisfaction of the US authorities that its overall regulatory regime regarding the taking of marine mammals was comparable to that of the US.

To meet this requirement, the country in question needed to prove that the average rate of incidental taking of marine mammals by its tuna fleet operating in the ETPO was not in excess of 1.25 times the average incidental taking rate of US vessels operating in the ETPO during the same period.

The MMPA additionally provided that ninety days after imports of yellow-fin tuna and yellow-fin tuna products from a country had been prohibited in accordance with the rules set out above, the import of such tuna and tuna products from any 'intermediary nation' would also be prohibited, unless the intermediary nation could prove that it too had acted to ban imports of such tuna and tuna products from the country of origin subject to the direct import embargo.

Finally, certification by the US Secretary of State to the President, which took place six months after the effective date of an embargo, triggered the operation of section 8(a) of the 1967 Fishermen's Protective Act (the 'Pelly Amendment'). This provides a discretionary authority for the US President to order a prohibition of imports of fish products 'for such duration as the President determines appropriate and to the extent that such prohibition is sanctioned by the [GATT]'. Under the MMPA, the US prohibited the import into its customs territory of yellow-fin tuna and yellow-fin tuna products from Mexico which were caught with purse-seine nets in the ETPO. An earlier embargo had been imposed on such tuna and tuna products in August 1990; a new embargo was put in place in March 1991, and from 24 May 1991 the US implemented an 'intermediary nations' embargo on products from several other countries, including those from the European Community.

The dispute also concerned labelling requirements. The 1990 Dolphin Protection Consumer Information Act (DPCIA) provided that, when a tuna product exported from or offered for sale in the US bears the optional label 'Dolphin Safe' or any similar label indicating it was fished in a manner not harmful to dolphins, this tuna product must not contain tuna harvested on the high seas by a vessel engaged in driftnet fishing, or harvested in the ETPO by a vessel using a purse-seine net, unless it is accompanied by documentary evidence showing that the purse-seine net was not intentionally deployed to encircle dolphins. The labelling provisions of the DPCIA took effect on 28 May 1991.

Tuna/Dolphin I (1991)

In January 1991, Mexico requested the GATT Council to establish a Panel to examine the compatibility of the MMPA and the DPCIA, and implementing regulations, with the GATT. The

Panel examined the compatibility with GATT (under Articles III, IX, XI and XIII, and the exemptions under Article XX)of:

1. the prohibition of imports of certain yellow-fin tuna and certain yellow-fin tuna products from Mexico imposed by the US and the provisions of the MMPA on which it was based;
2. the prohibition of imports of certain yellow-fin tuna and certain yellow-fin tuna products from 'intermediary nations' imposed by the US and the provisions of the MMPA on which it was based;
3. thepossibleextensionof each oftheseimport prohibitions to all fishproducts from Mexico and the 'intermediary nations', under the MMPA and the Pelly Amendment; and
4. the application to tuna and tuna products from Mexico of the labelling provisions of the DPCIA, as well as its provisions as such.

The Panel held that the US import restrictions were incompatible with the GATT and could not be justified under Article XX(b) or (g). The measures prohibiting Mexican imports were classed as quantitative restrictions under Article XI. The Panel rejected the US argument that the prohibitions were internal regulations under Article III, noting that, even if they were, the US import prohibitions were discriminatory and did not meet the requirements of Article III(4) which: calls for a comparison of the treatment of imported tuna as a product with that of domestic tuna *as a product*. Regulations governing the taking of dolphins incidental to the taking of tuna could not possibly affect tuna as a product. Article III.4 therefore obliges the [US] to accord treatment to Mexican tuna no less favourable than that accorded to [US] tuna, whether or not the incidental taking of dolphins by Mexican vessels corresponds to that of [US] vessels.

Since the direct import prohibitions were inconsistent with Article XI(1) of GATT (the US had not presented a contrary argument), it was not necessary to make a finding on the consistency of the measures under Article XIII.

At the heart of the case lay the question of whether these import prohibitions, which were contrary to Article XI, were permitted under Article XX(b) and (g). The Panel considered that the US was entitled to invoke Article XX, but noted that: the practice of panels has been to interpret Article XX narrowly, to place the burden on the party invoking Article XX to justify its invocation, and not to examine Article XX exceptions unless invoked.

The principal issue relating to Article XX(b) was whether it covered measures necessary to protect human, animal or plant life *outside US jurisdiction.* Since the GATT text did not provide a clear answer, the provision had to be analysed 'in the light of its drafting history, its purpose, and the consequences that the interpretations proposed by the parties would have for the operation of the GATT as a whole'. The Panel concluded that the concerns of the drafters focused on the use of measures 'within the jurisdiction of the importing country'.The Panel further considered that measures taken under Article XX(b) must be 'necessary' and should not 'constitute a means of arbitrary or unjustifiable discrimination' and that Article XX(b) was intended to allow restrictions 'to pursue overriding public policy goals to the extent that such inconsistencies were unavoidable'. The Panel held that to accept the US interpretation justifying measures under this provision would mean that: eachcontractingparty couldunilaterally determine the lifeor health protection policies from which other contracting parties could not deviate without jeopardising their rights under the General Agreement. The General Agreement would then no longer constitute a multilateral framework for trade among all contracting parties but would provide legal security only in respect of trade between a limited number of contracting parties with identical internal regulations.

Even if Article XX(b) were interpreted to permit extra-jurisdictional protection of life and health, the Panel held that the US had not shown that its measures were necessary, or that it had exhausted all other options reasonably available to it to pursue its dolphin protection objectives in a manner which was compatible with the GATT, in particular through the negotiation of international co-operative arrangements. Moreover, even if an import prohibition was the only measure reasonably available, the conditions adopted were too unpredictable to be regarded as necessary to protect the health or life of dolphins.

The Panel concluded that the direct import prohibitions were also unjustified under Article XX(g), which could not be interpreted to apply extra-jurisdictionally. It found that Article XX(g) required measures relating to the conservation of exhaustible natural resources to be taken 'in conjunction with restrictions on domestic production or consumption', which could only occur if the measure 'was primarily aimed at rendering effective these restrictions'.The Panel considered that a country can effectively control the production or consumption of an exhaustible natural resource only to the extent that the production or consumption is under its jurisdictionand that to accept the extra-jurisdictional interpretation of the US would mean that each contracting party could unilaterally determine the conservation policies from which other contracting parties could not deviate without jeopardising their rights under the General Agreement.

Finally, even if Article XX(g) could be applied extra-jurisdictionally, the US measures did not meet the conditions of the Article, since 'a limitation on trade based on such unpredictable conditions could not be regarded as being primarily aimed at the conservation of dolphins'.

The Panel also rejected the 'intermediary nations' embargo. It held that the embargo was a quantitative restriction subject to, and in this case inconsistent with, Article XI. It fell outside Article III, as argued by the US, since the domestic regulations were not applied to tuna as a product. For the reasons set out above, Article XX(b) and (g) also were not applicable. The Panel found that, since the US restrictions were inconsistent with the GATT, Article XX(d) was also not applicable.

The Panel found that the labelling provisions of the DPCIA relating to tuna caught in the ETPO were compatible with GATT. The labelling provisions did not make the right to sell tuna or tuna products, or the access to a government-conferred advantage affecting the sale of tuna or tuna products, conditional upon the use of tuna harvesting methods. Moreover, the legislation was consistent with Article I(1) of the GATT, since it did not discriminate against countries fishing in the ETPO (which was the only geographic area in which the harvesting of tuna by intentionally encircling dolphins with purse-seine nets occurred, by reason of the particular nature of the association between dolphins and tuna observed only in that area) and did not distinguish between products originating in Mexico and products originating in other countries.

Tuna/Dolphin II (1994)

In the second *Tuna/Dolphin* dispute, the EC and the Netherlands challenged provisions of the MMPA which placed an embargo on tuna imports from 'intermediary nations'. Although originally intended to prevent circumvention of the primary embargo by transhipment of dolphin-unsafe tuna through a third country, amendments made following a US court decision required each country which was identified as an 'intermediary nation' to prove that it had prohibited the import of any tuna that was barred from direct importation into the US, regardless of whether the tuna had in fact been caught in a dolphin-unsafe manner. The EC and the Netherlands maintained that the intermediary nations embargo violated Article XI of the GATT and could not be excused under the Article XX exceptions. The Panel agreed that the measures were inconsistent with Article XI(1) and proceeded to analyse their compatibility with Article XX(b) and (g).

In evaluating the compatibility of the US measures with Article XX(b) and (g), the Panel employed a three-step analysis. First, it had to be determined whether the policy underlying the measure fell within the range of policies mentioned in Article XX(b) or (g), i.e. policies to protect human, animal or plant life or health, or to conserve exhaustible natural resources. Secondly, it had to be determined whether the measure for which the exception was being invoked fulfilled the conditions of the relevant exception. Thirdly, it had to be determined whether the measure was applied in conformity with the requirement set out in the Preamble to Article XX, namely, that the measure not be applied in a manner which would constitute a means of arbitrary or unjustifiable discrimination between countries where the same conditions prevail or in a manner which would constitute a disguised restriction on international trade.

Examining Article XX(g), the Panel accepted that a policy to conserve dolphins was a policy to conserve an exhaustible natural resource since dolphin stocks could potentially be exhausted, and the basis of a policy to conserve them did not depend on whether their stocks were presently depleted. The EC and the Netherlands had argued (in line with the findings of the Panel in the first *Tuna/Dolphin* dispute) that the exhaustible natural resource to be conserved under Article XX(g) could not be located outside the territorial jurisdiction of the country taking the measure. However, this argument was firmly rejected by the Panel following an analysis of the text of the exception and the requirements of 'general international law'.

The panel then turned to the requirements of the exception itself, namely, that the measure be 'related to' the conservation of an exhaustible natural resource and be made effective 'in conjunction' with restrictions on domestic production or consumption. In line with previous GATT Panel decisions on Article XX(g), the Panel interpreted the phrases 'related to' and 'in conjunction with' to mean 'primarily aimed at'. The Panel then proceeded to examine whether the embargoes imposed by the United States could be considered to be primarily aimed at the conservation of an exhaustible natural resource, and primarily aimed at rendering effective restrictions on domestic production or consumption. The Panel noted that the intermediary nation embargo prohibited tuna imports from a country which imported tuna from countries maintaining harvesting practices and policies not comparable to those of the United States, whether or not the particular tuna was harvested in a dolphin-unsafe manner, and regardless of whether the country had tuna harvesting practices and policies that harmed or could harm dolphins. These observations might have led the Panel to conclude that the US measure was arbitrary or unjustifiably discriminatory in violation of the Article XX *chapeau*. Instead, the Panel decided that the 'primary aim' of embargo was to force changes in policy and practice in other countries, an objective which could not be justified under Article XX(g). The Panel held:

> If . . . Article XX were interpreted to permit Contracting Parties to take trade measures so as to force other Contracting Parties to change their policies within their jurisdiction, including their conservation policies, the balance of rights among Contracting Parties, in particular the right of access to markets, would be seriously impaired.

The Panel suggested that not only the intermediary nations embargo, but also the primary embargo could not be justified under Article XX(g) on this basis.The Panel applied similar reasoning in its analysis of the US measures under Article XX(b). Like Article XX(g), Article XX(b) was considered 'not [to] spell out any limitation on the location of the living things to be protected'. However, the Panel concluded that 'measures taken so as to force other countries to change their policies, and that were effective only if such changes occurred, could not be considered 'necessary' for the protection of animal life or health in the sense of Article XX(b).

ASSESSMENT

The GATT Panel decisions in the *Tuna/Dolphin* dispute placed significant limitations on the use of unilateral trade measures by states to achieve environmental goals. The *Tuna/Dolphin I* Panel rejected the use of trade restrictions seeking to give effect to national environmental protection measures relating to processes, operations cr activities carried out beyond the jurisdiction of the contracting party adopting the measures. It also stipulated that national environmental provisions must be 'necessary', which was defined to mean 'predictable' and 'unavoidable', the latter in the sense that all reasonably available international co-operative arrangements must have been exhausted. The application of these principles required the contracting parties to focus on the limited issue of the environmental effects in its territory of the product itself, and not the process which constituted the finished product.

The *Tuna/Dolphin II* Panel rejected the extra-jurisdictional limitation on Article XX(b) and (g) formulated by the first Panel, but went on to devise a further restriction on the use of these exceptions. The Panel held that unilateral trade measures which aim to change the environmental policies or practices of other contractingpartiesundermined the multilateraltrading system and could not be justified under Article XX. This interpretation, which has no apparent basis in the text of the GATT, created a test which could make it 'impossible for any nation to meet in the international trade arena'. The Panel's approach seemed to deny the availability of trade measures for environmental purposes, regardless of the geographic scope of the adverse environmental effects, and irrespective of a shared interest in the resource which is the subject of protective measures. Where the adverse environmental effects complained of by the importing country are the consequence of lax environmental process standards in the exporting country, the effectiveness of the measure to achieve its environmental goal could be dependent upon creating incentives for the exporting country to change its environmental policies in order to maintain access to the importing country's market.

The decisions of the GATT Panels in the *Tuna/Dolphin* dispute were apparently motivated by policy considerations, including concern at the prospect of the adoption of unilateral measures and growing disparities in national environmental standards, and a desire to encourage an international regulatory response to the trade problems posed by national environmental disparities. The concluding remarks of the first Panel included a call for the contracting parties, in the event that they decided to permit trade measures such as those adopted by the US, to do so by amending or supplementing the GATT, or waiving obligations thereunder, rather than by interpreting Article XX. The Panel suggested this would enable the contracting parties to impose limits on the range of environmental policy differences justifying trade responses and to develop criteria to prevent abuse. In the end, neither of the *Tuna/Dolphin* Panel decisions was adopted by the GATT Council. The findings of the Panels in the *Tuna/Dolphin* dispute must now be read in the context of the subsequent jurisprudence of the WTO Appellate Body, described below, which render both decisions of historical – rather than practical – interest.

Reformulated Gasoline Case (1996)

The *Reformulated Gasoline* case provided the new WTO Appellate Body with its first case, and its first opportunity to consider trade measures purporting to pursue environmental goals. The dispute arose out of a complaint brought by Brazil and Venezuela against regulations promulgated under the US Clean Air Act (CAA) dealing with the standards for reformulated and conventional gasoline. The function of the regulations, known as the 'Gasoline Rule', was to establish 'cleanliness' standards for gasoline sold throughout the US, based on 1990 pollution levels. The Gasoline Rule made provision for the establishment of 1990 baselines for refiners, blenders and importers as an integral part of the process of compliance assessment for the programme. Domestic entities were permitted to establish individual baselines; no provision was made, however, to allow foreign refiners to establish individual baselines. Instead, all foreign refiners were required to use statutorily determined baselines as a basis for determining whether their gasoline met the requirements of the Gasoline Rule. The US argued that statutory baselines for foreign refiners were necessary because of the overwhelming administrative difficulties its Environmental Protection Agency (EPA) would face if required to verify compliance of foreign refiners with individual baselines. The US also claimed that the measures were justified under the 'environmental exceptions' of Article XX as measures necessary for the protection of human health and relating to the conservation of an exhaustible natural resource (clean air).

The WTO Panel, at first instance, concluded that the Gasoline Rule was inconsistent with the national treatment obligation of Article III(4) and was not justified under Article XX(b) or (g). In reaching its conclusion in respect of ArticleXX(b), the Panel ruled that statutory base lines for foreign refiners were not 'necessary' because other GATT-consistent or less inconsistent measures, such as applying statutory baselines to domestic as well as foreign refiners or permitting foreign refiners to use individual baselines, were reasonably available to the US to achieve its policy goal. The Panel considered that the US had not discharged its burden of proving that reasons of administrative complexity precluded the effective use of individual baselines for foreign refiners, noting particularly that the US had not shown that a determination of origin of the gasolinecould notbe achieved bystandard meansof documentaryevidence and third party verification. In respect of Article XX(g), the Panel concluded that clear air was a 'natural resource' that could be 'depleted', and hence a policy to reduce the depletion of clean air was a policy to conserve an exhaustible natural resource within the meaning of Article XX(g). However, the Panel held that, as there was no direct connection between the less favourable treatment of imported gasoline and the US objective of improving air quality, the baseline establishment rules could not be 'primarily aimed at' the conservation of a natural resource. In reaching this conclusion, the Panel appeared to rely on its earlier conclusion in respect of Article XX(b), namely, that the baseline establishment rules were not necessary for the protection of human, animal or plant life or health. The Panel read into Article XX(g) a 'least restrictive means' test.

The appeal to the Appellate Body was limited to the Panel's rulings in respect of the application of Article XX(g). The Appellate Body found a number of legal errors in the Panel's approach to Article XX(g). First, the Appellate Body noted that the Panel should have examined whether it was the *measure,* rather than the *less favourable treatment,* which aimed at the conservation of resources.Secondly, the Panel had erred in applying a least restrictive means test (i.e. effectively whether the measure was 'necessary') rather than interpreting the actual words of the exception which simply required that the measure 'relate to' conservation. While the Appellate Body did not expressly overrule the interpretation of 'relating to' as equivalent to 'primarily aimed at' advanced in previous GATT Panel decisions, it noted that the phrase 'primarily aimed at' was not itself treaty language and 'was not designed as a simple litmus test for inclusion or exclusion from Article XX(g)'. In this regard, the Appellate Body had concluded that 'the General Agreement is not to be read in clinical isolation from public international law', opening up the possibility of its reaching out to other rules of international law arising outside the WTO, including those in the environmental field.

Overturning the Panel, the Appellate Body ruled that the Gasoline Rule was 'primarily aimed at' conservation as the baseline rules were necessary to allow scrutiny and monitoring of the level of compliance by refiners and others with the non-degradation requirements, which in turn were necessary to reach the objective of stabilising and preventing further deterioration of air quality. The Appellate Body noted that the requirement in Article XX(g) for the measures to be made effective in conjunction with restrictions on domestic production and consumption amounted to a requirement of even-handedness that was satisfied in respect of the US measure.

The Appellate Body then went on to analyse the US measure under the *chapeau* to Article XX. In doing so, it made the following general observations about the interpretation of the *chapeau:*

- It addresses not so much the questioned measure or its content but the manner in which the measure is applied.
- Its purpose and object are the prevention of abuse of the Article XX exceptions.
- It is animated by the principle that, while the exceptions of Article XX maybe invoked as a matter of legal right, they should not be so applied as to frustrate or defeat the legal obligations of the holder of rights under the substantive rules of the GATT.
- Measures falling within the particular exceptions must be

applied with due regard to the legal duties of the party claiming the exception and the legal rights of the other parties concerned.

- The burden of proof to justify the measure under the *chapeau* rests with the party advancing the measure.

The Appellate Body noted that the US had alternative courses open to it to achieve its policy goal, namely:

1. setting statutory baselines for domestic refiners; or
2. allowing foreign refiners to use individual baselines.

The Appellate Body did not accept that the use of individual baselines for foreign refiners was precluded by the administrative difficulties that would face the EPA. The Appellate Body noted that there are 'established techniques for checking, verification, assessment and enforcement of data relating to imported goods, techniques which in many contexts are accepted as adequate to permit international trade', and concluded that the US must have been aware that for these established techniques to work 'co-operative arrangements with both foreign refiners and the foreign governments concerned would have been necessary and appropriate'. It appeared to the Appellate Body that the US had not pursued the possibility of entering into co-operative arrangements with foreign governments, or, if it had, then it had not reached 'the point where it encountered governments that were unwilling to co-operate'.

In respect of the application of statutory baselines to domestic refiners, the US had argued that this would have been physically and financially impossible because of the magnitude of the changes required in almost all US refineries, causing substantial delay in implementing the programme. The Appellate Body noted, however, that similar considerations did not appear to have been taken into account *vis-a-vis* foreign refiners.

There had been two omissions on the part of the US, namely:

1. the failure to explore adequately the means (including, in particular, cooperation with the governments of Venezuela and Brazil) of mitigating the administrative problems relied on as justification by the US for rejecting individual baselines for foreign refiners; and
2. the failure to count the costs for foreign refiners that would result from the imposition of statutory baselines.

According to the Appellate Body, these resulted in the US measure giving rise to unjustifiable discrimination and amounting to a disguised restriction on international trade. The US measure thus could not be validated under Article XX(g). The Appellate Body went out of its way, however, to note that:

> It is of some importance that the Appellate Body point out what this does not mean. It does not mean, or imply, that the ability of any WTO Member to take measures to control air pollution or, more generally, to protect the environment, is at issue. That would be to ignore the fact that Article XX of the General Agreement contains provisions designed to permit important state interests – including the protection of human health, as well as the conservation of exhaustible natural resources – to find expression. The provisions of Article XX were not changed as a result of the Uruguay Round of Multilateral Trade Negotiations. Indeed, in the preamble to the WTO Agreement and in the Decision on Trade and Environment, there is specific acknowledgment to be found about the importance of co-ordinating policies on trade and the environment. WTO Members have a large measure of autonomy to determine their own policies on the environment (including its relationship with trade), their environmental objectives and the environmental legislation they enact and implement. So far as concerns the WTO, that autonomy is circumscribed only by the need to respect the requirements of the General Agreement and the other covered agreements.

SHRIMP/TURTLE CASES (1998 AND 2001)

D. Brack, 'The Shrimp-Turtle Case: Implications for the Multilateral Environmental Agreement–World Trade Organization Debate', 9 *Yearbook of International Environmental Law* 13 (1998); H. Mann, 'Of Revolution and Results: Trade and Environmental Law in the Afterglow of the Shrimp Turtle Case', 9 *Yearbook of International Environmental Law* 28 (1998); D. Wirth, 'Some Reflections on Turtles, Tuna, Dolphin and Shrimp', 9 *Yearbook of International Environmental Law* 40 (1998); R. Howse, 'The Appellate Body Rulings in the Shrimp/Turtle Case: A New Legal Baseline for the Trade and Environmental Debate', 27 *Columbia Journal of Environmental Law* 491 (2002).

The second 'environmental' case to come before the dispute resolution bodies of the WTO raised similar legal issues to those considered by GATT Panels in the *Tuna/Dolphin* dispute. The case concerned an import prohibition imposed by the US on certain shrimp and shrimp products from India, Malaysia, Pakistan and Thailand, on the ground that they were harvested in a manner which adversely affected endangered sea turtles. In 1987, the US had issued regulations (pursuant to its 1973 Endangered Species Act) requiring all US-registered shrimp trawl vessels to use approved turtle excluder devices (TEDs) in specified areas where there was a significant mortality of sea turtles in shrimp harvesting. TEDs allowed for shrimp to be harvested without harming other species, including sea turtles. The US regulations became fully effective in 1990, and were subsequently modified to require the general use of approved TEDs at all times and in all areas where there was a likelihood that shrimp trawling would interact with sea turtles. In 1989, the US enacted section 609 of Public Law 101-162, which addressed the importation of certain shrimp and shrimp products. Section 609 required the US Secretary of State to negotiate bilateral or multilateral agreements with other nations for the protection and conservation of sea turtles. Section 609(b)(1) imposed (not later than 1 May 1991) an import ban on shrimp harvested with commercial fishing technology which might adversely affect sea turtles. Further regulatory guidelines were adopted in 1991, 1992 and 1996, governing *inter alia* annual certifications to be provided by harvesting nations. In broad terms, certification was to be granted only to those harvesting nations which provided documentary evidence of the adoption of a regulatory programme to protect sea turtles in the course of shrimp trawling. Such a regulatory programme had to be comparable to the programme of the US, with an average rate of incidental taking of sea turtles by their vessels which should be comparable to that of US vessels. The 1996 guidelines further required that all shrimp imported into the US had to be accompanied by a shrimp exporter's declaration attesting that the shrimp was harvested either in the waters of the nation certified under section 609, or under conditions that did not adversely affect sea turtles, including through the use of TEDs. Section 609 also included a provision calling upon the US Secretary of State, in consultation with the Secretary of Commerce, 'to initiate negotiations as soon as possible for the development of bilateral or multilateral agreements with other nations for the protection and conservation of . . . sea turtles'. Acting under this provision, the US negotiated and concluded an Inter-American Convention for the Protection and Conservation of Sea Turtles with nations fishing for shrimp in the Western Atlantic. However, the US made no attempt to negotiate a similar agreement with the complainants prior to the imposition of the import ban.

From a WTO perspective, the difficulty with the approach taken by the US was that it was, in effect, applying its conservation laws extra-territorially to activities carried out within – or subject to the jurisdiction of – third states. This raises an issue of broader international legal interest, namely, the circumstances (if any) in which a state may apply its conservation measures to activities taking place outside its territory or jurisdiction, including by non-nationals. The US sought to justify its actions on the ground that the sea turtles it was seeking to protect were recognised in international law as being endangered.

The US legislation was challenged by India, Malaysia, Pakistan and Thailand. At first instance, a WTO Panel concluded that the import ban applied on the basis of section 609 was not consistent with Article XI(1) of GATT 1994 and could not be justified under any of the exceptions in Article XX of GATT 1994.

The US appealed to the WTO Appellate Body, invoking in particular Article XX(g) to justify the legality of its measures. In appraising section 609 under Article XX of GATT 1994, the Appellate Body followed a three-step analysis. First, the Appellate Body asked whether the Panel's approach to the interpretation of Article XX was appropriate; it concluded that the Panel's reasoning was flawed and 'abhorrent to the principles of interpretation we are bound to apply' (paras. 112–24). Secondly, the Appellate Body asked whether section 609 was 'provisionally justified' under Article XX(g). Invoking the concept of 'sustainable development', it found that it was so justified (paras. 125–45). Thirdly, it asked whether section 609 met the requirements of the *chapeau* of Article XX, and concluded that it did not because the US actions imposed an 'unjustifiable discrimination' and an 'arbitrary discrimination' against shrimp to be imported from India, Malaysia, Pakistan and Thailand. In relation to the second and third steps, the Appellate Body invoked the principle of 'sustainable development', as an aid to interpretation.

The Appellate Body's approach is premised upon an application of the 'customary rules of interpretation of public international law', as required by Article 3(2) of the DSU, which rules 'call for an examination of the ordinary meaning of the words of a treaty, read in their context, and in the light of the object and purpose of the treaty involved'. It is these customary rules which the Panel had failed to apply, leading to the conclusion at step one that the Panel's approach was flawed.

In relation to step two, the Appellate Body invoked the principle of sustainable development in determining whether the measures taken by the US were 'provisionally justified'. As a threshold question, the Appellate Body had to decide whether section 609 was a measure *concerned with* the conservation of 'exhaustible natural resources', in the face of the argument that the term refers only to finite resource such as minerals, and not biological or renewable resources such as sea turtles (which, it was argued, fall to be covered by Article XX(b)). The Appellate Body rejected the argument, ruling that Article XX(g) extended to measures taken to conserve exhaustible natural resources, whether living or non-living, and that the sea turtles involved here 'constituted "exhaustible natural resources" for the purpose of Article XX(g)'.In reaching that conclusion, the Appellate Body stated that Article XX(g) had to be read by a treaty interpreter 'in the light of contemporary concerns over the community of nations about the protection and conservation of the environment'.

Referring to the Preamble to the 1994 WTO Agreement, the Appellate Body noted that its signatories were 'fully aware of the importance and legitimacy of environmental protection as a goal of national and international policy' and that the Preamble 'explicitly acknowledges "the objective of *sustainable development*'. This, said the Appellate Body, was a concept which 'has been generally accepted as integrating economic and social development and environmental protection'. According to the Appellate Body, this conclusion was supported by modern international conventions and declarations, including the UN Convention on the Law of the Sea. It followed that the sea turtles at issue were an 'exhaustible natural resource' and highly migratory animals, passing in and out of the waters subject to the rights of jurisdiction of various coastal states on the high seas. The Appellate Body observed:

Of course, it is not claimed that all populations of these species migrate to, or traverse, at one time or another, waters subject to United States jurisdiction. Neither the appellant nor any of the appellees claims any rights of exclusive ownership over the sea turtles, at least not while they are swimming freely in their natural habitat – the oceans. We do not pass upon the question of whether there is an implied jurisdictional limitation in Article XX(g), and if so, the nature or extent of that limitation. We note only that in the specific circumstances of the case before us, there is a sufficient nexus between the migratory and endangered marine populations involved and the United States for the purpose of Article XX(g).

The concept of 'sustainable development' was not expressly invoked to justify this potentially far-reaching conclusion as to the nexus between the sea turtles and the United States. Nevertheless, the concept appeared to inform that conclusion, apparently establishing the necessary link between the interest of the United States in the proper conservation of a distant natural resource located from time to time outside its jurisdiction, and the finding that section 609 is 'provisionally justified' under Article XX(g). Although the Appellate Body claimed that it did 'not pass upon the question of whether there is an implied jurisdictional limitation in Article XX(g)', its conclusion appears hardly consistent with such a limitation. The concept of 'sustainable development' (and the need to integrate economic and social development and environmental protection) appears to have been implicitly invoked to extend (by interpretation) the jurisdictional scope of Article XX(g). This marks a significant move away from the approach of the earlier *Tuna/Dolphin* panels.

The third step of the Appellate Body's analysis addressed the issue of whether section 609 was consistent with the requirements of the *chapeau* to Article XX. Again, the Appellate Body invoked 'sustainable development', this time in the context of its conclusion that section 609 was an 'unjustifiable' discrimina-tion. The Appellate Body revisited the Preamble to the WTO Agreement, noting that it demonstrated that WTO negotiators recognised 'that optimal use of the world's resources should be made in accordance with the objective of sustainable development', and that the preambular language, including the reference to sustainable development must add colour, texture and shading to our interpretation of the agreements annexed to the WTO

Agreement, in this case the GATT 1994. We have already observed that Article XX(g) of the GATT 1994 is appropriately read with the perspective embodied in the above preamble.

In support of the relevance of 'sustainable development' to the process of interpretation of the WTO Agreements, the Appellate Body invoked the Decision of Ministers at Marrakesh to establish a permanent Committee on Trade and the Environment. That Decision refers, in part, to the consideration that 'there should not be . . . any policy contradiction between . . . an open, non-discriminatory and equitable multilateral trading system on the one hand, and acting for the protection of the environment, and the promotion of sustainable development on the other'. The Appellate Body noted that the terms of reference for the establishment by this Decision of the Committee on Trade and the Environment (which made further reference to the concept of sustainable development) specifically referred to Principles 3 and 4 of the Rio Declaration on Environment and Development.

It appears that 'sustainable development' informed the conclusion that the US measures constituted an unjustifiable discrimination: according to the Appellate Body, section 609 established a rigid standard by which US officials determined whether or not countries would be certified, and it was not acceptable 'for one WTO Member to use an economic embargo to require other Members to adopt essentially the same comprehensive regulatory programme, to achieve a certain policy goal, as that in force within that Member's territory, without taking into consideration different conditions which may occur in the territories of those other Members'. Shrimp caught using identical methods to those employed in the US had been excluded from the US market solely because they had been caught in waters of countries that had not been certified by the US, and the resulting situation was 'difficult to reconcile with the declared [and provisionally justified] policy objective of protecting and conserving sea turtles'. This suggested that the US was more concerned with effectively influencing WTO members to adopt essentially the same comprehensive regulatory regime as that applied by the US to its domestic shrimp trawlers. Moreover, the US had not engaged the appellees 'in serious, across-the-board negotiations with the objective of concluding bilateral or multilateral agreements for the protection and conservation of sea turtles, before enforcing the import prohibition'. The failure to have *a priori* consistent recourse to diplomacy as an instrument of environmental protection policy produced 'discriminatory impacts on countries exporting shrimp to the US with which no international agreements [were] reached or even seriously attempted'.The fact that the United States negotiated seriously with some but not other members that exported shrimp to the United States had an effect which was 'plainly discriminatory and unjustifiable'. Further, different treatment of different countries' certification was observable in the differences in the levels of efforts made by the US in transferring the required TED technology to specific countries. Moreover, the protection and conservation of highly migratory species of sea turtles demanded 'concerted and co-operative efforts on the part of the many countries whose waters [were] traversed in the course of recurrent turtle migrations'. Such 'concerted and co-operative efforts' were required by *inter alia* the Rio Declaration (Principle 12), Agenda 21 (para. 2.22 (i)), the 1992 Biodiversity Convention (Article 5) and the 1979 Berne Convention. Further, the 1996 Inter-American Convention for the Protection and Conservation of Sea Turtles provided a 'convincing demonstration' that alternative action was reasonably open to the US other than the unilateral and non-consensual procedures established by section 609. And finally, while the US was a party to the 1973 CITES, it had not attempted to raise the issue of sea turtle mortality in relevant CITES committees, and had not signed the 1979 Berne Convention or the 1982 UNCLOS, or ratified the 1992 Biodiversity Convention.

Shrimp/Turtle Case Phase II (2001)

The Appellate Body report in the *Shrimp/Turtle* dispute was adopted by the WTO's DSB on 6 November 1998, together with a recommendation that the

US bring the import prohibition into conformity with its obligations under the WTO Agreement. In implementing the recommendations and rulings of the DSB, the US did not amend section 609, leaving its import prohibition on shrimp from uncertified states in effect. However, the US Department of State issued 'Revised Guidelines for the Implementation of Section 609 of Public Law 101-162 Relating to the Protection of Sea Turtles in Shrimp Trawl Fishing Operation'. Under the Revised Guidelines, a country could apply for certification even if it did not require the use of TEDs, provided it demonstrates that it had implemented and was enforcing, a 'comparably effective' regulatory programme to protect sea turtles without the use of TEDs. Malaysia challenged the Revised Guidelines before another WTO panel, which found them to be in violation of Article XI but justified under Article XX as long as the conditions stated in the findings of the Panel's report, and in particular 'the ongoing serious good faith efforts to reach a multilateral agreement' remained satisfied.

Malaysia subsequently appealed the Panel's ruling to the Appellate Body, on two principal grounds: first, the duty of the US to pursue international co-operation in protecting and conserving endangered sea turtles prior to implementing unilateral trade measures, and, secondly, whether the Revised Guidelines were sufficiently 'flexible' to meet the requirements of the Article XX *chapeau*. In its rulings on these issues, the Appellate Body clarified its approach to unilateral trade measures taken to achieve environmental goals. In relation to the duty to pursue international co-operation, Malaysia asserted that the US should have negotiated *and concluded* an international agreement on the protection and conservation of sea turtles before imposing a unilateral import prohibition. In response, the US countered that it had made serious, good faith efforts to secure a multilateral sea turtle conservation agreement among Indian Ocean and South-East Asian states. The Appellate Body confirmed that the requirement for 'serious across-the-board negotiations' did not imply that agreements on environmental resources had to be actually concluded, since that would, in effect, grant a veto to individual states. The Appellate Body considered that such a requirement would not be reasonable:

> For a variety of reasons, it may be possible to conclude an agreement with one group of countries but not another. The conclusion of a multilateral agreement requires the co-operation and commitment of many countries. In our view, the United States cannot be held to have engaged in 'arbitrary or unjustifiable discrimination' under Article XX solely because one international negotiation resulted in an agreement while another did not.

Although the *conclusion* of an agreement with all affected countries was preferable, it was not required: what was necessary was that negotiations in different fora should be *comparable*. The Appellate Body ruled that the Panel had correctly concluded that the efforts made by the US in the Indian Ocean and South-East

Asia region constituted serious, good faith efforts to secure multilateral agreement on sea turtle conservation in that region, and the US measure was not being applied in a manner constituting unjustifiable or arbitrary dis-crimination.

On the issue of the 'flexibility' of the Revised Guidelines to takeaccount ofthe differing conditions prevailing in other members' territories, Malaysia argued that the Revised Guidelines breached the Article XX *chapeau* by 'unilaterally' imposing US domestic standards on exporters. The Appellate Body rejected this argument, noting that the Revised Guidelines contained provisions permitting the US authorities to take into account the specific conditions of Malaysian shrimp production, and of the Malaysian sea turtle conservation programme, should Malaysia decide to apply for certification. The Appellate Body found that the Revised Guidelines, on their face, permitted a degree of flexibility which would enable the US to consider the particular conditions prevailing in Malaysia if and when Malaysia applied for certification. The Appellate Body's approach appears to be intended to address concerns raised in the wake of its decisions in *Reformulated Gasoline* and the first phase of the *Shrimp/Turtle* dispute, to the effect that countries wishing to adopt unilateral trade measures for environmental purposes would face an extremely onerous task if required to consider the particular conditions prevailing in every potentially affected member before acting. It remains to be seen whether the changes to the US measure in issue will result in adequate consideration by US authorities of other countries' alternative approaches to achieving environmental goals, and the limitations those countries may face in addressing environmental concerns.

ASBESTOS CASE (2000)

D. A. Wirth, 'GATT – Technical Barriers to Trade Agreement – Asbestos Import Ban', 96 AJIL 435 (2002); S. Charnovitz, 'The Law of Environmental "PPMs" in the WTO: Debunking the Myth of Illegality', 27 *Yale Journal of International Law* 59 (2002).

The most recent trade/environment case to come before a WTO panel and the Appellate Body involved a challenge by Canada to a French decree concerning asbestos and products containing asbestos. In the *Measures Affecting Asbestos and Asbestos-Containing Products* case, Canada requested a WTO panel to consider the consistency of a French decree with the TBT Agreement, and Articles III and XI of the GATT. It also alleged, under Article XXIII(1)(b) of the GATT, that the French decree nullified or impaired advantages accruing to Canada directly or indirectly under the WTO Agreement, or impeded the attainment of an objective of that Agreement. The French decree law generally banned the use of asbestos and asbestos-containing products, subject to time-limited exceptions for certain existing materials, products or devices containing chrysotile fibres. In particular, chrysotile fibres and products containing them could continue to be used but only where no substitute was available which 'in the present state of scientific knowledge, poses a lesser occupational health risk than chrysotile fibre to workers handling those materials, products or devices' and 'provides all technical guarantees of safety corresponding to the ultimate purpose of the use thereof '.

In examining the French decree under the TBT Agreement, the Panel distinguished between its general prohibition in Article 1 of the decree and the exceptions established by Article 2, holding that the former did not fall within the scope of the TBT Agreement as the asbestos ban did not amount to a 'technical regulation'. The Panel did not consider whether the exceptions amounted to a technical regulation under the TBT Agreement, on the basis that no claim had been made by Canada in relation to Article 2 of the decree. The Panel found that the law violated Article III(4), but held that the French measures could be justified under Article XX(b). Canada appealed the Panel's decision to the Appellate Body, challenging the Panel's interpretations of the TBT Agreement, and Articles III, XX(b) and XXIII(1)(b) of the GATT.

In reviewing the Panel's interpretation of the term 'technical regulation' in the TBT Agreement, the Appellate Body stated that the proper legal character of the measure at issue could not be determined unless the measure were examined as a whole, including both the ban and its exceptions. The Appellate Body ruled that the French decree was a 'technical regulation' under the TBT Agreement, but did not go on to complete the analysis under the TBT Agreement as it concluded that it did not have an adequate factual basis in the findings of the Panel to enable it to do so. For present purposes, the most important aspect of the Appellate Body's ruling relates to its interpretation of the 'like products' requirement in Article III(4). The question raised was whether chrysotile asbestos fibres were 'like' certain other fibres, namely, PVA fibres, or cellulose and glass fibres (collectively referred to as PCG fibres), and whether cement-based products containing asbestos fibres were 'like' those containing one of the PCG fibres. The Panel had concluded that the two categories of products – one containing asbestos and the other containing PCG alternatives – were 'like' within the meaning of Article III(4). The EC appealed, arguing that the 'likeness' test in Article III(4) called for an analysis of the health objective of the regulatory distinction made in the measure between asbestos fibres and other fibres. The Appellate Body accepted the EC's arguments and reversed the Panel's finding.

The Appellate Body considered the term 'like products' in Article III(4) by reference to dictionary definitions, the surrounding GATT provisions, and the general principle articulated in Article III(1) that members should ensure equality of competitive conditions for imported products in relation to domestic products. It concluded that 'likeness' was 'a determination about the nature and extent of a competitive relationship between and among products', and had to be made on a case-by-case basis. The Appellate Body adopted the criteria taken by previous GATT panels, and the WTO Panel in the *Asbestos* case, to assess the question of likeness, namely: (1) the properties, nature and quality of the products; (2) the end-uses of the products; (3) consumers' tastes and habits in respect of the products; and (4) the tariff classification of the products.In this case, for asbestos fibres 'evidence relating to the health risks associated with a product' could be pertinent in an examination of 'likeness' and needed to be evaluated under the criteria of physical properties, and of consumers' tastes and habits, having regard to their carcinogenicity. The evidence had established that the products in issue were physically different, and, to overcome an indication that products were *not* 'like', 'a higher burden is placed on complaining members to establish that, despite the pronounced physical differences, there is a competitive relationship between the products such that *all* of the evidence, taken together, demonstrates that the products are 'like' under Article III: (4) of the GATT 1994'. Considering the health risks posed by asbestos products, and the implications of such for the physical properties of the products and consumers' preferences in respect of them, the Appellate Body found that the evidence relied on by the Panel in finding 'likeness' was insufficient, and reversed the Panel's finding on this point.

As to the meaning of 'necessity' under Article XX(b), the Appellate Body rejected Canada's three grounds of challenge. It ruled that Article XX(b) did not require the Panel to 'quantify' the risk associated with asbestos fibres: it was sufficient for the risk to be evaluated either in quantitative or qualitative terms. On the question of the level of health protection selected by France in its law, the Appellate Body reiterated that WTO members have an undisputed right to determine their own level of health protection, and that the 'controlled use' of asbestos fibres and asbestos-containing products (as proposed by Canada) was not an alternative measure that would achieve the end sought by France. In determining whether any alternative measure was 'reasonably available', several factors had to be taken into account, besides the difficulty of implementation, including the interests or values pursued by the measure. The health protection objective pursued by the measure was a value 'both vital and important in the highest degree', and France could not reasonably be expected to employ any alternative measure if the measure would involve a continuation of the very risk that the law sought to halt because the alternative measure would effectively prevent France from achieving its chosen level of health protection.

Finally, the Appellate Body made important observations about the standard of proof to be applied by Panels when evaluating scientific evidence advanced in justification of a measure taken under Article XX(b). It rejected Canada's argument that any such claim had to be made on the basis of the 'preponderant' weight of the evidence, ruling that it was sufficient for a member to rely, in good faith, on scientific sources which, at the time, may represent a divergent, but qualified and respected, opinion. Thus, a member was not obliged automatically to follow what, at any given time, constituted majority scientific opinion.

ASSESSMENT

Overall, the 'trade and environment' disputes decided under the new WTO dispute resolution system have tended to give greater weight to the environmental and health concerns reflected in the Article XX(b) and (g) exceptions. In interpreting the provisions of the GATT 1994 and other WTO Agreements, the Appellate Body has demonstrated a commitment to refer to general international law arising outside the WTO system, including multilateral environmental treaties. It has also proposed a clearer legal framework for analysis of measures under Article XX and has clarified that the purpose of the *chapeau* is to prevent protectionist abuse of the Article's exceptions, not to limit the use of measures which are genuinely intended to achieve environmental objectives. concerning end-uses and consumer preferences, and questioning the necessity or appro priateness of the majority's adoption of a 'fundamentally' economic interpretation of the 'likeness' criterion.

In the *Reformulated Gasoline* and *Shrimp/Turtle* cases, the Appellate Body has identified two preconditions necessary to ensure that a member's environmental measures do not fall foul of the requirements of the Article XX *chapeau*: first, the need to make serious efforts to secure a co-operative solution to the problem, prior to resorting to unilateral action; and, secondly, the need to consider the conditions prevailing in other members' territories in designing any trade-restricting measure. The *Asbestos* case provides important guidance on the meaning of 'likeness', indicating a willingness to permit greater consideration of potential health and environmental risks associated with a product in determining 'likeness' for the purpose of Article III(4).

Measures for health and safety protection

An increasingly important aspect of the relationship between trade and the environment in international law is that relating to the requirements for states to adopt trade measures in furtherance of national goals of human, animal or plant health and safety protection. Health and safety measures with the potential to impact trade are dealt with by the WTO's Agreement on Sanitary and Phytosanitary Measures (SPS Agreement). The SPS Agreement lays down the conditions governing sanitary and phytosanitary (SPS) measures enacted by members, amplifying Article XX(b) and confirming that measures consistent with the SPS Agreement are deemed to meet the requirements of that Article.

The SPS Agreement affirms the right of each WTO member to take SPS measures necessary for the protection of human, animal and plant life or health, subject to the provisions of the

Agreement, in particular their trade restrictive-ness and the need for scientific justification. Members must observe national treatment and non-discrimination principles in the design of their measures, must accept the SPS measures of other members as equivalent if the exporting member objectively demonstrates equivalency, and must not apply SPS measures in a manner that would constitute a disguised restriction on international trade. Members must also ensure that their SPS measures are applied only to the extent necessary, are based on scientific principles and are not maintained without sufficient scientific evidence. To promote the harmonisation of SPS measures, members are encouraged to base their SPS measures on international standards where they exist. SPS measures that 'conform to' international standards are deemed necessary to protect human, animal and plant life or health and are presumed to be consistent with the SPS Agreement. Members are not prevented from introducing or maintaining SPS measures which are stricter than those reflected in international standards 'if there is a scientific justification, or as a consequence of the level of sanitary or phytosanitary protection a Member determines to be appropriate in accordance with the relevant provisions of paragraphs 1 through 8 of Article 5'.

Article 5 provides that members are to ensure their SPS measures are based on a risk assessment which takes into account *inter alia* available scientific evidence and relevant processes and production methods, and relevant ecological and environmental conditions. In assessing risk and determining the measure to achieve its appropriate level of SPS protection, a member must take into account as relevant economic factors the potential damage in terms of loss of production or sales in the event of entry, the establishment or spread of the pest or disease, the costs of control or eradication and the relative cost-effectiveness of alternatives to limiting risks. Members must avoid arbitrary or unjustifiable distinctions in the levels of protection considered appropriate in different situations if the distinctions result in discrimination or a disguised restriction on international trade. They must also ensure that measures are not more trade-restrictive than is required to achieve the appropriate level of SPS protection, taking into account technical and economic feasibility. Where relevant scientific evidence is insufficient to allow a full risk assessment, Article 5.7 allows the adoption of provisional SPS measures by a member 'on the basis of available pertinent information' and subject to undertaking a subsequent risk assessment within a 'reasonable' period of time.

Disputes between members over SPS measures are dealt with under the dispute settlement procedures of the WTO. To date, there have been three disputes before WTO Panels and the Appellate Body which raised issues under the SPS Agreement: the *Australian Salmon*, *Japanese Varietals* and *Beef Hormones* cases. One dispute which has not yet been taken to WTO dispute settlement is that between the United States and the European Union, concerning the latter's *de facto* moratorium on the approval of new genetically modified crops, which has been in place since mid-1998, as well as various EU and other schemes designed to require the labelling of products which contain, or may contain, GMOs.

BEEF HORMONES

J. McDonald, 'Big Beef Up or Consumer Health Threat?: The WTO Food Safety Agreement, Bovine Growth Hormone and the Precautionary Principle', 15 *Environmental and Planning Law Journal* 115 (1998); D. A. Wirth, 'European Communities Restrictions on Imports of Beef Treated with Hormones', 92 AJIL 755 (1998); J. Pauwelyn, 'The WTO Agreement on Sanitary and Phytosanitary Measures as Applied in the First Three SPS Disputes', 2 *Journal of International Economic Law* 641 (1999); T. Christoforou, 'Settlement of Science-Based Trade Disputes in the WTO: A Critical Review of the Developing Case Law in the Face of Scientific Uncertainty', 8 *New York University Environmental Law Journal* 622 (2000).

Canada and the US challenged the EC measures primarily on the ground of the alleged failure of the EC to undertake a risk assessment, prior to adoption of the measures, as required by the SPS Agreement. The Panel upheld the challenges, holding that the EC measure was inconsistent with Article 5.1, and that the import prohibition was inconsistent with Articles 3.3 and 5.5 of the SPS Agreement. Beyond its conclusion on the relevance of the precautionary principle, the Appellate Body overturned the Panel's ruling that the SPS Agreement allocated the 'evidentiary burden' to the member imposing an SPS measure. It found that the complaining parties bore the initial burden of showing *prima facie* inconsistency of the challenged measures with the SPS Agreement; only after such a *prima facie* case was made did the burden shift to the other party to provide evidence and arguments to disprove the complaining party's claim. The standard of review was neither *de novo* review nor 'total deference' to national authorities, but rather the 'objective assessment of the matter' required by Article 11 of the DSU.

As to Article 3.1 and 3.3 of the SPS Agreement, the Appellate Body overturned the Panel, ruling that Article 3.1 did not require members to harmonise their SPS measures, by conforming those measures to international standards. Instead, a measure which was 'based on' international standards (such as *Codex Alimentarius* standards) may adopt some but not necessarily all of the elements of the international standard. Measures based on (rather than conforming to) international standards enjoyed no presumption of GATT consistency, but the burden was on the complainant to demonstrate *prima facie* inconsistency with the SPS Agreement. The Appellate Body noted that Article 3.3 gave members an 'autonomous right' (which was neither unqualified nor absolute) to establish their own levels of SPS protection, which may be stricter than international standards. In this regard it agreed with the Panel that a higher standard pursuant to Article 3.3 required a risk assessment (pursuant to Article 5.1).

As to Article 5.1, the Appellate Body considered that the function of the Panel was simply to determine whether the measures were sufficiently supported or reasonablywarranted bythe riskassessment. It wasnot necessary thatthe risk assessment come to a monolithic conclusion that coincided with the scientific conclusion or view implicit in the SPS measure. The SPS measure might be based on a qualified but divergent minority scientific view:

> The risk assessment could set out both the prevailing view representing the 'mainstream' of scientific opinion, as well as the opinions of scientists taking a divergent view. Article 5.1 does not require that the risk assessment must necessarily embody only the view of a majority of the relevant scientific community. In some cases, the very existence of divergent views presented by qualified scientists who have investigated the particular issue at hand may indicate a state of scientific uncertainty. Sometimes the divergence may indicate a roughly equal balance of scientific opinion, which may itself be a form of scientific uncertainty. In most cases, responsible and representative governments tend to base their

legislative and administrative measures on 'mainstream' scientific opinion. In other cases, equally responsible and representative governments may act in good faith on the basis of what, at a given time, may be a divergent opinion coming from qualified and respected sources. By itself, this does not necessarily signal the absence of a reasonable relationship between the SPS measure and the risk assessment, especially where the risk involved is life-threatening in character and is perceived to constitute a clear and imminent threat to public health and safety.

The Appellate Body also addressed the preparation and content of the risk assessment. It concluded that the EC's measures were not based on a risk assessment that reasonably supported or warranted the import prohibition. The various scientific studies the EC had adduced (produced by European committees, international organisations and individual scientists which it sought to rely upon as the basis for its measures) were too general in nature. Accordingly, the measures were inconsistent with Article 5.1 and consequently also with Article 3.3.

AUSTRALIAN SALMON

The *Salmon* dispute arose out of a Canadian complaint regarding Australia's prohibition on the importation of fresh, chilled or frozen salmon from Canada. The Australian restrictions, which had been in place since 1975, were maintained on the basis that importation of Canadian salmon could result in the introduction of exotic disease agents into Australia, with negative consequences for the health of fish in the country's waters. They prohibited the import of dead salmon into Australia unless, prior to importation, the fish had been 'subject to such treatment as in the opinion of the Director of Quarantine is likely to prevent the introduction of any infectious or contagious disease, or disease or pest affecting persons, animals or plants'. The Director of Quarantine had permitted the entry of commercial imports of heat-treated salmon products for human consumption as well as non-commercial quantities of other salmon (primarily for scientific purposes) subject to prescribed conditions. Australian authorities had conducted an import risk analysis for uncooked, wild, adult ocean-caught Pacific salmon which was initially set forth in a 1995 Draft Report, finalised in December 1996 (Final Report). The 1995 Draft Report had recommended allowing the importation of ocean-caught Pacific salmon under certain conditions but this was revised in the Final Report which recommended continuing the import prohibition for uncooked salmon products. Acting on the basis of the Final Report, the Director of Quarantine decided to prohibit the importation of uncooked ocean-caught Pacific salmon.

The WTO Panel found that the Australian prohibition was in breach of the SPS Agreement on the grounds that it was not based on a risk assessment and that the prohibition was more trade-restrictive than required to achieve Australia's chosen level of SPS protection. The Panel also held that Australia had adopted arbitrary or unjustifiable distinctions in the levels of SPS protection designated for salmon *vis-a'-vis* non-salmonids in breach of Article 5.5. Australia appealed the Panel's decision to the WTO Appellate Body, challenging the Panel's interpretation of Articles 5.1, 5.5 and 5.6 of the SPS Agreement.

As to Article 5.1, the Appellate Body conducted its own assessment of the consistency of the Australian measure withArticle 5.1. It first examined whether the risk analysis conducted by Australian authorities amounted to a risk assessment for the purpose of Article 5.1, holding that a risk assessment on which quarantine restrictions are based must satisfy three conditions, namely, it must:

1. *identify* the diseases whose entry, establishment or spread a member wants to prevent within its territory, as well as the potential biological and economic consequences associated with the entry, establishment or spread of these diseases;
2. *evaluate* the likelihood of entry, establishment or spread of these diseases, as well as the associated potential biological and economic consequences; and
3. *evaluate* the likelihood of entry, establishment or spread of these diseases according to the SPS measures which might be applied.

The Appellate Body stressed that it was not sufficient for a risk assessment to conclude that there was a possibility of entry, establishment or spread of diseases. Rather, a proper risk assessment had to evaluate the likelihood (i.e. the 'probability'), of entry, establishment or spread of diseases and associated biological and economic consequences, including by reference to the SPS measures which might be applied. The likelihood or probability of an event could be expressed quantitatively or qualitatively and there was no requirement for a risk assessment to establish a certain magnitude or threshold level of degree of risk. On this basis, the Appellate Body concluded that the 1996 Final Report was not a proper risk assessment within the meaning of Article 5.1. With regard to Article 5.5, the Appellate Body found that the different levels of SPS protection adopted by Australia for imports of different fish and fish products were arbitrary, and that the distinctions in the levels of protection imposed by Australia resulted in a disguised restriction on international trade.As to Article 5.6, the Appellate Body reversed the Panel's finding but made no final determination as to the consistency of the import prohibition with Article 5.6.

Japanese Varietals

The *Japanese Varietals* dispute concerned a challenge by the United States to a requirement imposed by Japan to test and confirm the efficacy of quarantine treatment for each variety of certain agricultural products prior to import.Under its Plant Protection Law and Regulation, Japan prohibited the importation of eight agricultural products (apples, cherries, peaches, walnuts, apricots, pears, plums and quince) from, *inter alia*, the United States on the ground that these fruits were potential hosts of the codling moth, a pest of quarantine significance to Japan. Pursuant to the Japanese regulations, the import prohibition could be lifted if an exporting country proposed an alternative quarantine treatment which would achieve a level of protection equivalent to the import prohibition. Japan issued administrative guidelines concerning the testing requirements which applied to initial lifting of the import prohibition on a product and also to import approval for additional varieties of the product. The testing requirement for additional varieties was the measure challenged by the United States in the dispute. A WTO Panel found that Japan's measure violated several provisions of the SPS Agreement, including Articles 2.2, 5.6 and 5.7.

The Panel found that Japan's varietal testing requirement (as applied to apples, cherries, nectarines and walnuts) was maintained without sufficient scientificevidenceand therefore inconsistent with Article 2.2. Japan appealed the Panel's findings, arguing that the requirement in Article 2.2 for a member not to maintain an SPS measure 'without sufficient scientific evidence' should be interpreted in light of the precautionary principle. The Appellate Body upheld the Panel's ruling, and reiterated its finding in *Beef Hormones* that the precautionary principle, while finding reflection in the Preamble, Article 3.3 and Article 5.7, 'has not been written into the SPS Agreement as a ground for justifying SPS measures that are otherwise inconsistent with the obligations of Members set out in particular provisions of the Agreement'.

The Panel had also rejected Japan's reliance on Article 5.7. Reviewing that provision, the Appellate Body found that it establishes four requirements for provisional SPS measures, all of which must be satisfied, namely, that the measure is:

1. imposed where 'relevant scientific information is insufficient';
2. adopted 'on the basis of available pertinent information';
3. not maintained unless the member 'seek[s] to obtain the additional information necessary for a more objective assessment of risk'; and
4. 'review[s] the . . . measure accordingly within a reasonable period of time'.

The Appellate Body upheld the Panel's finding that additional information collected by Japan had failed to 'examine the appropriateness' of the SPS measure at issue and had not addressed the core issue of whether 'varietal characteristics cause a divergency in quarantine efficacy'. It also confirmed that Japan had not conducted the necessary review within a 'reasonable period of time'.

ASSESSMENT

The decisions under the SPS Agreement indicate the extent of the limitations on the ability of WTO members to adopt SPS measures with potential trade effects. They emphasise the need for measures to be based on a scientific assessment of potential risks, which comprehensively evaluates the probability (not the mere possibility) of adverse effects, on a case-by-case basis. 'Real world' risks can be taken into account as part of the assessment but there must be a rational relationship between any SPS measure and the scientific evidence. As to Article 5.5, the Appellate Body has affirmed that members have an autonomous right to determine their appropriate level of SPS protection for different risks. The decisions in *Beef Hormones* and *Australian Salmon* emphasise the need for WTO members to pay greater attention to the issue of consistency between the SPS measures which they maintain for similar risks. In *Beef Hormones*, the Appellate Body appeared willing to accept differences in levels of SPS protection reflecting the socio-cultural environment of the adopting member state; the *Australian Salmon* case suggests that substantial differences between SPS measures for similar risks may be taken as an indication of a discriminatory or protectionist intent, especially in the absence of a scientific risk assessment justifying the measures adopted. With regard to Article 5.7, members must seek additional information germane to the conduct of a proper risk assessment and review any provisional measures within a reasonable period of time. The precautionary principle does not provide a separate basis for the adoption of SPS measures where the underlying science is uncertain, though a precautionary approach to risk assessment may be warranted in such circumstances. In particular, a member may be justified in basing its measures on qualified divergent scientific opinion 'where the risk involved is life-threatening in character and is perceived to constitute a clear and imminent threat to public health and safety'.

European Community

EC Commission, *1992: The Environmental Dimension – Task Force Report on the Environment and the Internal Market* (1990); P. Demaret, 'Trade-Related Environmental Measures (TREMs) in the External Relations of the European Community', in M. Maresceau (ed.), *The European Community's Commercial Policy After 1992: The Legal Dimension* (1993); A. Ziegler, *Trade and Environmental Law in the European Community* (1996); L. Gormley, 'Free Movement of Goods and the Environment', in J. Holder (ed.), *The Impact of EC Environmental Law in the United Kingdom* (1997); H. Temminck, 'From Danish Bottles to Danish Bees', 1 *Ye a r b o o k of European Law* 61 (2000); J. Scott, *EC Environmental Law* (2000), Chapter 4; J. Jans, *European Environmental Law* (2000), 121–34 and Chapter VI; L. Kra¨mer, *EC Environmental Law* (2000, 4th edn), 74–89; V. Heyvaert, 'Balancing Trade and Environment in the European Union: Proportionality Substituted?', 13 *Journal of Environmental Law* 392 (2001).

Similar provisions to those found in the GATT also exist in the EC Treaty, which was adopted in 1957 to create a 'common market' between the six original member states. Article 28 (formerly Article 30) of the EC Treaty prohibits quantitative restrictions on imports and all measures having equivalent effects (non-tariff barriers to trade). The express exceptions to Article 28, set out in Article 30 (formerly Article 36), include the protection of health and life of humans, animals or plants, provided that such prohibitions or restrictions do not constitute a means of arbitrary discrimination or a disguised restriction on trade between member states. Environmental protection is not expressly included as an exception. As set out in further detail in chapter 15 above, the EC began to legislate actively on environmental matters shortly after the 1972 Stockholm Conference, and in 1980the ECJ endorsed the use of the EC Treatyto legislate on environmental matters. In 1986, the EC Treaty was amended by the additionofa new Article100a(nowArticle 95) andthe specific provisionson environmental protection in Articles 130r to 130t (now Articles 174–176), but Article 30 was not amended to include environmental measures as a justifiable limitation on trade. Following the conclusion of the Treaty of Amsterdam in 1997, the EC Treaty was again amended to include a further provision relating to environmental protection. Article 6 (formerly Article 3c) of the Treaty now provides that:

Environmental protection requirements must be integrated into the definition and implementation of the Community policies and activities . . . in particular with a view to promoting sustainable development.

In relation to the trade and environment issue, the EC Treaty was amended to provide that where harmonisation measures are adopted by the EC under Article 95 (including environmental measures) to achieve the progressive establishment of the internal market then if a Member State deems it necessary to maintain national provisions on grounds of major needs referred to in Article 30, or relating to the protection of the environment or the working environment, it shall notify the Commission of these provisions as well as the grounds for maintaining them. Moreover, . . . if, after the adoption by the Council or by the Commission of a harmonisation measure, a Member State deems it necessary to introduce national provisions based on new scientific evidence relating to the protection of the environment or the working environment on grounds of a problem specific to that Member State arising after the adoption of the harmonisation measure, it shall notify the Commission of the envisaged provisions as well as the grounds for introducing them.

Where environmental protection measures are adopted under Article 175 of the EC Treaty, member states are not prevented from 'maintaining or introducing more stringent protective measures' which are compatible with the EC Treaty.Even after the amendments introduced in 1986, 1992, 1997 and 2001, the EC Treaty is silent as to the permissibility of national environmental measures which restrict or limit trade where no EC measures have been adopted on a particular environmental matter under Articles 95 or 175.

TRADE RESTRICTIONS ON ENVIRONMENTAL GROUNDS: THE ROLE OF THE ECJ

The ECJ has played an important role in delimiting the conditions under which environmental protection measures adopted by EC member states will be permitted. In 1983, the ECJ upheld French legislation which restricted the export of waste oils from France to other EC member states. Two years later, the ECJ held that the protection of the environment was one of the Community's 'essential objectives' which could, as such, justify certain limitations on the free movement of goods provided that they did not 'go beyond the inevitable restrictions which are justified by the pursuit of the objective of environmental protection'. This was followed by two landmark cases which provided significant guidance on the position of the ECJ: the 1989 judgment in the *Danish Bottles* case and the 1992 judgment in the *Belgian Waste Disposal* case.Since then, the ECJ has decided a number of cases dealing with both environmental protection measures and measures concerned with the related goal of ensuring public health and safety.

Danish Bottles Case

P. Kromarek, 'Environmental Protection and Free Movement of Goods: The Danish Bottles Case', 2 JEL 89 (1990); P. Sands, 'Danish Bottles and Mexican Tuna', 1 RECIEL 28 (1992).

The *Danish Bottles* case was the result of an action commenced by the EC Commission under Article 226 (formerly Article 169) against Denmark, for a declaration that a Danish beer and soft drinks container law breached Article 28 (formerly Article 30) of the EC Treaty. In 1978, Danish legislation had been introduced to allow the relevant minister to adopt rules limiting, prohibiting or requiring the use of certain materials and types of container for drinks. The legislation was presented as an anti-pollution measure, and empowered the National Agency for the Protection of the Environment (NAPE) to administer the law. In 1981, further legislation was adopted pursuant to the 1978 legislation requiring, first, that containers for gaseous mineral waters, lemonade, soft drinks and beer be subject to a compulsory deposit-and-return system, and, secondly, that such containers be approved by NAPE.

Producers of beverages and containers in other member states, and their trade associations, considered the Danish legislation to establish a non-tariff barrier to trade which restricted the import into Denmark of their products. Insofar as the Danish legislation affected production (bottling) techniques outside Danish jurisdiction, the legislation might be considered to have certain extra-territorial effects. The producers were supported in their view by the EC Commission, which called on the Danish Government to change its 1981 law. This led to a 1984 amendment to the 1981 legislation, which allowed beverages covered by the 1981 legislation to be sold in non-approved containers, provided that the quantity sold did not exceed 3,000 hectolitres per annum per producer, or that the beverage was being sold in the container normally used for that product in the country of production in order to 'test-market' it in Denmark. Additionally, the 1984 amendment required that no metal containers be used, that a return/recycling system for non-approved containers be set up, that the deposit for the container be equal to that normally charged on a similar approved container, and that the person marketing the product keep the NAPE fully informed to show compliance.

The EC Commission was not satisfied with the 1984 amendments and in 1986 brought Article 226 proceedings to have the compulsory deposit-and-return system and the NAPE bottle approval system declared incompatible with Article 28 of the EC Treaty. The United Kingdom intervened in support of the Commission. In his opinion, Advocate General Slynn supported the Commission's argument and found both the compulsory deposit-and-return system and the compulsory NAPE approval system to be in breach of Article 28. The ECJ did not follow the Advocate General's Opinion, holding that the deposit-and-return system was compatible with Article 28 but that the NAPE approval system was not compatible. In its first judgment after the 1986 Single European Act to address environmental limitations on free trade in the single market, but applying the pre-1986 rules, the ECJ stated that:

> in the absence of common rules relating to the marketing of the products concerned, obstacles to movement within the Community resulting from disparities between national laws must be accepted, in so far as such rules, applicable to domestic and imported products without distinction, may be recognised as being necessary in order to satisfy mandatory requirements of Community law. It is also necessary for such rules to be proportionate to the aim in view. If a member state has a choice between various measures to achieve the same objective, it should choose the means which least restrict the free movement of goods . . . The protection of the environment is a mandatory requirement which may limit the application of Article 30 of the Treaty.

The ECJ found that the deposit-and-return system established an obligation which was: an essential element of a system aiming to secure the re-use of containers and therefore appears to be necessary to attain the objectives of the disputed regulations. In view of this finding, the restrictions which they impose on the free movement of goods should not be considered as disproportionate.

However, as regards the NAPE approval system, the ECJ found that by restricting the quantity of beer and soft drinks which could be marketed by a single producer in non-approved containers to 3,000 hectolitres per year Denmark had adopted measures with disproportionate consequences: the existing system of return for approved containers guarantees a maximum percentage of re-use and therefore gives considerable protection to the environment because the empty containers can be returned to any retailer of beverages, whereas non-approved containers can only be returned to the retailer who sold the beverage because of the impossibility of setting up such a complete organisation for such containers also. However, the system for returning non-approved containers is capable of protecting the environment and, so far as imports are concerned, covers only limited quantities of beverages by comparison with the quantity consumed in the country because of the restrictive effect of the compulsory return of containers on imports. Under these conditions, limiting the quantity of products which can be marketed by importers is disproportionate to the objective.

In the absence of specific EC legislation establishing a rule of environmental protection, national environmental rules to restrict trade between member states will be permitted provided that

1. the rules are necessary to protect the environment;
2. the effect on trade is not disproportionate to the objective pursued; and
3. the rules are not discriminatory against producers in third countries.

The ECJ's approach is not dissimilar to the analysis applied to the Article XX *chapeau* by the Appellate Body in the *Shrimp/Turtle* dispute, although the Appellate Body speaks in terms of the need to maintain a balance between the right of a member to invoke an exception under Article XX and the rights of the other members under GATT's substantive provisions, rather than in terms of proportionality. The ECJ's approach recognises the widespread support for weight to be given to legal aspects of environmental protection, even if this results in disparities in environmental standards and justifiable interference with the sanctity of free trade ideals. It focuses primarily on the nature of the legislation at issue, rather than the consequences for the 'single market'. As required by EC law, there is no consideration of the intentions of the drafters (who are unlikely to have imagined these types of disputes back in the mid-1950s), and the 'extra-jurisdictional' consequences of the Danish legislation were ignored.

DEAD RED GROUSE CASE

The following year, the ECJ was called upon to consider the legality of a Dutch prohibition on the importation of red grouse lawfully killed in the United Kingdom. On an Article 234 (formerly Article 177) reference from the Netherlands, the Court held that the prohibition was incompatible with Article 30 (formerly Article 36) of the EC Treaty, read in conjunction with the 1979 EC Wild Birds Directive. Although Article 14 of the Directive permitted member states to introduce stricter protective measures than those provided under the Directive, the import prohibitions could not be justified for a species of bird which did not inhabit the territory of the legislating member state but could be found in another member state where it could be lawfully hunted under the Directive. Since the red grouse was neither a migratory species nor a seriously endangered species listed in Annex I to the Directive, and was not an endangered species under EC legislation implementing CITES, the Dutch prohibition was held to be unlawful under EC law.

BELGIAN WASTE DISPOSAL CASE

In July 1992, the ECJ ruled that Belgian legislation limiting the free movement of waste had been adopted in breach of an EC Directive but did not violate the provision on the free movement of goods. The judgment is an important one which established further principles to justify restrictions on free trade which are adopted for environmental protection purposes. The case was brought by the EC Commission against Belgium under Article 226 of the EC Treaty. The Commission took the view that legislation of the Wallonia region of Belgium which prohibited the disposal in Wallonia of waste originating from another state was incompatible with Directive 75/442/EEC (waste) and Directive 84/631/EEC (transboundary movement of waste), as well as Article 28 (formerly Article 30) and Article 30 (formerly Article 36) of the EC Treaty. The Court found that there had been no breach of Directive 75/442, since it did not include any provisions on trade in waste between member states or any express prohibition on adopting measures such as those taken by Belgium.

The Court did hold, however, that the Belgian legislation breached Directive 84/631, as amended. By introducing an absolute ban, the legislation went beyond the measures permitted by the Directive, which had established a 'complete system relating to transfrontier shipments ofhazardouswastes for disposal in specified establishments' including a system of notification and the possibility of banning certain shipments of hazardous wastes which posed a threat to the environment and health, or to public security; the Directive did not permit a blanket prohibition.

The question concerning the violation of Articles 28 and 30 raised interesting points which are analogous to issues raised in GATT/WTO disputes. It turned on whether the EC Treaty provisions governing the free movement of goods applied to wastes which could not be recycled or re-used. Belgium argued that such wastes were not goods within the meaning of Article 28, since they had no intrinsic commercial value and could not be the subject of a sale. The Court rejected this approach. It held that any objects which were transported across a boundary to give effect to a commercial transaction were subject to Article 28, whatever the nature of the transaction, and that recyclable or non-recyclable wastes were products subject to Article 28 whose free movement under that Article should not, as a matter of principle, be limited. The Court held that the distinction between recyclable and non-recyclable wastes created serious practical difficulties of application, particularly in the context of constantly evolving technical progress; whether waste was recyclable or not depended also on the cost of recycling and the usefulness of the re-use envisaged.

Having decided that wastes were covered by Article 28, the Court considered whether the prohibition imposed by the limitation could nevertheless be justified. It accepted that the protection of the environment could justify the Belgian legislation, and rejected the Commission's argument that the legislation should be declared unlawful on the grounds that it was discriminatory because it treated wastes from other member states more restrictively than the same wastes which might have been produced in Wallonia having regard 'to the differences between waste produced in one place and that in another and its connection with the place where it is produced'. The Court considered that wastehadaspecialcharacter and that theapplication ofArticle 174(2) (formerly Article 130r(2)) of the EC Treaty, which established the principle that environmental damage should as a priority be rectified at source, implied that it was a matter for each region, commune or other local authority to take appropriate measures to ensure the receipt, treatment and disposal of its own wastes: waste should be disposed of as close as possible to the place where it is produced in order to keep the transport of waste to the minimum practicable. The Court thus endorsed an environmentally-based limitation on the free movement of goods under EC law, justifying this on the grounds that it accorded with the principles of 'self-sufficiency' and 'proximity' as provided in the 1989 Basel Convention.

Belgian Pesticides Case

The *Belgian Pesticides* case was brought before the ECJ on an Article 234 preliminary ruling reference from Belgium. A Belgian law prohibited the sale of pesticides for non-agricultural use, where they had not been previously authorised by the Belgian authorities. A prosecution was brought under the Belgian law in respect of the sale of a prohibited pesticide which had nevertheless been approved in the Netherlands and satisfied all the requirements of existing EC Directives. The parties agreed that the Belgian law was incompatible with Article 28 (formerly Article 30) of the EC Treaty but sought guidance from the Court as to whether Belgium could rely on the public health exemption under Article 30 (formerly Article 36).

The ECJ found that Community legislation, as it stood, did not make any provision relating to the marketing of biocidal products. The Court noted that, since biocidal products are used to combat organisms harmful to human or animal health and organisms liable to damage natural or manufactured products, they inevitably contain dangerous substances and that in the absence of harmonising rules, the member states are free to decide on their intended level of protection of human health and life and on whether to require prior authorisation for the marketing of such products. The Court held that while a member state is free to require a product of the type in issue in the case, which had already received approval in another member state, to undergo a fresh procedure of examination and approval, the authorities of the member states are nevertheless required to assist in relaxing the controls existing in intra-Community trade and to take account of technical or chemical analyses or laboratory tests which have already been carried out in another member state.

Aher-Waggon Case

In the *Aher-Waggon* case, a German court made an Article 234 preliminary reference to the ECJ seeking a ruling as to whether certain German legislation was incompatible with Article 28 (formerly Article 30) of the EC Treaty. The German legislation, implementing Council Directive 80/51/EEC on the limitation of noise emissions from subsonic aircraft, made the first registration in Germany of aircraft previously registered in another member state conditional upon compliance with stricter noise standards than those laid down by the Directive, while exempting from those standards aircraft which obtained registration in Germany before the Directive was implemented. The ECJ noted that the EC Directive merely laid down minimum requirements for noise emissions from aircraft and did not prevent member states from imposing stricter noise limits. Moreover, the Court found that, while the measure restricted intra-Community trade, it could be justified by considerations of public health and environmental protection such as those put forward by the German Government, namely, that Germany, which is a very densely populated state, attaches special importance to ensuring that its population is protected from excessive noise emissions. The Court was satisfied that the measure was proportionate, accepting the explanation by the German Government that limiting noise emissions from aircraft was the most effective and convenient means of combating the noise pollution which they generate. The German Government argued that, without extremely costly investment, it was generally difficult to reduce noise emissions appreciably by carrying out works in the vicinity of airports.

As for the exemption from stricter noise emissions standards for aircraft registered in Germany before the Directive was implemented, this did not violate Article 28 since those aircraft were also required to comply with the stricter noise standards when they underwent technical modification, even if such modifications had no bearing on noise emissions, or when they were temporarily withdrawn from service. Furthermore, the Court noted, the number of such aircraft could readily be determined by the German authorities. The national authorities were thus entitled to consider that the number of aircraft not meeting the stricter noise standards was necessarily going to fall and that the overall level of noise pollution would diminish. Moreover, the ECJ held, the effectiveness of the German policy of progressively eliminating from the national fleet aircraft not meeting the stricter noise standards would be undermined if their number could be increased, to an extent not foreseeable by the national authorities, by aircraft from other member states.

Danish Bees Case

The *Danish Bees* case arose out of criminal proceedings brought against Ditlev Bluhme for the infringement of Danish legislation prohibiting the keeping on the Danish island of Laeso of bees other than those of the subspecies *Apis mel-lifera mellifera* (Laeso brown bees). The defendant argued that the legislation was a prohibition on importation, and constituted a measure having equivalent effect contrary to Article 28.

A preliminary ruling on the question was sought from the ECJ under Article 234 of the EC Treaty. The Danish Government argued that its measure applied to bees indiscriminately, whatever their state of origin, and was justified by the aim of protecting biological diversity, such an aim being recognised, *inter alia*, by the 1992 Habitats Directive.

The Danish Government argued that the measure was both necessary and proportionate as the Laeso brown bee sub-species was disappearing and could be preserved only on the island of Laeso. Moreover, the measure did not affect the possibility of carrying on bee-keeping on the island but merely regulated the species of bee which could be used for this purpose. These contentions were disputed by the defendant and the Commission on the basis of a lack of scientific consensus as to whether Laeso brown bees were a distinct sub-species or in fact in danger of extinction.

Notwithstanding the lack of conclusive scientific evidence establishing the nature of the sub-species and the risk of extinction, the Court considered that the threat of disappearance of the Laeso brown bee was 'undoubtedly genuine' if mating with golden bees occurred, given the recessive nature of the genes of the brown bee. The measure was justified on environmental protection grounds since: measures to preserve an indigenous animal population with distinct characteristics contribute to the maintenance of biodiversity by ensuring the survival of the population concerned. By so doing, they are aimed at protecting the life of those animals and are capable of being justified under Article 36 [now Article 30] of the Treaty.

From the point of view of such conservation of biodiversity, it is immaterial whether the object of protection is a separate subspecies, a distinct strain within any given species or merely a local colony, so long as the populations in question have characteristics distinguishing them from others and are therefore judged worthy of protection either to shelter them from a risk of extinction that is more or less imminent, or, even in the absence of such risk, on account of a scientific or other interest in preserving the pure population at the location concerned.

The Court noted that the conservation of biodiversity through the establishment of areas in which a population enjoys special protection was a method recognised by Article 8(a) of the 1992 Biodiversity Convention, and was already put into practice in Community law by the Directives on wild birds and habitat protection. Thus the establishment by Danish legislation of a protection area was a necessary and proportionate measure in relation to the aim pursued.

Belgian Foodstuffs Labelling Case

The *Belgian Foodstuffs Labelling* case was the result of an action commenced by the EC Commission under Article 226 (formerly Article 169) against Belgium for a declaration that a Belgian Royal Decree concerning the placing on the market of nutrients and foodstuffs to which nutrients had been added was contrary to Article 28. The Decree required the labelling of foodstuffs containing nutrients to include details of the notification number given to the product by the Inspection Service for Foodstuffs of the Ministry of Public Health and the Environment. Belgium sought to justify its labelling requirement on the ground of public health protection under Article 30 of the EC Treaty.

In its judgment, the ECJ reiterated that it had made clear in its case law that: in the absence of harmonisation of laws, Article 30 [now Article 28] of the Treaty prohibits, in principle, obstacles to intra-Community trade which are the consequence of applying, to goods coming from other Member States where they are lawfully manufactured and marketed, rules that lay down requirements to be met by such goods, such as those relating to presentation, labelling and packaging, even if those rules apply without distinction to domestic products and imported products.

The Court found that the Belgian labelling obligation was 'of a nature such as to hinder intra-Community trade' as it had the potential to 'force the importer to alter the packaging of his products on the basis of the place where they are marketed and therefore to incur additional packaging and labelling costs'.Notwithstanding the Belgian Government's contention that the extra costs associated with the packaging and labelling requirements would ultimately be borne by Belgian consumers, the Court found that 'the mere prospect of having to lay out those costs constitutes a barrier for traders since it is capable of acting as a disincentive to those of them who are contemplating marketing the products concerned in Belgium'. The Court concluded that the measure was not justified on the grounds of public health protection, nor was it proportionate.

Swedish Chemical Products Ban Case

In *Kemikalieinspektionen* v. *Toolex Alpha AB*, a Swedish court sought a preliminary ruling from the ECJ concerning whether a prohibition on the industrial use of the chemical trichloroethylene was consistent with Article 30 of the EC Treaty,even if it contravened Article28. TheSwedishmeasurein issue banned the industrial use of trichloroethylene chemical products subject to certain exemptions which applied to allow the continued use of the chemical where no feasible substitutes were available. Sweden argued that the measure was justified under Article 30 as being necessary for the protection of human health and/or the environment. While the chemical was not a known carcinogen, experimental and epidemiological studies had suggested a link between the chemical and cancer in humans.

The ECJ upheld the legislation as justified:

[T]aking account of the latest medical research on the subject, and also the difficulty of establishing the threshold above which exposure to trichloroethylene poses a serious health risk to humans, given the present state of the research, there is no evidence in this case to justify a conclusion by the Court that national legislation such as that at issue in the case in the main proceedings goes beyond what is necessary to achieve the objective in view.

Moreover, the exemptions established by the measure were appropriate and proportionate offering increased protection for workers while at the same time taking account of the difficulties faced by companies for which no feasible alternative for the chemical was available. This was ensured by strict conditions on the granting of exemptions which permitted use of the chemical only where no safer replacement product was available, and provided that the applicant continued to seek alternative solutions which were less harmful to public health and the environment. Furthermore, in no case could the concern to avoid causing disruption to an undertaking where there was no alternative solution justify the grant of an exemption unless workers' exposure to trichloroethylene was maintained at acceptable levels.

German Renewable Energy Case

The *German Renewable Energy* case arose out of an Article 234 reference to the ECJ concerning, *inter alia*, the compatibility with Article 28 of a German law obliging electricity supply undertakings, which operated a general supply network, to purchase the electricity produced in their area of supply from renewable sources of energy. The ECJ noted that, according to the well-known *Dassonville* formula, 'any national measure which is capable of hindering, directly or indirectly, actually or potentially, intra-Community trade' is inconsistent with Article 28. It recalled that its case law established that an obligation to obtain a certain percentage of supplies from a national supplier limited the possibility of importing the same product because purchasers are precluded from obtaining supplies, in respect of part of their needs, from suppliers situated in other member states. Consequently, the German law was 'capable, at least potentially, of hindering intra-Community trade', since it expressly stated that the purchase obligation imposed on electricity suppliers applied only to electricity produced from renewable energy sources within the respective supply area.

Notwithstanding this finding, the Court ruled that the German measure was not incompatible with Article 28 given its aim and the features of the electricity market. In particular, the Court noted that the: use of renewable energy sources for producing electricity, which a statute such as the amended *Stromeinspeisungsgesetz* is intended to promote, is useful for protecting the environment in so far as it contributes to the reduction in emissions of greenhouse gases which are among the main causes of climate change which the European Community and its Member States have pledged to combat.

In contrast to the *Danish Bottles* case, the Court did not rely on environmental protection as a 'mandatory requirement' justifying a departure from Article 28. Rather, it pointed to a number of considerations supporting its conclusion that, 'in the current state of Community law concerning the electricity market', legislation such as the German law was not incompatible with Article 28 of the Treaty. These included the obligations assumed by the Community and individual member states under the 1992 Climate Change Convention and the 1997 Kyoto Protocol to promote growth in the use of renewable energy; the requirements of Article 6 of the EC Treaty (environmental protection requirements must be integrated into the definition and implementation of EC policies); various recitals of Council Directive 96/92/EC concerning common rules for the internal market in electricity, which expressly state that it is 'for reasons of environmental protection' that the Directive authorises member states to give priority to the production of electricity from renewable sources; and the fact that once electricity has been allowed into the transmission or distribution system, it is difficult to determine its origin and, in particular, the source of energy from which it was produced necessitating a system of certificates of origin for electricity produced from renewable sources, capable of being the subject of mutual recognition, in order to make intra-Community trade in that type of electricity both reliable and possible in practice.

Canada–United States Free Trade Agreement

The Canada–United States Free Trade Agreement (FTA) aims to eliminate a large number of barriers to trade between the two countries. Although it has been superseded by the NAFTA (see below), the FTA merits consideration because of the case law it has generated. Under the FTA, the parties affirm the 1979 GATT Agreement on Technical Barriers to Trade and agree not to 'maintain or introduce standards-related measures or procedures for product approval that would create unnecessary obstacles to trade between the territories of the parties'.

'Unnecessary obstacles' are not deemed to be created if 'the demonstrable purpose of the measure or procedure is to achieve a 'legitimate domestic objective' and the measure or procedure does not exclude goods of the other party that meet such an objective. An objective whose purpose is to protect the environment is a legitimate objective. Exceptions are also made for trade in goods by Article 1201 of the FTA, which incorporates Article XX of the GATT. The FTA requires the parties to exchange full texts of proposed federal standards-related measures and product approval procedures prior to their adoption, except in urgent cases where delay would frustrate the achievement of a legitimate domestic objective.

The FTA has its own dispute settlement provisions, including the establishment of FTA Panels. In 1989, an FTA Panel interpreted Article XX(g) of the GATT in the *Salmon and Herring* case, and in 1990 an FTA Panel considered environmental issues the *Lobsters from Canada* case. The latter dispute concerned the enactment by the US of an amendment to the Magnuson Fishery Conservation and Management Act to prohibit, *inter alia*, the sale or transport in or from the US of whole live lobsters smaller than the minimum possession size in effect under US federal law. Canada considered that the application of this law to Canadian lobster exports to the US was contrary to Article 407 of the FTA, which incorporates Article XI of the GATT. The US agreed that even if the measures were contrary to Article XI, they fell within the exception under Article XX(g) of the GATT, which was incorporated by Article 1201 of the FTA. The Panel held, by a majority of three to two, that the US measures imposed on live US and Canadian lobsters were not covered by Article XI but by Article III of GATT, and that they came within the 'scope of laws, regulations and requirements affecting the internal sale, offering for sale, purchase, transportation, distribution or use of products'. The Panel did not determine whether these Article III measures were consistent with the national treatment requirements, since such determination lay outside its terms of reference. Accordingly, the majority did not consider the applicability of Article XX of the GATT.

The minority, however, found that Article XI was applicable and that the US measures conflicted with that provision, since they had the effect of totally denying access to the US market of Canadian live small lobsters. Accordingly, they considered whether the US measures were permitted by the conservation exception in Article XX(g). The minority relied on the interpretation of Article XX(g) adopted by the FTA Panel in the *Salmon and Herring* case, which had held that Article XX(g) must be narrowly construed and that to qualify for an exemption:

- the measure must relate to an exhaustible natural resource;
- domestic production of the resource must be likewise restricted;
- the measure must not involve arbitrary or unjustifiable discrimination between foreign countries; and
- the measure must be primarily aimed at conservation.

On this basis, the minority in the FTA *Lobsters from Canada* case concluded that the US measures were in the nature both of a conservation measure and of a trade restriction, and that therefore the 1989 Magnuson amendment was not 'primarily aimed at' conservation, since the US had not addressed the reasons why its conservation objections could not be met by alternative measures, such as the special marking of small Canadian lobsters, or the requirement that lobsters be sorted by size prior to importation into the US, or particular documentary requirements as to small lobsters of Canadian origin, or increased penalties for the possession of sub-sized lobsters, more vigilant enforcement efforts, or other requirements.

North America Free Trade Agreement

G. C. Hufbauer *et al*., *NAFTA and the Environment: Seven Years Later* (2000).

The North America Free Trade Agreement (NAFTA) between Canada, Mexico and the US entered into force in January 1994. The NAFTA establishes a free trade area between the parties in accordance with Article XXIV of the GATT, and is intended to establish principles and rules (including national treatment and most-favoured nation treatment, which will, *inter alia,* eliminate barriers to trade in goods and services and promote competition between the parties) in a manner which is consistent with environmental protection and conservation and which will promote sustainable development. In the event of inconsistencies between the NAFTA and the GATT, and except as otherwise provided in the NAFTA, the provisions of the NAFTA will prevail. The NAFTA's provisions on foreign investment protection are addressed in chapter 20 below.

Environmental considerations were and remain a controversial aspect of the NAFTA, due to strong lobbying by environmental groups and labour unions in the US who were concerned by the potential effect of weaker Mexican environmental standards on the more stringent US environmental standards, and on the implications for labour. The NAFTA addresses environmental issues, and further measures to strengthen its commitment to environmental protection were set forth in the 1993 Agreement on Environmental Co-operation (see below). It expressly provides that trade obligations under the 1973 CITES, the 1987 Montreal

Protocol (and its 1990 amendments), the 1989 Basel Convention (upon its entry into force for the parties), and the agreements set out in Annex 104.1 to the NAFTA, are to prevail to the extent of inconsistency 'provided that where a party has a choice among equally effective and reasonably available means of complying with such obligations, the party chooses the alternative that is least inconsistent with the other provisions of [NAFTA]'.Moreover, for the purposes of Part Two (Trade in Goods) and Part Three (Technical Barriers to Trade) of the NAFTA, Article XX of the GATT is incorporated on the understanding that 'the measures referred to in GATT Article XX(b) include environmental measures necessary to protect human, animal or plant life or health, *and* that GATT Article XX(g) applies to measures relating to the conservation of living and non-living exhaustible natural resources'.

The NAFTA requires each party to accord national treatment to the goods of the other parties in accordance with Article III of the GATT, and provides for the elimination of tariffs. Except as provided in the NAFTA, non-tariff measures such as prohibitions on imports or exports, which could include national environmental protection measures, are prohibited except in accordance with Article XI of the GATT. Prohibited non-tariff measures include customs user fees, country of origin marking, standards and labelling of distinctive products, and export taxes and other export measures. The NAFTA contains detailed provisions on sanitary and phytosanitary measures, and other non-technical barriers to trade, drawing a distinction between the rules applicable to each type of measure.

The NAFTA establishes a framework of rules and disciplines to guide the development, adoption and enforcement of sanitary and phytosanitary measures that may directly or indirectly affect trade between the parties which is virtually identical to that of the WTO SPS Agreement. The NAFTA SPS rules allow each party to adopt, maintain or apply any sanitary or phytosanitary measure which is 'necessary for the protection of human, animal or plant life or health in its territory, including a measure more stringent than an international standard, guideline or recommendation'. Under Article 712(2), each party may establish appropriate levels of protection in accordance with protecting human, animal or plant life or health, but must ensure that any sanitary or phytosanitary measure that it adopts, maintains or applies:

1. is based on scientific principles (including a risk assessment) (Article 712(3));
2. does not arbitrarily or unjustifiably discriminate between its goods and like goods of another party or between goods of another party and like goods of any other country where identical or similar conditions prevail (Article 712(4));
3. is applied only to the extent necessary to achieve its appropriate level of protection (Article 712(5)); and
4. does not create a disguised restriction on trade (Article 712(6)).

Under NAFTA, international standards, guidelines or recommendations are to be used as the basis for sanitary and phytosanitary conditions. The general objective of this section is to create equivalence in standards:

Without reducing the level of protection of human, animal or plant life or health, the parties shall, to the greatest extent practicable and in accordance with this Section, pursue equivalence of their respective sanitary and phytosanitary measures.

Article 715 sets out the factors which are to be taken into account in conducting risk assessments. These include: relevant techniques and methodologies of international standardising organisations; relevant scientific evidence; relevant processes and production methods and inspection and testing methods; the prevalence of relevant diseases or pests; relevant ecological or other environmental conditions; relevant treatments such as quarantine; certain specified economic factors; and the objective of minimising negative trade effects and arbitrary or unjustifiable restrictions on trade which discriminate or constitute a disguised restriction on trade.

NAFTA provides for adaptation to regional conditions and the procedures for dealing with control, inspection and approval, and for the notification and publication of information on federal measures, and establishes an advisory Committee on Sanitary and Phytosanitary Measures to facilitate the enhancement of food safety and the improvement of sanitary and phytosanitary conditions, activities under Articles 713 and 714, technical co-operation and consultation.

NON-TECHNICAL BARRIERS TO TRADE

Chapter 9 of the NAFTA (Articles 901 to 915) establishes rules for any standards-related measure of a party other than sanitary and phytosanitary measures, that may directly or indirectly affect trade in goods or services between the parties, and to measures of the parties relating to such standards. This includes environmental measures other than those related to agriculture. Further to Article 103, the parties affirm their existing rights and obligations relating to standards-related measures under the 1979 GATT Agreement on Technical Barriers to Trade and all other international agreements, including environmental and conservation agreements, to which they are party.

Under Article 904(1), the parties are allowed to adopt, maintain or apply any standards-related measure, which is defined as a standard, technical regulation, or conformity assessment procedure, including those 'relating to safety, the protection of human, animal and plant life or health, the environment or consumers, and any measure to ensure its enforcement or implementation'.

Article 904(1) provides that such measures include those to prohibit the importation of a good of another party that fails to comply with the applicable requirements of those measures. Since the definition of standard and technical regulation includes 'processes and production methods' related to goods, Article 904 would appear to permit US legislation prohibiting the import of yellow-fin tuna from Mexico on the ground that it was caught in a way which violated US environmental and fisheries standards, in effect superseding the ruling of the GATT Panel in the *Yellow-Fin Tuna* case.

This would appear to be the correct interpretation, since in pursuing its legitimate environmental objectives each party may establish the level of protection that it considers appropriate, provided that those measures: avoid arbitrary or unjustifiable distinctions between similar goods or services in the level of protection it considers appropriate, where the distinctions:

(a) result in arbitrary or unjustifiable discrimination against goods or service providers of another party;

(b) constitute a disguised restriction on trade between the parties; or

(c) discriminate between similar goods or services for the same use under the same conditions that pose the same level of risk and provide similar benefits.

Goods and service providers are entitled to national treatment and treatment no less favourable than that accorded to goods or service providers of any other country. Standards-related measures are prohibited if they create an unnecessary obstacle to trade, but no such unnecessary obstacle will be deemed to be created if the demonstrable purpose of such measures is to achieve a legitimate objective and they do not exclude goods of another party that meet that legitimate objective. However, the parties must use established international standards (or international standards whose completion is imminent) as a basis for their standards-related measures, except where such standards would be ineffective or inappropriate to fulfil legitimate objectives, including their failure to achieve a 'level of protection that the party considers appropriate'.Measures based on international standards will be presumed to be consistent with Article 904(3) and (4). Moreover, and crucially, Article 905(1) is not to be construed to prevent a party, in pursuing its legitimate objectives, from adopting, maintaining or applying any standards-related measure that results in a higher level of protection than would be achieved if the measures were based on the relevant international standard.

In this context (and recognising the 'crucial role of standards-related measures in promoting and protecting legitimate objectives'), the parties agree to work jointly to enhance the level of the protection of the environment; without reducing such protection, and taking into account international standardisation activities, NAFTA commits the parties 'to the greatest extent practicable, [to] make compatible their respective standards-related measures'. To that end, the parties undertake to seek to promote the compatibility of specific standard or conformity assessment procedures. Each importing party agrees to treat technical regulations adopted or maintained by an exporting party as equivalent to its own where the exporting party demonstrates to the satisfaction of the importing party that its technical regulation adequately fulfils the importing party's legitimate objectives. In pursuing their legitimate objectives, a party may conduct a risk assessment on a good or service, which is to include: consideration of available scientific evidence; intended end uses; processes or production and other methods; and environmental conditions. Chapter 9 of NAFTA also provides for rules establishing the compatibility of conformity assessment, the notification and publication of proposals adopting or modifying technical regulations, inquiry points and technical co-operation. A Committee on Standards-Related Measures is established to, *inter alia*: monitor implementation; facilitate the compatibility of measures and enhance the development, application and enforcement of measures; and consider non-governmental regional and multilateral developments regarding standards-related measures, including those under the WTO/GATT.

COMPETITION

The rules on competition are far less detailed than their equivalent in the EC and are unlikely, in the short or medium term, to provide a basis for the further development of international law rules on competition and the environment. The NAFTA requires each party to adopt or maintain measures to proscribe anticompetitive business conduct. A monopoly must not act in a manner which is inconsistent with a party's obligations under the NAFTA, must act solely in accordance with commercial considerations, and must not use its monopoly position to engage in anti-competitive practices in a non-monopolised market in its territory. The NAFTA establishes a Working Group on Trade and Competition, but has no rules on subsidies. National laws on anti-dumping and countervailing duties are retained.

INSTITUTIONS AND DISPUTE SETTLEMENT

NAFTA's principal organ is the Free Trade Commission, which is responsible for supervising implementation, overseeing its further elaboration, resolving disputes concerning interpretation and application, supervising the work of committees established under the Agreement and considering any other matters which arise. The Commission, which comprises cabinet-level representatives or their designees, is assisted by a secretariat. The system for the settlement of disputes under the NAFTA provides for a number of options. First, disputes arising under both the NAFTA and the GATT may be settled in either forum at the discretion of the complaining party. However, where the responding party claims that its action is subject to Article 104

(Relation to Environmental and Conservation Agreements) and requests that the matter be dealt with under the NAFTA, only the procedures available under the NAFTA will be available. Similar provisions apply in respect of disputes arising under the provisions on sanitary and phytosanitary measures and standards-related measures concerning, *inter alia,* measures to protect the environment or factual issues concerning the environment and directly related scientific matters. If consultations between the parties and the good offices of the Free Trade Commission fail to resolve the matter, an arbitral panel of five members will be established by the Commission at the request of any consulting party.

The Panel's initial report will be based on the parties' submissions and arguments, and on information from experts and Scientific Review Boards, and may contain findings of fact, determinations, and recommendations for the resolution of the dispute. Unless the parties agree otherwise, the Panel will present a final report within thirty days of the initial report, which will be published fifteen days after its transmission to the Commission. The parties will then agree on the resolution of the dispute, which 'normally shall conform with the determinations and recommendations of the panel', and either not implement a measure or remove a measure which does not conform with the NAFTA, or provide compensation. If no agreement is reached within thirty days, the complaining party may suspend the application to the party in breach of benefits of equivalent effect until agreement is reached. Agreed interpretations of the NAFTA by the Commission may be submitted to national courts or bodies, but the NAFTA excludes rights of action before domestic courts on the ground that a measure by another party is inconsistent with the NAFTA.

NORTH AMERICAN AGREEMENT ON ENVIRONMENTAL CO-OPERATION

To counter criticisms of the inadequate provisions of the NAFTA on environmental matters, in September 1993 the three NAFTA parties adopted a supplementary North American Agreement on Environmental Co-operation to support the environmental goals and objectives of NAFTA. The Agreement's general objectives include protecting and improving the environment, promoting sustainable development, enhancing compliance with environmental laws and regulations, and promoting pollution prevention. The Agreement's general commitments address information, education, environmental assessment and promoting the use of economic instruments; it does not affect rights and obligations under other applicable international environmental agreements.Marginally more substantive are the obligations which require each party to 'ensure that its laws and regulations provide for high levels of environmental protection'and toeffectivelyenforcethese lawsandregulationsthroughgovern-mental action and the availability of judicial and administrative enforcement proceedings to sanction or remedy violations. Each party is also required to ensure that 'persons with a legally recognised right under its law in a particular matter' have appropriate access to enforcement proceedings, and to ensure that such proceedings are fair, open and equitable and subject to procedural guarantees.

The Agreement creates a Commission for Environmental Co-operation to oversee implementation of the Agreement and further development, comprising a Council, secretariat and Joint Public Advisory Committee. The Council has limited powers to adopt non-binding recommendations on a wide range of matters, although it has a more substantive role in the enforcement process. The secretariat may consider submissions from any non-governmental organisation or person asserting that a party is 'failing to effectively enforce its environmental law' and can request a response from the party concerned if it determines that the submission so merits. The secretariat may be instructed by the Council, by a two-thirds vote, to prepare a 'factual record' which may be made public by the Council. The Council may also, upon request of any party and by a two-thirds vote, establish an Arbitral Panel to address an 'alleged persistent pattern of failure by the party complained against to effectively enforce its environmental law' involving companies or sectors which produce goods or provide services which are traded between the parties or which compete with the goods or services of another party. Panel reports should lead to an agreement between the disputing parties on a mutually satisfactory action plan which will normally conform with the Panel's recommendations.Non-implementation of the action plan may lead to the Panel being reconvened and a monetary enforcement assessment being imposed, the non-payment of which may lead to the suspension of benefits.

BORDER ENVIRONMENT CO-OPERATION COMMISSION, AND NORTH AMERICAN DEVELOPMENT BANK

The United States and Mexico also adopted an Agreement Concerning the Establishment of a Border Environment Co-operation Commission and a North American Development Bank. The Commission's purpose is to preserve, protect and enhance the environment of the border region by developing environmental infrastructure projects and arranging public and private financing for such projects. The Bank will provide financing for projects certified by the Commission or for community adjustments and investments supporting the purposes of NAFTA which have been endorsed by the United States or Mexico. The Bank is capitalised at US$3 billion, which is divided in equal shares between Mexico and the United States.

African Economic Community

The Treaty Establishing the African Economic Community was adopted in 1991 to promote interrelated objectives, including: economic, social and cultural development and the integration of African economies; co-operation in all fields of human endeavour to raise the standards of living of African peoples; and to 'co-ordinate and harmonise policies among existing and future economic communities in order to foster the gradual establishment of the [African Economic] Community'. The Treaty sets forth a range of measures which are to be taken towards theachievementofthoseobjectives. Attheirheartis thecommitment to abolish customs duties and non-tariff barriers among member states, together with a commitment to the 'harmonisation and co-ordination of environmental protection policies'. The Treaty is silent as to how it will address those environmental laws of its member states which are also non-tariff barriers, and it does not propose a basis upon which the balance between environmental objectives and free trade objectives is to be struck. It does, however, include several provisions which suggest that the environment will not necessarily be accorded a significantly lower status. By Article 58, the member states undertake to 'promote a healthy environment' and, to that end, agree to adopt national, regional and continental policies, strategies and programmes, and to establish institutions for the protection and enhancement of the environment. Moreover, member states commit themselves to accelerating the process leading to 'ecologically rational, economically sound and socially acceptable development policies', to take every appropriate step to ban the importation and dumping of hazardous wastes in their territories, and to co-operate in accordance with the yet-to-be-negotiated Protocol on the Environment.

The Treaty therefore provides a basis for the development of regional and continental environmental policies, much in the same way that the original EC Treaty served, in the name of economic integration, as the basis for the development of an extensive body of environmental laws aimed both at establishing basic standards and at removing barriers to trade.

UNCED

Trade and the environment was one of the most controversial legal issues at UNCED. Four of the five instruments there adopted contain provisions on the permissibility of unilateral environmental measures. The most detailed is the consensus language adopted by 176 states in Agenda 21, which has served as an important point of reference in 'trade and environment' disputes. It commits states:

To promote, through the gradual development of universally and multi-laterally negotiated agreements or instruments, international standards for the protection of the environment that take into account the different situations and capabilities of countries. States recognise that environmental policies shoulddeal withthe root causes of environmental degradation, thus preventing environmental measures from resulting in unnecessary restrictions to trade. Trade policy measures for environmental purposes should not constitute a means of arbitrary or unjustifiable discrimination or a disguised restriction on international trade. Unilateral actions to deal with environmental challenges outside the jurisdiction of the importing country should be avoided. Environmental measures addressing international environment problems should, as far as possible, be based on an international consensus. Domestic measures targeted to achieve certain environmental objectives may need trade measures to render them effective. Should trade policy measures be found necessary for the enforcement of environmental policies, certain principles and rules should apply. These could include, *inter alia*, the principle of non-discrimination; the principle that the trade measure chosen should be the least trade-restrictive necessary to achieve the objectives; an obligation to ensure transparency in the use of trade measures related to the environment and to provide adequate notification of national regulations, and the need to give consideration to the special conditions and development requirements of developing countries as they move towards internationally agreed environmental objectives.

Principle 12 of the Rio Declaration is compatible with the text of Agenda 21, but shorter, incorporating the central elements, but excluding reference to the principles. The text is drawn from Agenda 21, with oneexception: 'international environmental problems' in the Agenda 21 text is replaced by 'transboundary or global environmental problems' in the Rio Declaration. Principle 12 and the Agenda 21 language were adopted by consensus, subject to the written statement of the US that trade measures may provide an effective and appropriate means of addressing environmental concerns, including those 'outside national jurisdiction, subject to certain disciplines'. While establishing a pre-sumptioninfavour of free tradeobligationsandagainst nationalenvironmental measures, these formulations nevertheless leave open the possibility that unilateral measures may be adopted, even where they may have 'extra-jurisdictional effect'.

The other instruments adopted at UNCED are less specific. The 1992 Climate Change Convention provides that measures to combat climate change 'should not constitute a means of arbitrary or unjustifiable discrimination or a disguised restriction on international trade', which also suggests that trade measures are permissible in certain circumstances. The Forest Principles also address trade issues, calling for international trade in forest products to be facilitated on the basis of non-discriminatory and multilaterally agreed rules and procedures consistent with international trade law and practices. The Forest Principles also provide that '[u]nilateral measures, incompatible with international obligations or agreements, to restrict and/or ban the international trade in timber or other forest products, should be removed or avoided'.

Taken together, the UNCED instruments suggest the emergence of a consensus, reinforced in the subsequent WTO/GATT jurisprudence, that unilateral measures should be avoided but that they are not, *per se*, prohibited. The *Shrimp/Turtle (Phase II)* decision of the WTO Appellate Body provides particular guidance in this regard, suggesting that unilateral measures will be permissible where preceded by serious, though not necessarily successful, attempts to secure international agreement on an environmental issue, and provided that the measures are designed in such a manner that there is sufficient flexibility to take into account the specific conditions prevailing in any exporting WTO member. The WSSD Plan of Implementation restates the language of Agenda 21 and the Rio Declaration, suggesting that states did not feel the need to revisit their approach in the light of WTO case law since 1992. to achieving sustainable development' (para. 91), and to promote 'mutual supportiveness between the multilateral trading system and the multilateral environmental agreements, consistent with sustainable development goals . . . while recognizing the importance of maintaining the integrity of both sets of systems' (para. 92).

COMPETITION AND SUBSIDIES

S. Budlong, 'Article 130r(2) and the Permissibility of State Aids for Environmental Compliance in the EC', 30 *Columbia Journal of Transnational Law* 431 (1992); OECD, *Subsidies and Environment: Exploring the Linkages* (1996); D. Geradin, 'EC Competition Law and Environmental Protection', 2 *Yearbook of European Environmental Law* 117 (2002).

Closely related to international trade obligations are the emerging rules which prohibit anti-competitive behaviour which distorts trade. These rules, established by the WTO/GATT and the EC, are potentially significant for environmental issues. They are intended, in large part, to supplement free trade obligations by limiting anti-competitive practices which might distort competition and consequently affect trade between states. As was seen in chapter 15 above, the development of environmental law in the EC was in large part justified by the desire to remove environmentally related distortions to competition and b arriers to trade. Competition law has intersected with the environment in at least three ways. First, environmental considerations influence the application of rules prohibiting or limiting the grant by governments and other public authorities of subsidies (state aids). Secondly, environmental considerations are beginning to be taken into account in applying competition rules to agreements between companies, including 'environmental agreements'. Thirdly, the failure to integrate environmental costs into production costs has led to charges of 'environmental dumping' in international trade. A fourth aspect of the relationship concerns the international instruments addressing the economic aspects of environmental policies,whichhave long recognised therelationship between environmental protection and competition. The development and application of the polluter-pays principle, described in chapter 6 above, is closely related to competition rules, since it is intended in part to ensure that the costs of the environmental measures necessary to protect the environment should be reflected in the costs of goods and services which cause pollution in production or consumption; as early as 1972, the OECD Council recommended that environmental protection measures should not be accompanied by subsidies that would create significant distortions in international trade and investment, although exceptions or special arrangements may occur.

Subsidies

The introduction of environmental considerations into the law of subsidies has at least two consequences. It may allow the grant of subsidies which would otherwise be prohibited for activities which are environmentally beneficial. And it may allow enforcement bodies to prevent subsidies from being granted to activities which are particularly harmful to the environment. Although Agenda 21 called for the removal or reduction of subsidies that do not conform with sustainable development objectives, international legal developments have so far focused on the first of these two aspects. In 1974, the OECD Council recommended that in application of the polluter-pays principle the state should not, as a general rule, assist polluters in bearing the costs of pollution control whether by means of subsidies, tax advantages or other measures. The OECD Council further recommended that the grant of such assistance for pollution control should be strictly limited and be notified to OECD member countries, and must comply with three conditions:

1. it should be selective and restricted to those parts of the economy, such as industries, areas or plants, where severe difficulties would otherwise occur;
2. it should be limited to well-defined transitional periods, laid down in advance and adapted to the specific socio-economic problems associated with the implementation of a country's environmental programme; and
3. it should not create significant distortions in international trade and investment.

The OECD rules have influenced the EC. Article 87 (formerly Article 92) of the EC Treaty prohibits state aids (subsidies) which distort competition and affect tradebetweenmemberstates unlessithasasocialcharacter,makesgooddamage caused by natural disasters or other exceptional occurrences, or is 'aid granted to the economy of certain areas of the Federal Republic of Germany affected by the division of Germany, insofar as such aid is required in order to compensate for the economic disadvantages caused by that division'. However, state aid may be held compatible with the common market by the EC Commission if it:

1. promotes economic development in certain areas where the standard of living is abnormally low or where there is serious underemployment;
2. promotes the execution of an important project of common European interest;
3. remedies a serious disturbance in the economy of a member state;
4. facilitates the development of certain economic activities and does not adversely affect trading conditions to an extent contrary to the common interest;
5. promotes culture and heritage conservation where such aid does not affect trading conditions and competition in the Community to an extent that is contrary to the common interest; or
6. is otherwise decided by the EC Council.

The EC Council Recommendation on cost allocation and action by public authorities on environmental matters allows exceptions to the polluter-pays principle, including: financial contributions for the construction of public installations for the protection of the environment which could not be wholly covered in the short term from charges paid by polluters using them; financing to meet particularly heavy costs to achieve 'an exceptional degree of environmental cleanliness'; and contributions towards research and development on processes and products causing less pollution.

The EC approach is now governed by its 2001 Guidelines, although since 1975 the grant of environmental aid in the EC has been the subject of special rules and practice. The original principles provided that aid had to specify the industry and geographical areas for which it was to be granted and should facilitate the adaptation of firms to new obligations for the elimination of pollution imposed by public authorities, with the aim of carrying out research and development or new investments. Moreover, aid could be granted only where a 'sudden major change' in pollution-related obligations and constraints had occurred and only to plant in service at the time of the change, unless international competition is such that their activities would be 'seriously handicapped by being subjected to differing obligations from those imposed in given non-member countries or where non-member countries are themselves granting environmental protection aid'. This approach was justified as a compromise to reconcile the need to accelerate urgent pollution control investment with the requirement of undistorted competition, and applied until the mid-1990s.

Practice under the earlier rules was extensive. Examples of projects in which state aid had been granted for which the Commission did not raise objections included a Danish law on aid for environmental investments; aid by the state of Baden-Wu¨rttemberg in Germany to encourage air pollution control measures going beyond statutory requirements; reductions in a Dutch special consumer tax for less-polluting cars; a Spanish draft government programme to create an industrial, energy and environmental technology base; a Catalonian regional aid scheme to reduce atmospheric pollution; and Dutch tax incentives for the purchase of buses and lorries that comply with stricter noise and exhaust emissions standards. In 1992, the Commission approved, subject to the fulfilment of certain conditions, an aid scheme financed by a levy to stimulate the environmentally acceptable disposal of surplus manure, to prevent the contamination of surface and subterranean water supplies, gaseous emissions, and residual heavy metals. Although the aid did not fall within the

Commission's 1974 and 1980 guidelines, since it was not designed to finance investments, it was exempted under Article 87(3)(c) as it facilitated the economic development of Dutch animal husbandry by creating a system for an environmentally-sound disposal of its surplus manure. Having due regard to Article 130r of the Treaty the Commission notes that the environmental policy pursued by the Netherlands Government, in so far as it reduces manure pollution, is in the interest of the Community as a whole.

However, the Commission did not always accept arguments by governments to approve the grant of aid on environmental grounds. For example, in 1989, the Commission objected to a French aid scheme providing grants of up to 50 per cent of investment costs with a total budget of FFr90 million, on the ground that the 'intensity of the aid and the size of the budget were liable to distort competition and affect intra Community trade'.

In 1994, the Commission adopted new guidelines on state aid for environmental protection, which remained in force until new guidelines were adopted at the start of 2001, having regard to (1) developments in the field of the environment; (2) state aid being granted more frequently in the energy sector; and (3) new forms of operating aid. The 2001 Guidelines apply to aid to protect the environment in all sectors governed by the EC Treaty, including those subject to specific Community rules on state aid (e.g. steel processing, transportandfisheries)withtheexception ofagriculture.The Guidelinesseekto encourage energy efficiency and the use of renewable energies. They identify the Commission's policy on the control of state aid for environmental purposes as having a double imperative, namely:

1. to ensure the competitive functioning of markets; and
2. to ensure that the requirements of environmental protection are integrated into the definition and implementation of competition policy, to promote sustainable development, recognising that the internalisation of costs is a priority objective.

The 2001 Guidelines mark a significant shift in approach. The 1994 Guidelines had permitted aid either to encourage firms to adapt to new environmental standards, ortoact as an incentive toimprove on standardsor undertake further investment to reduce pollution. The 2001 Guidelines reflect the Commission's position that aid will only now be justified on the second ground and will no longer be used to make up for the absence of cost internalisation, so that aid will no longer be justified for investments to bring companies into line with new or existing standards. The 2002 Guidelines set out the general and detailed conditions for authorising aid (pursuant to Article 87(3)(c) of the EC Treaty) of three kinds:

1. investment aid;
2. aid to small and medium-sized enterprises for advisory and consultancy services in the environmental field; and
3. operating aid.

The Commission maintains a register of state aid decisions on environmental aid.

Article XVI(1) of the GATT has a similar objective to Article 87 of the EC Treaty, although the former does not prohibit subsidies or declare them void *per se*. Rather, Article XVI(1) requires any contracting party to notify the other contracting parties on the nature and extent of any subsidisation and its estimated effect on imports or exports, and requires discussions between the parties concerned, or with the contracting parties, about the possibility of limiting subsidies which are determined to cause or threaten serious prejudice to the interests of any other contracting party. To date,the provision has not apparently led to any disputes between contracting parties over environment-related subsidies. The increased attention being given by states to their international competitiveness in the face of increased national and international environmental regulation makes it likely, however, that Article XVI(1) could become a contentious issue.

Under the auspices of the GATT Uruguay Round, a Subsidies Agreement was negotiated which is binding on all WTO members. The Agreement defines certain 'non-actionable' subsidies, including those related to environmental protection. It states, quite specifically, that non-actionable environmental subsidies cover: assistance to promote adaptation of existing facilities to new environmental requirements imposed by law and/or regulations which result in greater constraints and financial burden on firms, provided that the assistance:

(i) is a one-time non-recurring measure; and

(ii) is limited to 20 per cent of the cost of adaptation; and (iii) does not cover the cost of replacing and operating the assisted investment, which must be fully borne by firms; and

(iv) is directly linked to and proportionate to a firm's planned reduction of nuisances and pollution, and does not cover any manufacturing cost savings which may be achieved; and

(v) is available to all firms which can adopt the new equipment and/or production processes.

ANTI-COMPETITIVE AGREEMENTS

The second area of competition law with environmental implications relates to rules which prohibit anti-competitive agreements and practices by companies and other persons. The WTO does not yet have rules on this subject, but Article 81 (formerly Article 85) of the EC Treaty prohibits agreements, decisions and concerted practices which affect trade between member states and prevent, restrict or distort competition. Under Article 82 (formerly Article 86), similar prohibitions apply to abuses by companies of dominant positions, such as price-fixing and limiting markets and technical developments. Under Article 81(3), the EC Commission may find that the Article 81 prohibition is not applicable to agreements, decisions or practices, or categories thereof, which are considered to bring public benefits; these public benefits include improving the production or distribution of goods or promoting technical or economic progress, while allowing consumers a fair share of the resulting benefit, provided that the agreement does not impose restrictions which are not indispensable to the attainment of these objectives or eliminate competition in respect of a substantial part of the products in question. This is broad enough language to justify exemptions for technical or economic progress which contributes to environmental protection, thereby benefiting consumers. In *Cali* v. *Servizi ecologici porto di Genova SpA*, the ECJ ruled that Article 82 (formerly Article 86) of the EC Treaty is not applicable to anti-pollution surveillance with which a body governed by private law has been entrusted by the public authorities in an oil port of a member state, even where port users must pay dues to finance that activity. The EC Commission has been willing to take into account environmental considerations in applying Articles 81 and 82, and has also applied Article 81 to 'environmental agreements' between companies.By way of example, in *Re Independent Power Generators*, which concerned a joint venture agreement in the energy sector which included certain restrictive practices (agreement not to compete), one of the factors the Commission took into account in deciding not to object to a long-term exclusive purchase agreement, which might otherwise have been caught, was the intended use by the joint venture of combined cycle gas turbine generators or clean coal-fired systems, which was considered to be efficient generating technology offering environmental advantages.

CONCLUSIONS

As this chapter shows, a large body of international legislation and case law has developed over the past ten years as the international community seeks, at the regional and global level, to find an acceptable balance between trade liberalisation objectives and environmental objectives. If anything, the legal situation has become increasingly complex. On the one hand, the international community has furthered its efforts to liberalise and deregulate international trade; on the other hand, it has redoubled efforts to develop international environmental agreements, many of which rely upon trade sanctions to achieve their objectives. These international initiatives have been accompanied by domestic legislation, mostly in industrialised countries, which tightens up national environmental regulations, including restrictions on imports. In the midst of these political and legal controversies, international courts and other bodies find themselves increasingly being called upon to adjudicate on the basis of bilateral, regional and global legal arrangements, and it is hardly surprising that they will apply different tests and reach different conclusions on the appropriate balance between environmental objectives and trade objectives. It is one of the ironies of the trade/environment tension that the free trade ideal based upon deregulation has required a new layer of international regulation to set minimum standards; the experience in each region and globally has been that free trade inevitably points to a degree of harmonisation of environmental standards, at least in the sense that minimum standards are to be met. The challenge for the international community is to ensure that those harmonised standards do not lead to a general weakening of environmental protection. In this regard, it is notable that many international environmental agreements explicitly recognise the right of a party to maintain more stringent standards, subject to certain requirements. While it can be argued that the GATT/WTO rules do not give adequate weight to the environment, the jurisprudence of, in particular, the new WTO Appellate Body has significantly expanded the potential for the 'environmental exceptions' available under Article XX of the GATT. This development reflects a recognition that legitimate environmental measures can, in certain circumstances, lawfully restrict international trade, provided that certain conditions are met.

The international community faces two challenges here. One relates to standards, the other to institutions. With regard to standards, further efforts will be needed to refine and clarify (through practice, presumably) the emerging rules to assist governments, international organisations and adjudicative bodies to determine when environmental considerations can be allowed. In view of the approach taken by the Appellate Body, it may no longer be necessary to reconsider and modernise Article XX of the GATT, as the previous edition of this book suggested. It is apparent that the WTO Appellate Body has been inspired by rules of international law arising outside the WTO, including the approach taken by the ECJ in the *Danish Bottles* and *Belgian Waste Disposal* cases, and reflected in Principle 12 of the Rio Declaration. With regard to institutions, significant advances have been made with the establishment of the WTO and the conclusion of new agreements relating to SPS measures and technical barriers to trade. However, the concept of sustainable development (and its practical consequences) remains to be defined, and the relationship between international trade law and multilateral environmental agreements remains less certain than it should be. The level of controversy and debate stimulated by the

Appellate Body's decision in *Beef Hormones* suggested that the interaction of international trade obligations with domestic health and environmental standards may be a new frontier on which the 'trade and environment' battle is fought out in the twenty-first century.

In many ways, the trade/environment debate reflects a broader issue as to how far environmental considerations can go in bringing about a restructuring of established international economic organisations, how far environment and development can (as a matter of law) be integrated, and whether it is the environment which will ultimately be subsumed into economic approaches, or whether it will be the other way round.

In the meantime, if the late 1980s to the early years of the new millennium were about trade and environment, the next related international legal issue looming on the horizon is the relationship between competition law and the environment. It is likely that environmental arguments will increasingly be raised to justify commercial agreements which might otherwise be caught by anti-trust laws. It is equally foreseeable that the law on subsidies and the environment will expand, and that environmental dumping (selling goods whose prices do not fully reflect their environmental costs and impacts) will be subject to international legal scrutiny. It is at this interface between international environmental law and international economic law that the effectiveness of the standards which have been meticulously developed to protect flora, fauna and other environmental resources will be judged.

5

Financial Resources, Technology and Intellectual Property

INTRODUCTION

The establishment by the 1990 amendments to the 1987 Montreal Protocol of a financial mechanism to address ozone depletion marked an important turning point in international environmental law. In the subsequent decade the rules on finance and technology transfer have developed significantly and substantively, together with legislative and judicial consideration of the relationship between intellectual property rights and environmental protection.

This has occurred notwithstanding the early concerns of some industrialised countries that the establishment of the Montreal Fund would adversely prejudice future developments. Financial resources, technology transfer and intellectual property were central issues at UNCED and of the two treaties signed at UNCED. As described in this chapter, the 1992 Climate Change and Biodiversity Conventions – as well as subsequent instruments on drought and desertification (1994), climate change (1997), biosafety (2000) and persistent organic pollutants (2001) have further elaborated the principles established under the Montreal Protocol and its amendments.

Related developments – particularly in the context of the activities of the multilateral development banks, the WTO Agreement on Trade Related Aspects of Intellectual Property Rights (TRIPs), the European Patent Convention, and the 2001 International Treaty on Plant Genetic Resources for Foodand Agriculture –have added to the broadening range of legal issues which are touched by, and increasingly integrated with, international environmental concerns.

These three subjects – financial resources, technology and intellectual property – occupy a central place in the legal arrangements of international environmental law, at the regional and global levels, and will determine to a considerable extent whether the substantive protections put in place can be achieved (in that regard, the experience with the Montreal Protocol provides some grounds for optimism). The consequence is that international environmental lawyers will necessarily find themselves facing the complex (and often black letter) legal issues which emerge as a result of an increasingly integrated approach to environmental protection and economic development. It remains to be seen, in the process of cross-fertilisation, what the nature of the integrated relationship will be, and the manner in which balance will be achieved.

FINANCIAL RESOURCES AND MECHANISMS

The provision of international financial resources related to the environment has two main aspects. The first concerns the extent to which overseas development assistance granted bilaterally by states (or collectively by a group of states) or by international organisations is subject to compliance with international environmental law. The second relates to the body of international institutional and substantive law which has arisen out of the establishment and development of international mechanisms to provide financial assistance for global environmental objectives. These include the Global Environment Facility (GEF) and the Montreal Protocol Multilateral Fund, as well as earlier mechanisms such as the Wetlands Fund, the World Heritage Fund, and the International Fund for Plant Genetic Resources. Complex legal issues have also arisen in the context of the relationship between the GEF and international conventions on biodiversity, climate change, desertification and POPs. Other efforts to support international conservation include 'debt-for-nature swaps', trust funds and endowments.

Chapter 33 of Agenda 21, 'Financial Resources and Mechanisms', deals with the financing of Agenda 21 and the global consensus integrating environmental considerations into an accelerated development process. In the context of the estimated

US$600 billion annual cost over the period 1993–2000 of implementing in developing countries the activities set out in Agenda 21, Chapter 33 identifies three objectives for the international community: adopting measures concerning financial resources and mechanisms for the implementation of Agenda 21; providing new and additional financial resources that are adequate and predictable; and seeking full use and improvement of the funding mechanisms to be utilised for the implementation of Agenda 21, including the provisions on environmental protection. The main sources of financial resources will be bilateral overseas development aid and funds from the multilateral development banks and specialised environmental funds; other sources are likely to include private funding, debt relief, direct foreign investment and what Agenda 21 terms 'innovative financing', including debt swaps, the use of economic and fiscal incentives and tradeable permits. Agenda 21 also supports the reallocation of resources committed to military purposes.

Overseas development assistance

J. Hornberry, 'The Accountability of Development Assistance Agencies: The Case of Environmental Policy', 12 *Ecology Law Quarterly* 675 (1985); P. Muldoon, 'The International Law of Eco-Development: Emerging Norms for Development Assistance Agencies', 22 *Texas International Law Journal* 1 (1987); P. Kohona, 'UNCED – The Transfer of Financial Resources to Developing Countries', 1 RECIEL 307 (1992).

At UNCED – and again at the WSSD – the developed countries reaffirmed their political commitment to reach the accepted UN target of 0.7 per cent of GNP for overseas development assistance (ODA) and, to the extent that they had not yet reached that target, agreed to augment their aid programme to reach that target as soon as possible. The developed countries have not, however, accepted any international legal obligations or other international commitments to apportion ODA, or any part of it, to environmental programmes and projects. As a matter of domestic policy, a number of developed countries have committed themselves to the objective of allocating a proportion of ODA to environmental activities. The grant of ODA is subject to any obligations which the granting state may have under relevant international environmental law, including treaty obligations. Such obligations might include compliance with certain minimum standards, and the conduct of environmental assessments in respect of projects likely to damage the environment. Several bilateral and regional development assistance treaties include specific environmental obligations, which either require assistance to be directed towards environmental protection programmes or projects, or that development assistance should be subjected to some form of environmental assessment. Thus, environment and development are closely interwoven throughout the 1989 Lome´ Convention, whichprovided that the support to be provided in theACP–ECco-operation for the ACP states' efforts to achieve comprehensive self-reliant and self-sustained development must be based on development which achieves a 'sustainable balance between its economic objectives, the rational management of the environment and the enhancement of natural and human resources'. To the extent that overseas development assistance is subject to compliance with the national environmental laws of the assisting state, the possibility arises that such assistance could in effect apply national environmental laws extra-territorially.In practice, the political and economic requirements of the assisted state have limited the scope of making such types of 'green conditionality' arguments, and Principle 4 of the Rio Declaration provides a powerful basis for arguing that environmental protection must be an integral part of all development assistance.

The OECD Council has recommended that development assistance projects and programmes which could significantly affect the environment should be subjected to an environmental assessment at an early stage. The Recommendation identifies the issues which should be considered in an environmental assessment, and requires an in-depth environmental assessment for certain very fragile environments, such as wetlands, mangrove swamps, coral reefs, tropical forests and semi-arid areas. Other projects or programmes in need of environmental assessment include substantial changes in renewable resource use or farming and fishing practices, exploitation of hydraulic resources, infrastructure, industrial activities, extractive industries and waste management and disposal. Similar requirements have been applied in relation to public schemes aiming to insure or guarantee foreign investments from political and other risks, including regulatory change.

Multilateral development banks

R. E. Stein and B. Johnson, *Banking on the Biosphere? Environmental Procedures and Practices of Nine Multilateral Development Agencies* (1979); B. Rich, 'The Multilateral Development Banks, Environmental Policy and the United States', 12 *Ecology Law Quarterly* 69 (1985); S. Schwartzmann, *Bankrolling Disasters: International Development Banks and the Global Environment* (Sierra Club, 1986); V. Nanda, 'Human Rights and Environmental Considerations in the Lending Policies of International Development Agencies: An Introduction', 17 DJILP 29 (1988); Z. Plater, 'Damming the Third World: Multilateral Banks, Environmental Diseconomies, and International Reform Pressures on the Lending Process', 17 DJILP 121 (1988); B. Rich, 'The Emperor's New Clothes: The World Bank and Environmental Reform', 10 *World Policy Journal* 305 (1990); I. Shihata, *The World Bank in a Changing World: Selected Essays* (1991) (especially Chapter 4); I. Shihata, 'The World Bank and the Environment: A Legal Perspective', 16 *Maryland Journal of International Law and Trade* 1 (1992); K. Piddington, 'The Role of the World Bank', in A. Hurrell and B. Kingsbury (eds.), *The International Politics of the Environment* (1992), 212; 'Financial Mechanisms for the Protection of the Environment', 3 RECIEL 81 (1994); C. Redgwell, *Intergenerational Trusts and Environmental Protection* (1999); G. Handl, *Multilateral Development Banking: Environmental Principles and Concepts Reflecting General International Law and Public Policy* (2001).

The World Bank and the six regional development banks have played an important role in the elaboration of rules of international environmental law. In 1980, largely as a result of strong criticism targeted at their environmentally unsound lending activities, the World Bank, five of the regional development banks, the EC, the OAS, UNEP and UNDP adopted a Declaration of Environmental Policies and Procedures Relating to Economic Development. The Declaration reaffirmed their support for the principles and recommendations of the Stockholm Conference and agreed to institute procedures for the 'systematic examination' of all development activities under consideration for financing to ensure that appropriate measures are proposed for compliance with the Stockholm instruments. They also undertook to provide technical assistance to developing countries on environmental matters, and, if appropriate, to support project proposals which protect, rehabilitate or otherwise enhance the human environment. This early commitment to achieving environmental protection is now reflected in more detailed requirements forming part of the internal laws of multilateral development banks and other funding agencies.

The World Bank and the regional banks are established by international treaty. As such, and having been endowed by their constituent instruments with certain capacities and functions on the international plane, they have a degree of international personality from which certain consequences flow: the power to make treaties and, to undertake legal proceedings; and certain privileges and immunities under international law.

As international legal persons, the multilateral development banks may also have rights and obligations under international law. In the *Reparations for Injuries* case, the ICJ ruled that the UN was 'a subject of international law and capable of possessing international rights and duties, and that it has the capacity to maintain its rights by bringing international claims'. From the Advisory Opinion of the Court, it is clear that the multilateral development banks will have a sufficient degree of international personality to subject them to certain duties under international law, including duties which arise under the operation of general and specific rules of international environmental law.

Multilateral development banks are under an obligation to comply with general principles of international law relating to the protection of the environment, and any failure to comply with such obligations might entail their international responsibility, as well as liability for damages.

This possibility is important in the context of the attention which has been given to the development lending activities of multilateral development banks which have contributed to environmental despoliation and which have led to the adoption of measures to limit and prevent the adverse effects of their activities, including requirements for environmental impact assessment and environmental audits. Other, emerging approaches to dealing with the potential liability of the multilateral lender for the adverse environmental consequences of its activities include the use of 'environmental covenants'and agreements channelling liability to the recipient.

WORLD BANK (WWW.WORLDBANK.ORG)

The World Bank group comprises the International Bank for Reconstruction and Development (IBRD), the International Development Association (IDA) and the International Finance Corporation (IFC). The IBRD was established in 1945 to promote the international flow of financial resources for productive purposes and to assist in the reconstruction of states after the Second World War. Its Articles of Agreement do not include any provisions specifically referring to environmental protection objectives or to the sustainable or rational use of natural resources. Its main objective today is to provide financial support, usually in the form of loans, for productive projects or to finance reform programmes which will lead to economic growth in its less developed member countries. By the end of 2002, its outstanding disbursed loans totalled US$371 billion, with loans of US$11.5 billion in 2002.

The IDA was established in 1959 to promote economic development in the least-developed countries by providing concessionary finance on more concessionary terms than the conventional loans provided by the IBRD. The IDA finances projects and reform programmes in countries which would otherwise not be able to service loans from the IBRD. The IDA's resources come from contributions from developed and developing countries, including original subscriptions and nine replenishments, amounting to total resources of US$135 billion by the end of 2002. The IDA is subject to the World Bank's Directive on Environmental Assessment, and, in 1989, the Ninth Replenishment called for all IDA recipients to complete Environmental Action Plans by June 1993. The IDA has just been subject to its thirteenth replenishment.

The IFC was established in 1956, and became a specialised agency of the UN in 1957. The IFC is affiliated to the IBRD but has separate legal personality and maintains its capital separately from the IBRD. The IFC invests in private or partly governmental enterprises together with private investors, with a commitment to providing finance in the private sector; its Environment and Social Development Department ensures that IFC-financed projects meet the IFC's environmental policies and guidelines. Since its founding, the IFC has committed more than US$34 billion of its own funds and has arranged US$21 billion in syndications for 2,825 companies in 140 developing countries.

The World Bank group provides financial support for a wide range of projects, some of which have had notorious adverse environmental consequences. Large infrastructure projects, particularly relating to energy, transport and other infrastructure, such as the construction of the Polonoreste dam in Brazil, have often resulted in significant environmental damage at the national and regional levels. Smaller-scale projects, including in particular those relating to agriculture, transportation and energy, have also been criticised for failing to take into accountlong-term environmental costs,andfor contributing to environmental degradation and unsustainable development in developing countries. In the late 1980s, the Bank embarked on a programme of restructuring, which included the creation of an Environment Department and the adoption of a number of Operational Directives (now Operational Policies, accompanied by Bank Policies) related to the environment. These included Directives on involuntary resettlement, indigenous people, the involvement of non-governmental organisations in World Bank supported activities, and environmental assessment. In 1992, new environmental Operational Directives were issued in relation to National Environmental Action Plans and agricultural pest management, and subsequently policies have been adopted on natural habitats, forests, the safety of dams, and projects on international waterways. Also in 1992, the Executive Directors of the World Bank established a Rainforest Trust Fund, for which the Bank will act as trustee, to support a Pilot Programme to Conserve the Brazilian Rainforest. In 2001, the Bank's directors adopted a five-year Environment Strategy. One of the Bank's eleven thematic groups is 'Environment and Natural Resources Management'.

REGIONAL AND SUB-REGIONAL DEVELOPMENT BANKS

The regional development banks also provide large-scale financial support in the form of loans to developing countries, which are used on a range of projects. Agenda 21 limits itself to calling for these banks and funds to play 'an increased and more effective' role in providing resources on concessional or other favourable terms to implement the activities set out in Agenda 21.

The African Development Bank was established in 1963 under the auspices of the UN Economic Commission for Africa to 'contribute to the economic development and social progress of its members – individually and jointly'. In 1987, an Environment Unit was established, and in 1990 the Board of Directors approved the Bank's Environment Policy Paper, which established guidelines for the environmental impact assessment of project and non-project loans.

The Inter-American Development Bank was established under the auspices oftheEconomicConferenceoftheOAS in1959to'contribute totheacceleration of the process of economic and social development of the regional developing member countries'. The Bank has a Sustainable Development Department (formerly an Environment Committee and an Environmental Protection Division established in 1990) to ensure that the Bank's operations comply with the environmental legislation of recipient countries and its own environmental impact assessment and related requirements.

The Asian Development Bank was established in 1965 under the auspices of the predecessor organisation to ESCAP. It has had an Office of the Environment for some time, and in November 2002 adopted a new Environmental Policy paper which recommends means to adopt the new environmental policy.It has guidelines for incorporating environmental impact assessments into its project cycles.

The Caribbean Development Bank was established in 1970 under the auspices of UNDP 'to contribute to the harmonious economic growth and development of the member countries in the Caribbean and to promote economic co-operation and integration among them, having special attention and urgent regard to the needs of the less developed member countries of the region'. The Bank requires its borrowers to undertake an impact assessment of project proposals to ensure that they are environmentally sound and sustainable, and that any environmental consequences are taken into account in the project design.

The Islamic Development Bank was established in 1973 to foster the economic development and social progress of member countries and Muslim communities in accordance with the principles of *Shari' ah* (Islamic law). The Bank participates in equity capital and grants loans for projects and enterprises and provides financial assistance to members for economic and social development. It requires the prior environmental assessment of projects before funds will be disbursed.

The European Bank for Reconstruction and Development was established in 1990 to contribute to the economic progress and reconstruction of the countries of Central and Eastern Europe and to apply the principles of multi-party democracy, pluralism and market economics. The EBRD is the first multilateral development bank to include in its constitution a specific commitment to environmental protection. The EBRD is required to 'promote in the full range of its activities environmentally sound and sustainable development'.This language implies that all of its activities must comply with environmental standards, although the Articles of Agreement do not specify the source of these standards. Possible sources of environmental standards include those established by general international law, those established by the national law of donor and/or recipient countries, or any applicable regional rules such as those of EC environmental law. In performing its functions, the Bank is expressly mandated to make loans and to provide technical assistance for the reconstruction or developmentof infrastructure, includingenvironmentalprogrammes.The Bank is also required to report annually on the environmental impact of its activities. The Bank has an Environmental Department, and since January 1992 the Bank has adopted detailed environmental procedures, including the use of environmental assessments, environmental audits and environmental covenants. The Bank administers three funds for nuclear safety.

In the context of the EC, financial support of a general nature is provided to projects both inside and outside the member states by the European Investment Bank, and to projects in EC member states by the general programme on structural funds. The European Investment Bank is established by the EC Treaty and has as its task to contribute to the 'balanced and steady development of the common market' in the interest of the EC. It operates on a non-profit-making basis and provides loans and guarantees to facilitate the financing of three categories of projects: for developing less developed regions; for modernising or converting companies or developing fresh activities where these projects are too large or complex to be financed by individual member states; and projects of common interest to several member states which cannot be financed entirely by those member states. The protection of the environment is stated to be one of its five operational priorities, and it currently has an Environmental Assessment Group, an Environmental . . . Unit and . . . an Environmental Steering Committee. As an institution of the EC, the Bank is subject to compliance with the standards and procedures established under EC environmental law.

Environment funds

The establishment of the Multilateral Fund (under the 1990 amendments to the 1987 Montreal Protocol) and the Global Environmental Facility highlights the growing connection between the development and application of environmental rules and standards and the provision of financial resources to ensure their implementation, particularly by developing countries. In fact, the provision of international financial resources dedicated to international environmental protection goals, and the establishment of the necessary mechanisms, dates back at least to 1972 when the World Heritage Convention established the World Heritage Fund. This was followed in 1972 by the creation of the voluntary UNEP Environment Fund, and subsequently by funds established under the UNEP Regional Seas Programme. In 1990, a Wetlands Fund was established under the 1971 Ramsar Convention, and the 1989 Basel Convention allows the parties to decide on the establishment of 'appropriate funding mechanisms of a voluntary nature' and to consider the establishment of a revolving fund to assist on an interim basis in case of emergency situations to minimise damage from accidents. The EC has a financial instrument (LIFE) and a cohesion financial instrument which is to provide financial assistance for environmental projects; both instruments supplement the activities of the EC Structural Funds, the European Investment Bank and funds dedicated to Central and Eastern Europe under the PHARE programme. Other funds which provide financial resources in the form of compensation for environmental damage include the Kuwait Compensation Fund, and the International Oil Pollution Fund.

UNEP ENVIRONMENT FUND

The voluntary Environment Fund established by General

Assembly Resolution 2997 was established to enable the UNEP Governing Council to fulfil its policy guidance role for the direction and co-ordination of activities. It finances the whole or partial costs of new environmental initiatives within the UN system, including monitoring and data-collection, environmental research, information exchange, research on appropriate technologies, and such other programmes as the Governing Council may decide upon. In 2002, the Fund received contributions of about US$45 million.

WORLD HERITAGE FUND

The Fund for the Protection of the World Cultural and Natural Heritage was established under Article 15 of the World Heritage Convention. It is a trust fund which grants financial assistance to protect cultural and natural heritage of outstanding universal value, and is administered by the World Heritage Committee. In 2002, the Fund administered a budget of approximately US$3.5 million, raised by a combination of voluntary and compulsory contributions. The majority was spent on technical co-operation and training, with the remainder spent on preparatory assistance and regional studies, emergency assistance and advisory services.

WETLANDS FUND

The Wetland Conservation Fund was established in 1990 by the conference of the parties to the 1971 Ramsar Convention to assist developing country parties to implement theirobligations under the Convention. The Fund is operated in a similar way to the World Heritage Fund, and provides assistance to developing countries, upon their request, to support wetland conservation in one of four fields: improving the management of sites on the Ramsar List; designating new sites; promoting 'wise use'; and supporting regional and promotional activities. Developing countries which are not parties may request support for the designation of a site for the List, which is a condition for becoming a party. The Fund is administered by the Standing Committee to the Convention and by the Bureau.

MONTREAL PROTOCOL MULTILATERAL FUND

R. Bowser, 'History of the Montreal Protocol's Ozone Fund', 14 *International Environmental Reporter* 6356 (1991); P. Lawrence,

'Technology Transfer Funds and the Law: Recent Amendments to the Montreal Protocol on Substances that Deplete the Ozone Layer', 4 JEL 15 (1992); J. Patlis, 'The Multilateral Fund of the Montreal Protocol: A Prototype for Financial Mechanism in Protecting the Global Environment', 25 *Cornell International Law Journal* 181 (1992); F. Biermann, 'Financing Environmental Policies in the South: Experiences from the Multilateral Ozone Fund', 9 *International Environmental Affairs* 179 (1997).

The 1990 amendments to the 1987 Montreal Protocol established a mechanism, including a Multilateral Fund, to provide financial and technical co-operation, including the transfer of technologies, to developing country parties to enable their compliance with the control measures established under the Protocol.The Multilateral Fund operates under the authority of the parties who decide on its overall policies. The Fund meets on a grant or concessional basis the 'agreed incremental costs' of developing country parties in order to enable their compliance with the control measures of the Montreal Protocol; finances clearing-house functions to assist in identifying co-operation needs, to facilitate technical co-operation, to distribute information and relevant materials, to hold workshops, and to facilitate and monitor other co-operation available; and finances the secretarial services of the Fund. An Executive Committee, comprising seven developed and seven developing country parties, implements specific operational policies guidelines and administrative arrangements, including the disbursement of resources, with the co-operation and assistance of the World Bank, UNEP, UNDP and UNIDO. The Fund is administered by the World Bank as the implementing agency under the agreement between the Fund's Executive Committee and the World Bank. The Fund is financed by countries not operating under Article 5(1) (i.e. by developed countries) in currency or in kind on the basis of the United Nations scale of assessments, and allows bilateral and agreed regional co-operation to be considered as a contribution to the Fund provided that such co-operation, as a minimum, relates to compliance with the Montreal Protocol, provides additional resources and meets incremental costs. The concurrence of the beneficiary party is required, and decisions taken under the Fund are to be taken by consensus whenever possible, but otherwise by a two-thirds majority of the parties present and voting, including a 'double majority' of developed country parties and of developing country parties.

GLOBAL ENVIRONMENT FACILITY

J. Helland-Hansen, 'The Global Environment Facility', 3 *International Environmental Affairs* 137 (1991); L. Boisson de Chazournes, 'Le Fonds pour l'environnement mondial: recherche et conqueˆ te de son identite´', AFDI 612 (1995).

The Global Environment Facility (GEF) was established in 1990 as a three-year 'experiment' to provide grants for investment projects, technical assistance and research to developing countries to protect the global environment and to transfer environmentally benign technologies. The establishment of the GEF followed a proposal by France in September 1989 and materials prepared in 1990 by the World Bank in consultation with UNEP and UNDP, on the understanding that no new institutional structures would be created and only minimal changes would be made to the three implementing agencies. The first meeting of participating countries was held in May 1991. The resolution provided for the establishment of the GEF, comprising the Global Environment Trust Fund(GET),co-financingarrangementswith theGET,the OzoneProjects Trust Fund and such other trust funds and agreements as the World Bank may from time to time establish or agree to administer under the GET.

In March 1994, representatives of the then seventy-three states participating in the GEF's pilot phase and of other states wanting to participate in the restructured GEF accepted an Instrument for the Establishment of the Restructured GEF. The Instrument entered into force through subsequent adoption by the governing bodies of UNDP, UNEP and the World Bank. The World Bank serves as trustee of the GEF Trust Fund, which receives and administers con-tributions. Any member of the UN or its specialised agencies may become a participant in the restructured GEF. The arrangements for the governance of the GEF reflect the complexities of dividing responsibilities between donor and recipient participant states: it comprises an Assembly, a Council and a secretariat, and a Scientific and Technical Advisory Panel (STAP) provides advice.The Assembly consists of representatives of ali of the participants, and has responsibility for reviewing the general policies of the GEF and its operation, and for adopting amendments to the Instrument. The Council has responsibility for operational policies and programmes, and consists of thirty-two members (sixteen from developing countries, fourteen from developed countries, and two from countries from Central and Eastern Europe and the former USSR), some of which represent a constituency of states. The Implementing Agencies are UNDP, UNEP and the World Bank (which collaborate in accordance with an inter-agency agreement), and they are accountable to the Council for their GEF-financed activities, which is itself under an obligation to ensure that the GEF operate, *inter alia*, in conformity with the policies, programme priorities and eligibility criteria decided by the conferences of the parties of the conventions which it supports. To that end, the Council has approved co-operative arrangements or agreements with the conferences of the parties to the conventions.

According to the Instrument, the GEF is to provide 'new and additional grant and concessional funding to meet the agreed incremental costs of measures to achieve agreed global environmental benefits' in the following areas: climate change; biodiversity; international waters; and ozone layer depletion. Also eligible for funding are the agreed incremental costs of activities concerning land degradation, primarily desertification and deforestation. The GEF has been designated as the financial mechanism under three conventions (the 1992 Climate Change Convention, the 1992 Biodiversity Convention and the 2001 POPs Convention); it funds projects that combat desertification and protect international watercourses and the ozone layer; and it has been designated to manage other funds, such as the Adaptation Fund, the Least Developed Countries Fund and the Special Convention Fund (all under the 1992 Climate Change Convention).

The restructured GEF was originally capitalised at US$2 billion (over three years); in August 2002, thirty-two donor states pledged nearly US$3 billion to finance the GEF over the following four years. Allocation of the GEF's resources has been principally directed towards climate change and biodiversity.

UNCED AND THE RELATIONSHIP WITH THE BIODIVERSITY AND CLIMATE CHANGE CONVENTIONS

On an interim basis and subject to its restructuring, the GEF was confirmed as the financial mechanism for Agenda 21 and the

Climate Change and Biodiversity Conventions. Agenda 21 identified the GEF as the financial mechanism to cover the 'agreed incremental costs of relevant activities under Agenda 21' subject to the fulfilment of six conditions. The GEF should: be restructured to encourage universal participation; have sufficient flexibility; ensure transparent and democratic governance; ensure new and additional financial resources on grant and concessional terms; ensure predictability in the flow of funds; and ensure access to and disbursement of funds under mutually agreed criteria without introducing new forms of conditionality. The 1994 Instrument achieved that restructuring.

The 1992 Biodiversity Convention requires developed country parties to provide 'new and additional' financial resources to enable developing country parties to meet the agreed full incremental cost of implementing their commitments under the Convention, and links such implementation with the effective implementation by developed country parties of their financial commitments under the Convention. The Convention establishes a mechanism for the provision of financial resources to developing countries on a grant or concessional basis which' shall function under the authority andguidance of, andbeaccount-able to, the conference of the parties for the purpose of this Convention'. The conference of the parties designated the GEF as the institutional structure to carry out the operations of the mechanisms and will determine the 'policy, strategy, programme priorities and eligibility criteria' relating to access to and use of the resources.

The 1992 Climate Change Convention also requires the developed country parties to provide new and additional financial resources to developing country parties, and links the implementation by developing country parties of their commitments to the fulfilment by developed country parties of their financial commitments. It establishes a mechanism for the provision of financial resources on a grant or concessional basis which shall function 'under the guidance of and be accountable to' the conference of the parties, which will decide on its policies, programme priorities and eligibility criteria related to the Convention. The financial mechanism under the Climate Change Convention is not defined as being under the 'authority' of the conference of the parties, unlike the financial mechanism to be established by the Biodiversity Convention. The financial mechanism of the Climate Change Convention is to have an 'equitable and balanced representation of all parties within a transparent system of governance', and the conference of the parties and the entity entrusted with the operation of the mechanism will agree upon the working arrangements, including: the modalities to ensure that funded projects conform with the policies, programme priorities and eligibility criteria established by the conference of the parties and that particular funding decisions may be reconsidered; the provision of regular reports to the conference of the parties on funding operations; and the determination of the amounts of funding necessary and available in a predictable and identifiable manner. The conference of the parties has designated the GEF as the international entity entrusted with the operation of the financial mechanism.

The 2001 POPs Convention similarly requires developed country parties to provide new and additional financial resources to enable developing country parties and economies in transition to 'meet the agreed full incremental costs of implementing' measures required by the Convention, as agreed between the recipient party and the financial mechanism. The GEF is entrusted with the operations of the financial mechanisms (pending designation by the conference of the parties), which is to provide 'adequate and sustainable financial resources . . . on a grant or concessional basis'.

An important issue which has emerged is the legal relationship between the conferences of the parties of the various Conventions and the GEF Participants' Assembly, and in particular whether the conferences of the parties will have the final say on individual funding decisions or more general decisions taken by the GEF. Under the Conventions, the ultimate decision-making power rests with the conferences of the parties, which are granted the right to decide on the 'policies, programme priorities and eligibility criteria' of the financial mechanism (the Biodiversity Convention also grants power over 'strategies'), and in the event that the financial mechanism is not being operated to the satisfaction of the conferences of the parties each will be free to take a decision redesignating the international institution operating the mechanism.

In that sense, the GEF and its Participants' Assembly are, ultimately, accountable to the conferences of the parties and, in the case of the Biodiversity and POPs Conventions, under the 'authority' of the respective conferences of the parties. Whether the GEF and the Participants' Assembly are accountable to the conferences of the parties for each individual funding decision is less clear, but the ultimate sanction of 'redesignation' provides an incentive to the GEF to ensure that the wishes of the conferences of the parties are followed, or at least of those parties comprising the particular majority of parties which may be required to adopt a decision on the designation or redesignation of the financial mechanism.

EC FINANCIAL RESOURCES

Apartfrom thegeneralprogramme on structural funds (which are not dedicated to environmental-protection-related issues), the EC has created two specialised instruments to provide financial resources for environmental protection. The financial instrument for the environment (LIFE) was created in 1992 and, as revised in 2000, aims to contribute to 'the implementation, updating and development of Community environment policyandof environmental legislation, in particular as regards the integration of the environment into other policies, and to sustainable development in the Community'. It is divided into three components – LIFE-Nature, LIFE-Environment and LIFE-Third Countries – and provides financial assistance in those three fields. Assistance is provided in the form of co-financing of actions and interest rebates, with 640 million euros available for the period 2000–4 (LIFE III).

The second instrument established by the EC is a cohesion financial instrument established in 1993 to provide financial contributions to projects in the field of the environment and trans-European transport infrastructures in low-income EC member states (Greece, Spain, Ireland and Portugal). The instrument was established on an interim basis pending the establishment of the Cohesion Fund envisaged in ex Article 104c of the Treaty on European Union.The cohesion financial instrument now provides assistance of approximately 2.6 billion euros per annum, for the period 2000–6, *inter alia,* for environmental projects contributing to the achievement of the objective of Article 174 (formerly Article 130r) of the EC Treaty. Assistance for projects will be provided at a rate of 80–85 per cent of public or similar expenditure, and financial projects must be in conformity with the provisions of the EC Treaty, including those concerning environmental protection.

TECHNOLOGY TRANSFER AND TECHNICAL ASSISTANCE

C. Okolie, *Legal Aspects of the International Transfer of Technology to Developing Countries* (1975); C. P. Jeffries, 'Regulation of the Transfer of Technology: An Evaluation of the UNCTAD Code of Conduct', 18 *Harvard International Law Journal* 309 (1977); S. K. Agrawala, 'Transfer of Technology to LDCs: Implications of the Proposed Code', 23 *Indian Journal of International Law* 246 (1983); M. A. Bent, 'Exporting Hazardous Industries: Should American Standards Apply?', 20 NYUJILP 777 (1988); R. E. Lutz, 'The Export of Danger: A View from the Developed World', 20 NYUJILP 629 (1988); M. Blakeney, *Legal Aspects of Technology Transfer to Developing Countries* (1989) (and bibliography cited at 190–202); T. A. Cinti 'The Regulator's Dilemma: Should Best Available Technology or Cost Benefit Analysis Be Used to Determine the Applicable Hazardous Waste Treatment, Storage, and Disposal Technology?', 16 *Rutgers Computer and Technology Law Journal* 145 (1990); M. Lachs, 'Thoughts on Science, Technology and World Law', 86 AJIL 673 (1992); G. MacDonald, 'Technology Transfer: The Climate Change Challenge', 1 *Journal of Environment and Development* 1 (1992); L. Gundling, 'Compliance Assistance in International Environmental Law: Capacity Building Through Financial and Technology Transfer', 56 ZaöRV 796 (1996).

One of the major problems facing the international community is the use of obsolete, environmentally damaging techniques by industry in many countries. The wider dissemination and use of state-of-the-art technologies, including 'clean technologies', would go a long way to reducing the damaging effects of certain activities, and international law is now grappling with the problem of how to encourage or require the transfer of environmentally-sound technologies, particularly to developing countries. Until recently, the provisions of international environmental treaties concerning the transfer of technology and know-how, as well as the provision of technical assistance, particularly from developed to developing countries, established only vague and general commitments of limited value and effect. The inadequacy of many treaty provisions on technology transfer has been widely recognised, and developments reflected in the provisions of recent treaties suggest that technology transfer provisions are acquiring an enhanced legal and practical significance, with renewed efforts to address the issues properly.

A first development is the broad recognition of the need to ensure that financial resources are available to meet the costs of transferring environmentally-sound technologies and know-how, which has contributed to the establishment of the international mechanisms to channel resources. A second development is the linkage which has been made between the implementation by developing country parties of their treaty commitments with the transfer of technology and know-how from developed country parties in fulfilment of their treaty obligations. A third development, which seeks to address the problem that the application of intellectual property rights might raise barriers to the transfer of environmentally sound technologies, is considered in a later section of this chapter.

As early as 1972, Principle 12 of the Stockholm Declaration recognised the need to make international technical assistance available to developing countries, and Principle 20 called for 'environmental technologies to be made available to developing countries on terms which would encourage their wide dissemination without constituting an economic burden'. Twenty years later, Agenda 21 devoted an entire chapter to the subject of technology transfer and related issues.

Technology transfer is a term which is frequently used, with little consideration given to what it actually means. In general terms, 'technology transfer' describes the specific communication of a body of knowledge which is enshrined in a particular transaction, comprising an integrated sequence of commercial or non-commercial transactions, which might include the following: the grant or assignment of industrial property rights; the communication of technical know-how in a documentary form; the communication of technical or other know-how in the supply of services; assistance in the commissioning of an industrial plant; the sale or lease of machinery or the provision of services in relation to the sale or lease of machinery; providing services to assist in the recruitment and training of staff and the institutions of managerial and accounting procedures; providing services in relation to the marketing and distribution of the product of the plant.

In the context of international environmental agreements, technology transfer could include each one of these aspects, as well as larger infrastructure projects and technologies and services specifically related to environmental know-how.

Treaty provisions

The lack of real progress in establishing practical and effective means to ensure the transfer of environmentally-sound technology is evident from the unsuccessful efforts of the international community to elaborate an International Code of Conduct on the Transfer of Technology to establish basic rules of general application governing the transfer of technology, under the auspices of UNCTAD and the World IntellectualProperty Organization (WIPO).Progress on the subject was equally limited under early international environmental agreements. Early treaties included general language on the exchange of information on appropriate technologies. UNCLOS included a more detailed commitment to technology transfer, in particular to developing countries. Part XIV contains thirteen Articles on the development and transfer of marine technology, and adopts language subsequently relied upon in the UNCED instruments. UNCLOS calls for the development and transfer of science and marine technology on 'fair and reasonable terms and conditions' as a principal objective, taking into account the capabilities of states with regard to, *inter alia*, the conservation and management of marine resources and the protection and preservation of the marine environment, and should seek to accelerate the social and economic development of the developing states. Under UNCLOS, states commit themselves to: foster favourable economic and legal conditions for technology transfer for the benefit of all parties concerned on an equitable basis; promote the acquisition, evaluation and dissemination of marine technological knowledge; facilitate access to information and data; develop appropriate marine technology; and develop the necessary infrastructure to facilitate the transfer of technology. Under Article 269, states are required to endeavour to, *inter alia*: establish programmes of technical co-operation for the effective transfer of all kinds of marine technology to states which may need and request technical assistance in this field, particularly thedevelopingland-locked and geographically disadvantaged states, as well as other developing states which have not been able either to establish or develop their own technological capacity inmarinescience and in the exploration and exploitation ofmarine resources or to develop the infrastructure of such technology and to promote 'favourable conditions for the conclusion of agreements, contracts and other similar arrangements, under equitable and reasonable conditions'. Further commitments are adopted to foster international cooperation and to establish national and regional marine scientific and technological centres whose function will include compiling information on the marketing of technology and on contracts and other arrangements concerning patents. The UNEP Regional Seas Conventions include rather more general commitments on scientific and technical co-operation. Other conventions providing for the promotion of clean technologies include the 1994 Desertification Convention and, in relation to technical assistance, the 2001 POPs Convention.

The ozone regime

More concrete legal developments in relation to the transfer of technology occurred under the regime established by the 1985 Vienna Convention and the 1987 Montreal Protocol. The earlier treaty required parties to facilitate and encourage the exchange of scientific, technical, socio-economic, commercial and legal information and to co-operate, in consistency with their national laws, in promoting the 'development and transfer of technology and knowledge'.The original 1987 Montreal Protocol provided for co-operation in information exchange and in promoting technical assistance to developing countries to facilitate participation in and implementation of the Protocol. It was only with the 1990 amendments that the Montreal Protocol required each party to take steps to ensure that the 'best available, environmentally safe substitutes and related technologies are expeditiously transferred to' developing country parties and that those transfers occur under 'fair and most favourable conditions'.The establishment of the Multilateral Fund, providing financial resources to meet the incremental costs of enabling compliance by developing country parties with their obligations, has provided significant funds to meet the cost of supplying substitutes to controlled substances. The Montreal Protocol may also be interpreted as prohibiting the transfer of technologies which do not satisfy the standards of being 'environmentally safe', without expressly stating that commitment.

Biodiversity Convention

The 1992 Biodiversity Convention establishes a range of provisions which will go some way to encouraging, but still not actually requiring, the transfer of technology. The Convention also addresses the relationship between technology transfer and intellectual property rights. The Convention links the effective implementation by developing countries of their commitments with the effec-tiveimplementation bydevelopedcountrypartiesof theircommitmentsrelated to, *inter alia*, transfer of technology. The appropriate standard which technologies should satisfy are also elaborated: parties must provide and/or facilitate access for and transfer to other parties of 'technologies that are relevant to the conservation and sustainable use of biological 'diversity or make use of genetic resources and do not cause significant damage to the environment'. The access and transfer to developing country parties of those technologies should take place under 'fair and most favourable terms, including on concessional and preferential terms where mutually agreed' and on terms which recognise

and are consistent with the adequate and effective protection of intellectual property rights. Technologies which make use of genetic resources provided by parties, in particular developing country parties, are to be accessed by and transferred to those parties on 'mutually agreed terms', including technology protected by patents and other intellectual property rights, where necessary, through the provision of the Convention relating to financial resources and the financial mechanism. Moreover, each party must take appropriate measures with the aim that the private sector facilitates access to, joint development of and transfer of these technologies. The Convention's financial mechanism should meet some of the costs of technology transfer as 'agreed full incremental costs'.

Climate Change Convention

Similar provisions appear in the 1992 Climate Change Convention, which requires all parties to promote and co-operate in 'full, open and prompt' exchange of relevant scientific, technical, socio-economic and legal information related to the climate system and climate change. The provision of financial resources by developed country parties includes resources for the transfer of technology, and those parties undertake to take 'all practicable steps to promote, facilitate, and finance, as appropriate, the transfer of, or access to, environmentally sound technologies and know-how to other parties, particularly developing country parties, to enable them to implement the provisions of the Convention'.This process includes support for the enhancement of endogenous capacities and technologies of developing country parties. Developing country parties are also encouraged to voluntarily propose projects, including specific technologies needed to implement projects. The Clean Development Mechanism established under Article 12 of the 1997 Kyoto Protocol will go a considerable way towards facilitating the transfer of environmental technologies, particularly in the energy sector.

UNCED and WSSD

Chapter 34 of Agenda 21 ('Transfer of Environmentally Sound Technology, Co-operation and Capacity-Building') reflects the commitment, albeit a limited one, of the international community concerning technology transfer and technical assistance. The main objectives of Agenda 21 in this regard are to help ensure access to scientific and technological information, and to: promote, facilitate and finance, as appropriate, the access to and the transfer of environmentally sound technologies and corresponding know-how, in particular to developing countries, on favourable terms, including on concessional and preferential terms, as mutually agreed, taking into account the need to protect intellectual property rights as well as the special needs of developing countries for the implementation of Agenda 21.

Further objectivesinclude: promoting environmentally sound indigenous technologies; supporting endogenous capacity-building; and promoting long-term partnerships between holders of technologies and potential users. Similar provisions are reflected in Principle 9 of the Rio Declaration, which declares that: states should co-operate to strengthen endogenous capacity-building for sustainable development by improving scientific understanding through exchanges of scientific and technological knowledge, and by enhancing the development, adaptation, diffusion and transfer of technologies, including new and innovative technologies.

Both of these instruments set out 'safe' commitments, and it will be left for more formal treaty arrangements to translate the objectives into the actual transfer of technology. The WSSD Plan of Implementation does little more than restate the 1992 commitments.

INTELLECTUAL PROPERTY

S. Lall, 'The Patent System and the Transfer of Technologies to Less Developed Countries', 10 *Journal of World Trade Law* 1 (1976); W. R. Cornish, *Intellectual Property: Patents, Copyright, Trade Marks and Allied Rights* (1990); M. Gollin, 'Using Intellectual Property to Improve Environmental Protection', 4 *Harvard Journal of Law and Technology* 193 (1991); N. Atkinson and B. Sherman, 'Intellectual Property and Environmental Protection', 13 *European Intellectual Property Review* 165 (1991); G. Winter, 'Patent Law Policy in Biotechnology', 4 JEL 167 (1992); R. Margulies, 'Protecting Biodiversity: Recognizing International Intellectual Property Rights in Plant Genetic Resources', 14 *Michigan Journal of International Law* 322 (1993); D. Alexander, 'Some Themes in Intellectual Property and the Environment', 2 RECIEL 113 (1993); F. Yamin and D. Posey, 'Indigenous Peoples, Biotechnology and Intellectual Property Rights', 2 RECIEL 141 (1993); M. Footer, 'Intellectual Property and Agrobiodiversity: Towards Private Ownership of Genetic Commons', 10 *Yearbook of International Environment Law* 48 (1999); G. Dutfield, *Intellectual Property Rights, Trade and Biodiversity: Seeds and Plant Varieties* (2000); UK Department for International Development, *Integrating Intellectual Property*

Rights and Development Policy: Report of the Commission on Intellectual Property Rights (2002); P. Drahos and M. Blakeney, *Intellectual Property, in Biodiversity and Agriculture* (2001).

'Intellectual property' refers to property rights protected by laws which protect the application of thoughts, ideas and information which are of commercial value, including the law relating to patents, copyrights, trademarks, trade secrets and other similar rights. Legal issues arising out of the application of patent and other intellectual property rights have been raised in the development of international environmental law and policy, in three broad areas: first, the extent to which intellectual property rights granted, for example, in accordance with the WTO Agreement on Trade-Related Aspects of Intellectual Property

Rights (TRIPs), may limit the transfer of environmentally sound technology as required by international conventions; secondly, whether intellectual property rights should begranted topotentiallyenvironmentally damaging technologies, for example the grant of patents in respect of living organisms (biotechnology); and, thirdly, the extent to which intellectual property rights can or should protect indigenous environmental knowledge which has been in the public domain for decades or more.

Technology transfer

The first issue concerns the claim by developed states, in the negotiation of international environmental agreements, that they are precluded from imposing technology transfer requirements on persons within their jurisdiction or control because of their obligations under national and international laws for the protection of intellectual property, patents and biotechnology.

This issue has been particularly acute in the context of the development of biotechnology and the conservation of biodiversity, and is also addressed by Agenda 21 in relation to technology transfer, where the international community declared the need to consider the role of patent protection and intellectual property rights and to examine their impact on the access to and transfer of environmentally sound technology, particularly to developing countries.Significantly, Agenda 21 recognises the bar which intellectual property rights might place on the transfer of technologies: ina passage which balances competing interests, Agenda 21 calls for measures to be taken (including acquisition through compulsory licensing and the provision of 'equitable and adequate compensation') which are in 'compliance with and under the specific circumstances recognised by the relevant international conventions adhered to by states'.

The 1992 Biodiversity Convention was the first international environmental treaty to tackle the issue of intellectual property, its provisions reflecting a concern about the possible threat to intellectual property rights posed by technology transfer obligations, as well as the need to ensure the equitable allocation of 'ownership' rights in biological materials. Taken together, the various provisions are inconclusive as to which rights will prevail in the event of a conflict. The Biodiversity Convention recognises the need to protect property rights, providing in Article 16(2) that the access to and transfer of technology which is subject to patents and other intellectual property rights is to be provided 'on terms which recognise and are consistent with the adequate and effective protection of intellectual property rights'. However, in Article 16(5) the Convention also recognises that rights in intellectual property may have an influence on the implementation of the Convention, and calls on parties to co-operate on intellectual property rights 'subject to national legislation and international law in order to ensure that such rights are supportive and do not run counter to [the Convention's] objectives'. In this regard, the conference of the parties has recognised that intellectual property rights may have implications for the implementation of the Convention and the achievement of its objectives. Finally, the language of Article 22 of the Convention suggests that intellectual property rights and obligations deriving from an existing international agreement might actually be overridden 'where the exercise of those rights and obligations would cause a serious damage or threat to biological diversity'. The language of this latter provision, if interpreted to provide for the supremacy of the Biodiversity Convention, raises the possibility that it might conflict with the international treaties protecting intellectual property rights, which conflict would fall to be resolved by recourse to the ordinary rules of public international law. In the meantime, the Biodiversity Convention introduces a note of uncertainty into the debate about the primacy of intellectual property rights which caused sufficient concern to the United States to contribute to a delay in signing and an unwillingness to ratify. The United States may be reassured by the ECJ decision declining to recognise an inherently adverse link between the patentability of certain inventions and compliance with obligations to promote technology transfers, under the 1992 Biodiversity Convention.

The 2001 Treaty on Plant Genetic Resources aims to ensure the conservation and sustainable use of plant genetic resources and the fair and equitable sharing of benefits. It includes provisions designed to facilitate the transfer of technologies for the conservation of genetic resources. The heart of the Treaty is a 'Multilateral System' of access and benefit-sharing in respect of plant genetic resources for the food and agriculture listed in Annex I to the Convention and which are under the management and control of parties and in the public do-main. The parties agree to facilitate access to resources forming part of the Multilateral System, and to that end recipients agree not to claim any intellectual property or other rights that limit access to the resources or their genetic parts or components. Access to resources protected by intellectual and other property rights are to be consistent with relevant international agreements and with relevant national laws. The Treaty also provides that benefits accruing from the Multilateral System are to be shared fairly and equitably, including through the exchange of information and access to and transfer of technology. Additionally, the parties undertake to provide and facilitate access to technologies for the conservation and use of resources under the Multilateral System and, recognising that some technologies can only be transferred through genetic material, to do so in conformity with the requirements of Article 12 'while respecting applicable property rights and access laws'. Technology which is protected by intellectual property rights is to be transferred to developing countries and countries with economies in transition under fair and most favourable terms, in particular in the case of technologies for use in conservation as well as technologies for the benefit of farmers in developing countries . . . including on concessional and preferential terms where mutually agreed. Such access and transfer shall be provided on terms which recognise and are consistent with the adequate and effective protection of intellectual property rights.

Patents and other rights

A second – and related – issue raised by intellectual property rights in the context of international environmental law concerns the extent to which environmental considerations may limit or prevent the grant of patent (or other intellectual property rights) to products which may have adverse consequences for the environment. The 1973 European Patent Convention (establishing the European Patent Office (EPO)) provides that European patents will not be granted for inventions the publication or exploitation of which would be contrary to *ordre public* or morality, provided that the exploitation shall not be deemed to be so contrary merely because it is prohibited by law or regulation in some or all of the parties. It also prohibits the grant of patents in respect of 'plant or animal varieties or essentially biological processes for the production of plants or animals'.

The jurisdiction to refuse patent protection for environmentally damaging technologies as contrary to *ordre public* also receives indirect support from the Opinion of Advocate General Jacobs, in a case challenging the validity of the Biotechnology Directive (see below). He said:

Preservation of the environment must be regarded in the present state of Community law as one of the fundamental interests of society. That was recognised by the Court as long ago as 1988 in *Commission* v. *Denmark* . . . and is now enshrined in Article 2 of the Treaty which includes the promotion of 'a high level of protection and improvement of the quality of the environment among the Community's tasks. The 'fundamental interests of society' referred to by the Court in *Bouchereau* . . . must to my mind now be understood as extending to the environment. A genuine and sufficiently serious threat to the environment would thus fall squarely within the concept of *ordre public*.

The case law relating to Article 53 of the 1973 European Patent Convention illustrates the circumstances in which there may exist a certain tension between the grant of patents and the protection of the environment. In *Lubrizol Genetics Inc.*, objections were made to the grant of a patent on the grounds, among others, that such a grant would lead to a loss of biodiversity. The EPO stated that environmental arguments could be addressed within the *ordre public*/morality exception, and decided that a 'fair test to apply is to consider whether it is probable that the public in general would regard the invention as so abhorrent that the grant of a patent right would be inconceivable', noting that Article 53(a) was 'likely to be invoked only in rare and extreme cases'. On the facts, the EPO rejected the challenge, noting in respect to the loss of biodiversity argument that biotechnology increased genetic diversity by increasing new plant varieties, that traditional breeding techniques could also result in loss of biodiversity, andthat biotechnology should notbesingled out among various factorscausing loss of biodiversity. The EPO also expressed the view that 'patent law is not an appropriate instrument for regulating the development of new technologies and that the legislature should determine whether a certain technology is so dangerous and unacceptable to the public that it should be suppressed'.

In *Hormone Relaxin*, the test applied by the EPO in relation to the morality test was whether the grant of a patent for an invention 'would universally be regarded as outrageous', and noting that the existence of a draft EU Biotechnology Directive indicated that the patenting of human gene sequences was not universally considered to be outrageous. That case was appealed to the EPO Technical Board of Appeal since the passing of the EU Biotechnology Directive 98/44/EC of 6 July 1998, and the earlier decision was upheld in light of the interpretation provided by the Directive of the concept of *ordre public.*

In *Plant Genetic Systems,* Greenpeace challenged the grant of a patent in respect of an invention for developing plants and seeds resistant to certain types of herbicide, on the grounds that such plants and seeds would be environmentally harmful. The EPO's Technical Board of Appeal confirmed that *ordre public* encompasses environmental protection and that 'inventions, the exploitation of which is not in conformity with the conventionally accepted standards of con-ductpertainingto [the cultureinherent inEuropean society andcivilisation] are to be excluded from patentability as being contrary to morality'. The Board of Appeal ruled that the revocation on environmental grounds of a patent under Article 53(a) of the 1973 Convention required the environmental hazards to be sufficiently substantiated, that the evidence submitted by Greenpeace demonstrated possible risk, but that it would not be possible to deny a patent 'on the basis of possible, yet not conclusively documented hazards'. The Board of Appeal also confirmed earlier case law to the effect that seeds and plants shall not *per se* constitute an exception to patentability on the ground that plant genetic resources should remain the 'common heritage of mankind'.

The *Oncomouse/Harvard* case has attracted particular attention. The applicants sought the grant of a European patent for the US-patented Harvard oncomouse, the genetic make-up of which had been manipulated by the introduction of a single specified oncogene making it abnormally sensitive to carcinogenic substances and stimuli and, consequently, prone to develop tumours, which necessarily caused suffering. The patent was challenged on the grounds that it was incompatible with Article 53(a) of the 1973 Convention. On appeal, the Examining Division of the European Patent Office considered that the invention was not immoral or contrary to public order. The Examining Division held that each individual invention requires the question of morality to be examined, and that the possible detrimental effects and risks, including those of an environmental nature, had to be weighed and balanced against the merits and advantages. Three different interests were involved and required balancing in deciding whether to grant a patent: there is a basic interest of mankind to remedy widespread and dangerous diseases, on the other hand the environment has to be protected against the uncontrolled dissemination of unwanted genes and, moreover, cruelty to animals has to be avoided. The latter two aspects may well justify regarding an invention as immoral and therefore unacceptable unless the advantages, i.e. the benefit to mankind, outweigh the negative aspects.

The Examining Division decided that the invention was useful to mankind, that it contributed to the reduction of the overall extent of animal suffering, and that animal test models were at present indispensable. As to 'possible risks to the environment', the Examining Division found that:

No release is intended into the general environment. Therefore the risk of an uncontrolled release is practically limited to intentional misuse or blatant ignorance on the part of the laboratory personnel carrying out the tests. The mere fact that such uncontrollable acts are conceivable cannot be a major determinant for deciding whether a patent should be granted or not. Exclusion of patentability cannot be justified merely because technology is dangerous.

The grant was followed by renewed challenge, in proceedings that lasted several years and which were only concluded after the coming into force of the EU Biotechnology Directive. In November 2001, the EPO Examination Division decided to maintain the 'oncomouse' patent in amended form.

However, the cases indicate that, although it is possible to raise arguments against the grant of a patent based upon environmental grounds, the prospects of success are limited. The decisions indicate a tendency to focus on the environmental consequences flowing from the intended use, rather than the environmental consequences of misuse, whether accidental or otherwise. They also indicate a relatively high threshold of proof of environmental damage, in terms not dissimilar to the approach taken by the ICJ in the *Gabcikovo-Nagymaros* case. Further, no decision appears, thus far at least, to have invoked the precautionary principle (or approach), at least expressly.

The EPO adjudicatory bodies have been careful to avoid establishing general rules of wholesale application, thus requiring each case to be dealt with on its own merits. The 1973 Convention has been joined by a number of new international instruments since the first edition of this book appeared. It remains to be seen what their influence might be on the EPO's approach, although (as will be seen) their thrust is broadly neutral in seeking to achieve a balance between the protection of the environment, on the one hand, and of intellectual property rights, on the other.

At the global level, the 1994 WTO TRIPs Agreement establishes a regime requiring WTO members to make patents available for any inventions, whether products orprocesses, in all fields oftechnology withoutdiscrimination,subject to the normal tests of novelty, inventiveness and industrial applicability. It also requires that patents be available and patent rights be enjoyable without discrimination as to the place of invention and regardless of whether products are imported or locally produced.

Like the 1973 European Convention, the TRIPs Agreement allows exceptions to the general rule on patentability, of which two are environmentally relevant. The first is that patents should not be granted to inventions which are contrary to *ordre public*ormorality (including inventions dangerous to human, animal or plant life or health or seriously prejudicial to the environment). The second exception is that members may exclude plants and animals other than microorganisms and essentially biological processes for the production of plants or animals other than non-biological and microbiological processes.

Neither of these exceptions have yet been the subject of proceedings in an environmental case, but it is likely that the term *ordre public* would be held to mean the same in the TRIPs Agreement as in the 1973 European Patent

Convention from which it derives. If so, it will remain open to states bound by TRIPs to deny patent protection to environmentally damaging inventions.

A second new instrument is EC Directive 98/44/EC on the legal protection of biotechnological inventions, which commits member states to protecting biotechnological inventions under national patent law, without prejudice to their obligationsunderinternationalagreements,inparticular theTRIPsAgree-ment and the 1992 Biodiversity Convention. The Directive, which took over a decade to legislate, and which seeks in part to clarify the application of the '*ordre public* and morality' exception in the 1973 European Patent Convention, provides that new inventions which are susceptible of industrial application are patentable 'even if they concern a product consisting of or containing biological material or a process by means of which biological material is produced, processed or used'. However, plant and animal varieties and 'essentially biological processes for the production of plants or animals' are not patentable unless, in respect of inventions which concern plants or animals, the technical feasibility of the invention is 'not confined to a particular plant or animal vari-ety'. And inventions the commercial exploitation of which would be contrary to *ordre public* or morality remain unpatentable.

The Netherlands challenged the legality of the Directive on the basis, among other grounds, that its provisions violated the TRIPs Agreement and the 1992 Biodiversity Convention. The ECJ ruled that Article 4 of the Directive did not violate Article 27(3)(b) of the TRIPs Agreement, which allows (but does not require) member states not to grant a patent for plants and animals other than micro-organisms. The Court also rejected the Dutch argument that the Directive's purpose – of making biotechnological inventions patentable in all the member states – was counter to the principle of equitable sharing of the benefits arising out of the utilisation of genetic resources, one of the objectives of the 1992 Biodiversity Convention. The Court ruled:

> It cannot be assumed, in the absence of evidence, which is lacking in this case, that the mere protection of biotechnological inventions by patent would result, as is argued, in depriving developing countries of the ability to monitor their biological resources and to make use of their traditional knowledge, any more than it would result in promoting single-crop farming or in discouraging national and international efforts to preserve biodiver-sity.

The Court also found that, while the Article 1 objective of the 1992 Convention is the fair and equitable sharing of the benefits arising out of the utilisation of genetic resources, including by appropriate access to genetic resources and by appropriate transfer of relevant technologies, the provision specifies that this must be done taking into account all rights over those resources and technologies. The Court identified no provision of the Convention which requires that 'the conditions for the grant of a patent for biotechnological inventions should include the consideration of the interests of the country from which the genetic resource originates or the existence of measures for transferring technology'.

Traditional knowledge

It is broadly recognised that traditional knowledge may contribute to the conservation of the environment, biodiversity and sustainable agricultural prac-tices. However, the international community has only now begun to consider whether there is a need to take steps to protect such knowledge, and whether the existing system of intellectual property or new forms of protection will be required.

In 1996, the conference of the parties to the 1992 Biodiversity Convention called for case studies on the impact of intellectual property rights on the achievement of the Convention's objectives, including relationships between such rights and the knowledge, practices and innovations of indigenous and local communities embodying traditional lifestyles relevant for the conservation and sustainable use of biological diversity.

There has also been extensive work by WIPO in the field of traditional knowledge, but there has been no international harmonisation of standards of protection in this area and none is in sight. Practice differs among national jurisdictions: in some traditional knowledge may be protected by regular intellectual property rights, and in others *sui generis* regimes have been put in place. Recent international developments include the introduction of farmers' rights into the FAO International Undertaking on Plant Genetic Resources and the 2001 Treaty, and Article 8(j) of the 1992 Biodiversity Convention.

These efforts provide a starting point for the development of international rules governing the protection of traditional knowledge, recognising the tension between the objective of facilitating access to environmental benefits, on the one hand, and providing appropriate financial and other benefits to the holders of the knowledge, including through sharing of the monetary and other benefits of commercialisation.

CONCLUSIONS

The legal relationship between environmental protection and financial resources, technology transfer, and intellectual property rights is well established and becoming increasingly complex. This results from the developments at the regional and global levels in the period shortly before UNCED, and is now reflected in the two conventions and other international acts adopted at UNCED, andsubsequent legislative andjudicial developments. Theconsequenceis atwo-way interchange, also reflected in recent developments relating to the interplay of trade and environment: on the one hand, international environmental law and lawyers must take account of, and apply, legal concepts and rules deriving from the rules relating to the international economic system, including the protection of intellectual property rights; on the other hand, international economic institutions and their legal systems must integrate environmental considerations across the range of their activities.

This is a logical step in the progressive development of international environmental law, and follows earlier phases in which standards were set, institutions created, and procedural requirements put in place. There are four fundamental challenges which will need to be properly addressed if environmental considerations are to be moved from the periphery of international legal and institutional arrangements to their centre. First, international development assistance resources, and in particular those provided by the multilateral development banks, must be subjected to a regime which: (1) sets forth clear international legal obligations which ensure that adequate environmental standards are applied; (2) ensures that procedural obligations relating to environmental information and assessment are put in place and complied with; and (3) allows efficient and effective mechanisms to be put in place which will ensure that decisions which do not satisfy basic environmental requirements are reviewed and rejected if found wanting. With regard to review mechanisms, the system of international administrative tribunals provides an independent forum for reviewing employment decisions taken by international organisations and is a useful mechanism which has been tried and tested over time and found to be effective. To a significant extent these objectives have been met in the past decade. The second challenge for the law is posed by the creation of new mechanisms which have been established to provide financial resources dedicated to addressing regional or global environmental objectives, such as the GEF, the Ozone Fund and the EC Cohesion and LIFE Funds. Others may follow, under the NAFTA and possibly even under the WTO. The creation of these new arrangements raises complex constitutional issues, as the early wrangling over the establishment of the GEF illustrates. It will therefore be important to ensure that their creation takes a long-term view; that their activities reflect the needs of the communities which they are intended to serve; that their decision-making structures continue to be broadly acceptable to donors and recipients and allow the effective participation of interested and affected members of the international community; and that they target real environmental needs on the basis of internationally agreed environmental obligations. The considerations outlined above for bilateral and multilateral development assistance apply equally to the new, dedicated environmental funds, the successful operation of which will play a large part in determining whether new international environmental obligations are implemented.

The third challenge, which is closely linked to the need to provide international funds, will be the development of effective modalities to ensure the transfer of environmentally sound technologies which will allow developing countries to 'leapfrog' the dirty and obsolete technologies which have been used to underwrite mass industrialisation. Without international funding, it is unlikely that the technology transfer provisions set forth in recent environmental agreements can amount to very much. Additionally, however, international institutional questions will need to be addressed. One of the major institutional gaps, which UNCED did not fill, has been the absence of international institutional arrangements which can identify and assess appropriate technologies, provide information to buyers and sellers, and act as a conduit for independent advice on appropriate technologies. The idea of aninternational'clearinghouse' is now reflected in the 1997 Kyoto Protocol, the 1998 Chemicals Convention and the 2000 Biosafety Protocol. These arrangements, and others such as the Kyoto Protocol's Clean Development Mechanism and the 2001 Plant Treaty's Multilateral System, should go some way towards achieving greater transfers of clean technologies.

Finally, the fourth challenge relates to intellectual property rights which raise a variety of international legal issues of relevance to the environmental agenda. The challenge here will be to construct a system which can fulfil at least three environmental functions: to ensure that technologies or practices which are likely to lead to significant damage to the environment will not be granted protected status; to contributetothe efficienttransfer ofenvironmentally sound technologies;andto allowtheknowledge ofindigenous peoplestobeadequately protected.

6

Foreign Investment

R. Buckley, 'International Trade, Investment and Environmental Regulation: An Environmental Management Perspective', 27 *Journal of World Trade Law* 101 (1993); H. Ward and D. Brack, *Trade, Investment and the Environment* (1999); Permanent Court of Arbitration/Peace Palace Papers, *International Investments and the Protection of the Environment* (2000); T. Waelde and A. Kobo, 'Environmental Regulation, Investment Protection and "Regulatory Taking" in International Law', 50 ICLQ 811 (2001); R. Barsh, 'Is the Expropriation of Indigenous Peoples' Land Gatt-able?', 10 RECIEL 13 (2001); E. Neumayer, *Greening Trade and Investment: Environmental Protection Without Protectionism* (2001); Symposium on Regulatory Takings in National and International Law, 11 *New York University Environment Law Journal* 1 (2003).

INTRODUCTION

Foreign direct investment is now the largest source of external finance for developing countries, having outstripped public sector overseas development assistance since the early 1990s. In 2002, the WSSD Plan of Implementation called on states to:

> [f]acilitate greater flows of foreign direct investment so as to support sustainable development activities, including the development of infrastructure, of developing countries, and enhance the benefits that developing countries can draw from foreign investment, with particular actions to:
>
> (a) Create the necessary domestic and international conditions to facilitate significant increases in flows of [foreign direct investment] to developing countries . . .
>
> (b) Encourage foreign direct investment in developing

countries and countries with economies in transition through export credits that could be instrumental to sustainable development.

The objective of increasing foreign investment in areas of environmental need is reflected in mechanisms established under various environmental agreements, such as the Clean Development Mechanism established by the 1997 Kyoto Protocol, as well as in provisions of various environmental agreements promoting the transfer of technology. Among the international mechanisms available to encourage foreign direct investment, two are especially important for present purposes: the first comprises investment treaties – bilateral and multilateral – which seek to protect foreign investments against certain governmental acts, in particular expropriation and unfair treatment; the second comprises arrangements – domestic and international – which seek to provide guarantees (insurance and other) against the acts prohibited by investment treaties. Both mechanisms are becoming increasingly connected to international environmental rules, in the sense that they may impact upon states' abilities to adopt certain environmental measures at the national level or through multilateral environmental agreements, or encourage states to reduce their environmental standards in order to attract foreign investment. In recent international cases (discussed below) the principal issue has been the manner in which the protections that investment treaties are intended to afford against expropriation and other prohibited acts are applied when such acts are motivated by environmental (or other social) objectives, including those which are taken in accordance with international environmental obligations. In relation to export credit insurance, the principal issues concern the extent to which such arrangements should be available to projects which may be environmentally harmful, and what mechanisms are available to identify such projects at an early stage of their development.

INVESTMENT TREATIES

The rules of international law protecting the property rights of foreigners (traditionally referred to as 'aliens') are well established. Customary international law grants states a broad measure of discretion in relation to the treatment they accord to the property of aliens on their territory, including foreign investment. According to one leading commentator, 'far-reaching interference with private property, including that of aliens, is common in connection with such matters as taxation, measures of police, public health, the administration of public

utilities and the planning of urban and rural development'. To the list may be added measures intended to protect the environment, which could have the effect of limiting the economic benefits of an investment, or of bringing such benefits to an end altogether. It is accepted, however, that the state's discretion is not unlimited, and customary law requires a state to observe certain minimum international standards in respect of alien property. These standards are relatively well developed in relation to acts of expropriation and due process rights (including a right of access to courts and the principle of equality before the law). In assessing the legality of such acts, it is apparent that a balance must be struck between the legitimate interests of the state hosting the investment and the need to protect such investments from excessive interference.

The minimum standards set by customary international law are supplemented by more specific rules established by treaties. More than 2,000 bilateral investment treaties (BITs) have now been adopted, and they have recently been joined by a growing number of multilateral agreements applicable within a region or to a particular economic activity, such as the 1994 North American Free Trade Agreement (NAFTA) and the 1994 Energy Charter Treaty. Efforts to establish a global regime – in the mid-1990s under the auspices of the OECD – failed, although these have recently been renewed under the auspices of the WTO. Bilateral and multilateral treaties establish specific rules providing substantive protections, together with procedures for resolving disputes between foreign investors and host states, usually in the form of international adjudica-tory arrangements.

Substantive rules

Each BIT and multilateral agreement establishes its own substantive rules governing the extent of the protection to be granted to foreign investments. In general terms, however, the protection extends to two kinds of act: a prohibition on acts or measures which expropriate or relatedly interfere with the investment, and a prohibition on acts or measures which constitute 'unfair treatment'. In relation to rules prohibiting expropriation, it is important to note that the obligations imposed on the host state will not be identical in each bilateral treaty, so that each one must be considered on its own merits and interpreted and applied in accordance with the normal rules of treaty interpretation. As one leading commentary has put it: The most common terms . . . are expropriation and nationalization, but in addition some BITs refer to 'dispossession', 'taking', 'deprivation' or 'privation'. These latter terms are considered quite wide in scope and would include expropriation, nationalization and the transfer of property to nationals of the host state (i.e. indigenisation). BITs generally do not define the term expropriation or any of the other terms denoting similar measures of forced dispossession . . . Such apparent reluctance to attempt a definition of 'expropriation' in the BITs may be explained by the fact that a host state, as is well known, can take a number of measures which have a similar effect of expropriation or nationalization, although they do not *de jure* constitute an act of expropriation; such measures are generally termed 'indirect', 'creeping', or 'de facto' expropriation. The expropriation clause in most BITs therefore commonly includes expropriation and nationalization as well as a reference to indirect measures, and accords to them all the same legal treatment.

In broad terms, the approach taken by bilateral treaties is followed by multilateral agreements seeking to promote and protect foreign investments. The approach taken by Chapter 11 of the NAFTA is not unusual in this regard, although its language has led to varied approaches from the growing number of arbitral tribunals charged with resolving disputes. Article 1102 imposes a 'national treatment' requirement, and Article 1106 prohibits certain 'performance requirements'. Additionally, Article 1105(1) provides:

Each Party shall accord to investments of investors of another Party treatment in accordance with international law, including fair and equitable treatment and full protection and security.

And Article 1110(1) provides: No Party may directly or indirectly nationalize or expropriate an investment of an investor of another Party in its territory or take a measure tantamount to nationalization or expropriation of such an investment ('expropriation'), except:

(a) for a public purpose;

(b) on a non-discriminatory basis;

(c) in accordance with due process of law and Article 1105(1); and

(d) on payment of compensation in accordance with paragraphs 2 through 6.

Article 1114(1) of NAFTA (Environmental Measures) provides that nothing in Chapter 11 shall be construed to prevent a Party from adopting, maintaining or enforcing any measure otherwise consistent with this Chapter that it considers appropriate to ensure that investment activity in its territory is undertaken in a manner sensitive to environmental concerns.

This language indicates a hierarchy between the Article 1105 and 1110 obligations of the NAFTA parties and their rights in relation to environmental protection measures, and does not suggest that environmental objectives can inform the interpretation or application of Article 1105 and 1110 obligations. However, Article 1114(2) directs parties not to relax their environmental rules to attract foreign investment, indicating the parties' recognition that:

it is inappropriate to encourage investment by relaxing domestic health, safety or environmental measures. Accordingly, a Party should not waive or otherwise derogate from, or offer to waive or otherwise derogate from, such measures as an encouragement for the establishment, acquisition, expansion or retention in its territory of an investment of an investor. If a Party considers that another Party has offered such an encouragement, it may request consultations with the other Party and the two Parties shall consult with a view to avoiding any such encouragement.

The 1994 Energy Charter Treaty reflects a similar approach, although it is limited to investments relating to the energy sector. Part 3 addresses investment promotion and protection, and Article 10(1) provides:

Each Contracting Party shall, in accordance with the provisions of this Treaty, encourage and create stable, equitable, favourable and transparent conditions for Investors of other Contracting Parties to make Investments in its Area. Such conditions shall include a commitment to accord at all times to Investments of

Investors of other Contracting Parties fair and equitable treatment. Such Investments shall also enjoy the most constant protection and security and no Contracting Party shall in any way impair by unreasonable or discriminatory measures their management, maintenance, use, enjoyment or disposal. In no case shall such Investments be accorded treatment less favourable than that required by international law, including treaty obligations. Each Contracting Party shall observe any obligations it has entered into with an Investor or an Investment of an Investor of any other Contracting Party.

Article 13(1) provides: Investments of Investors of a Contracting Party in the Area of any other Contracting Party shall not be nationalized, expropriated or subjected to a measure or measures having effect equivalent to nationalization or expropriation (hereinafter referred to as 'Expropriation') except where such Expropriation is:

(a) for a purpose which is in the public interest;
(b) not discriminatory;
(c) carried out under due process of law; and
(d) accompanied by the payment of prompt, adequate and effective com-pensation.

Dispute settlement: Beyond the substantive obligations imposed in the bilateral and multilateral agreements, the arrangements almost always provide a means for internationalising the settlement of disputes. The investor will usually wish to avoid the national courts of the host state, and the host state will wish to avoid the national courts of the investor, or of a third state. The preferred option is therefore to provide for the settlement of disputes relating to claims of expropriation or unfair treatment to be addressed by international arbitration. Numerous options are available, but the tendency is either resort to the World Bank's International Centre for Settlement of Investment Disputes (ICSID) or recourse to arbitration under the rules of the United Nations Commission on International Trade Law (UNCITRAL). The attraction of ICSID is that it provides an established institutional structure, which the UNCITRAL rules do not. It is to be noted that initiation of the procedure is almost invariably at the instigation of the investor alone; since the host state generally has no express rights granted under the BIT or the multilateral treaty, *vis-a'-vis* the investor, no right is generally granted to it to invoke proceedings. The NAFTA and the Energy Charter Treaty illustrate the options. Under Article 1120(1) of the NAFTA, once six months have elapsed since the events giving rise to a claim a disputing investor may submit the claim to arbitration under:

(a) the ICSID Convention, provided that both the disputing Party and the Party of the investor are parties to the Convention;

(b) the Additional Facility Rules of ICSID, provided that either the disputing Party or the Party of the investor, but not both, is a party to the ICSID Convention; or

(c) the UNCITRAL Arbitration Rules.

Article 26 of the 1994 Energy Charter Treaty allows the investor to choose to submit dispute to a marginally wider choice of procedures. Three months after the parties' failure to settle a dispute amicably, the investor may submit the dispute: to the courts or administrative tribunals of the state party to the dispute; to any applicable, previously agreed dispute settlement procedure; or to international arbitration or conciliation under the ICSID rules, or the ICSID Additional Facility rules (where the state is not a party to the ICSID Convention), or UNCITRAL rules, or an arbitral proceeding under the Arbitration Institute of the Stockholm Chamber of Commerce.

Global rules: In 1995, negotiations began under the auspices of the OECD towards agreeing a Multilateral Agreement on Investment (MAI), which would establish investment rules of global application. The negotiations foundered in 1998, by which time considerable progress had been made towards agreement on the rules relating to investment protection and the procedures to govern the settlement of disputes between an investor and a contracting party. On both of these aspects, the draft text generally followed the approach taken in the NAFTA and the Energy Charter Treaty. However, one of the central sticking points concerned the relationship between the obligation not to expropriate or otherwise interfere with an investment, on the one hand, and the maintenance, adoption or enforcement of domestic environmental standards, on the other. By the time the negotiations collapsed in 1998, four draft texts sought to address the general agreement that states should not lower environmental standards; other draft texts addressed related environmental matters. One of the draft texts proposed a 'general exception Article' (reflecting Article XX(b) and (g) of the GATT 1994) stating:

Subject to the requirement that such measures are not applied in a manner which would constitute a means of arbitrary or unjustifiable discrimination or a disguised restriction on investment, nothing in this agreement shall be construed to prevent the adoption, maintaining or enforcement by any Contracting party of measures:

(a) necessary to protect human, animal or plant life or health;

(b) relating to the conservation of living or non-living exhaustible natural resources.

Another state (unnamed) proposed a full-scale 'environmental review' of the MAI, addressing *inter alia* the following questions:

1. Could MAI obligations affect parties' implementation and enforcement of their existing national and regional environmental laws?
2. Could the MAI affect a party's ability to address environmental problems in the future (i.e. the creation of new policy means to tackle new problems or the creation of new policies/regulations to deal with problems yet to be identified)?
3. Would MAI obligations conflict with any existing obligations under existing multilateral environmental agreements?
4. Could MAI obligations constrain the future development of existing or new multilateral environmental agreements?
5. Could the MAI encourage either MAI parties or non-parties to slacken environmental regulation in order to attract investment?

The MAI negotiations did not lead to agreement on these or other issues. In 2001, however, the Doha WTO Ministerial Declaration revived the idea of global rules, within the framework of the WTO. Ministers recognised 'the case for a multilateral framework to secure transparent, stable and predictable conditions for long-term cross-border investment, particularly foreign direct investment,that will contribute to the expansion of trade', and agreed that negotiations would commence in 2003 with a view to concluding the negotiations by 1 January 2005. It is unlikely that the environmental issues raised in the MAI negotiation will not re-emerge in future WTO negotiations.

Case law: Within the past five years a number of cases have been arbitrated internationally that address the relationship between domestic environmental protection measures and obligations to protect foreign investments from expropriatory and other practices. The cases have largely – but not exclusively – arisen in the NAFTA context, and in certain respects mirror the case law of the European Court of Human Rights in relation to the protection of property rights. A number of NAFTA cases are of particular interest for their implications on national and international environmental rules.

Ethyl Corporation v. *Canada* was the first arbitral decision under Chapter 11 of NAFTA, although it settled after the jurisdiction phase. The United States investor challenged Canada's ban on inter-provincial trade in and commercial imports of MMT, a manganese-based compound which enhances the octane value of unleaded gasoline. Ethyl Corporation claimed that the ban (which had been adopted on environmental grounds) violated *inter alia* national treatment requirements and represented an act 'tantamount to an expropriation' without compensation, as required by Article 1110 of NAFTA, and claimed damages of US$251 million. After the arbitrators found that the NAFTA/ UNCITRAL tribunal had jurisdiction, and after a Canadian procedure had found that the ban violated Canada's Agreement on Internal Trade, the parties settled the dispute, with Canada paying Ethyl US$13 million. It is not clear why Canada settled the case. The settlement indicated that the claim might have had some merit, and apparently encouraged other Article 1110 claims premised on the view that domestic environmental regulations could unlawfully interfere with investors' rights under NAFTA.

In *S. D. Myers, Inc.* v. *Canada,* the United States investor challenged a Canadian legislative order banning exports of PCBs and PCB wastes, on the ground *inter alia* of violations of Articles 1102, 1105, 1106 and 1110 of NAFTA. The Canadian ban had been adopted in November 1995 purportedly on the ground of 'a significant danger to the environment and to human life and health'; government views supporting the ban included a statement to the effect that Canada was obliged by the terms of the 1989

Basel Convention to dispose of its own PCBs. The ban was lifted in 1997, while the proceedings were pending. The arbitral tribunal found that the ban was intended primarily to protect the Canadian PCB disposal industry from US competition and that 'there was no legitimate environmental reason for introducing the ban'.

In interpreting the NAFTA rules, the arbitral tribunal had regard to a range of environmental agreements, including the 1986 US-Canada Agreement Concerning the Trans-boundary Movement of Hazardous Waste, the 1989 Basel Convention and the 1994 North American Agreement on Environmental Co-operation, stating that: the NAFTA should be interpreted in the light of the following general principles:

- Parties have the right to establish high levels of environmental protection. They are not obliged to compromise their standards merely to satisfy the political or economic interests of other states;
- Parties should avoid creating distortions to trade;
- Environmental protection can and should be mutually supportive.

The tribunal considered that the logical corollary of these principles was that:

Where a state can achieve its chosen level of environmental protection through a variety of equally effective and reasonable means, it is obliged to adopt the alternative that is most consistent with open trade. This corollary also is consistent with the language and the case law arising out of the WTO family of agreements.

Taking into account these principles, the arbitral tribunal held that Canada had violated Article 1102 of NAFTA by not treating US and Canadian companies involved in the destruction of PCBs in 'like circumstances', an assessment of which should take into account circumstances that would justify governmental regulations that treat entities differently in order to protect the public interest (i.e. the environment). A majority of the arbitral tribunal ruled that the breach of Article 1102 additionally gave rise to a breach of Article 1105, by failing to provide 'fair and equitable treatment'. However, the arbitraltribunal found no breach of Articles 1106 and 1110. The tribunal awarded the claimant US$6.05 million in damages, with interest.

Metalclad Corporation v. *Mexico* is the most notorious of the NAFTA environmental cases. The facts bear careful consideration, indicating the context of environmental and federalism issues against which the arbitral tribunal's approach is to be assessed. A Mexican company (COTERIN) owned a site in the valley of La Pedrera in the municipality of Guadalcazar, located in the Mexican state of San Luis Potosi.

COTERIN began operating a hazardous waste transfer station at the site in 1990, pursuant to an authority granted by the federal government of Mexico. However, 20,000 tons of waste were unlawfully deposited on the site without treatment or separation, and in September 1991 the federal government ordered the closure of the transfer station, which remained in effect until February 1996. Also in 1991, COTERIN applied to the municipality for a permit to construct a hazardous waste landfill at the site, but the application was refused, and the municipality's opposition to any further use of the site for the storage of hazardous wastes was reaffirmed in 1992.

In 1993, COTERIN received two federal permits in respect of a hazardous waste landfill at the site, two federal environmental impact authorisations in respect of the construction and operation of the landfill, and a land use permit issued by the state of San Luis Potosi. In 1993, Metalclad Corporation (a US investor) purchased COTERIN (and the site), without a municipal construction permit having been granted, or a decision having been given by the Mexican courts that no such permit was needed. It was well aware of the municipal permit issue, having made three-quarters of the purchase price contingent upon its resolution. COTERIN commenced construction of the landfill at the site without a municipal construction permit (although a further federal construction permit was issued in January 1995).

In October 1994, the municipality issued a 'stop work' order due to the lack of a municipal permit. COTERIN applied for a municipal construction permit in November 1994, but it was denied by the municipality in December 1995. By March 1995, construction of the landfill facility at the site had been completed. In November 1995, Metalclad entered into an agreement (*convenio*) with two sub-agencies of the Secretariat of the Environment of the Mexican Government, permitting operation of the landfill for an initial period of five years. In February 1996, the federal authorities issued a further permit to COTERIN increasing the annual permitted capacity of the facility from 36,000 tons to 360,000 tons. In April 1996, the municipality rejected a renewed application for a construction permit. The refusal was challenged in the Mexican federal court but dismissed on the ground that COTERIN had not exhausted its administrative remedies. An appeal to the Mexican Supreme Court was subsequently abandoned. In October 1996, Metalclad initiated NAFTA arbitration proceedings, alleging breaches of Articles 1105 and 1110 of NAFTA. On 20 September 1997, the governor of the state of San Luis Potosi issued an ecological decree declaring an area of 188,758 hectares within the municipality, including the site, to be an ecological preserve for the protection of cacti.

The arbitral tribunal found that Mexico could be internationally responsible for the acts of the municipality and the state of San Luis Potosi. As to Article 1105, it found thatMexico had not treated Metalclad fairlyand equitably,having regard to the requirements of transparency imposed by Articles 102 and 1802 of NAFTA. The tribunal ruled that the denial of the construction permit by the municipality– by reference to environmentalimpactand otherconsiderations – was improper, since the federal authority's jurisdiction was controlling and the authority of the municipality extended only to 'appropriate construction considerations'. It found that Mexico had failed to ensure the transparent and predictable framework for Metalclad's investment, and that the lack of orderly process and timely disposition was inconsistent with the investor's expectation that it would be treated fairly and justly. With regard to Article 1110, the tribunal ruled that Mexico had indirectly expropriated Metalclad's investment:

By permitting or tolerating the conduct of Guadalcazar in relation to Metal-clad which the Tribunal has already held amounts to unfair and inequitable treatment breaching Article 1105 and by thus participating or acquiescing in the denial to Metalclad of the right to operate the landfill, notwithstanding the fact that the project was fully approved and endorsed by the federal government, Mexico must be held to have taken a measure tantamount to expropriation in violation of NAFTA Article 1110(1) . . . [The municipality's denial of a construction permit], taken together with the representations of the Mexican federal government, on which Metalclad relied, and the absence of a timely, orderly or substantive basis for the denial by the Municipality of the local construction permit, amount to an indirect expropriation.

For good measure, the tribunal added: Although not strictly necessary for its conclusion, the Tribunal also identifies as a further ground for a finding of expropriation the Ecological Decree issued by the Governor of [San Luis Potosi] on September 20, 1997. The Decree covers an area of 188,758 hectares within the 'Real de Guadalcazar' that includes the landfill site, and created therein an ecological preserve. This Decree had the effect of barring forever the operation of the landfill . . . The Tribunal need not decide or consider the motivation or intent of the adoption of the Ecological Decree. Indeed, a finding of expropriation on the basis of the Ecological Decree is not essential to the Tribunal's finding of a violation of NAFTA Article 1110. However, the Tribunal considers that the implementation of the Ecological Decree would, in and of itself, constitute an act tantamount to expropriation.

The tribunal awarded Metalclad US$16.685 million in damages. Mexico challenged the award before the Supreme Court of British Columbia (which had jurisdiction on the basis that Vancouver, British Columbia, had been the place of arbitration and on British Columbia's International Arbitration Act 1996). The Supreme Court annulled that part of the award relating to Article 1105, on the ground that by incorporating principles and obligations concerning transparency under Chapter 18 into Article 1105 the Tribunal had made a decision which went beyond the scope of the submission to arbitration (limited to Chapter 11). The Supreme Court found that the tribunal's analysis of Article 1105 infected its analysis of Article 1110, so that by relying on transparency to conclude that there had been an expropriation the tribunal had also gone beyond the scope of the submission to arbitration. The Supreme Court did not, however, consider that the tribunal's decision on the effects of the 1997 Ecological Decree had been infected by its analysis of Article 1105. It noted that the tribunal had given 'an extremely broad definition of expropriation for the purposes of Article 1110', but that the definition of expropriation was a question of law which the Supreme Court was not entitled to interfere with under section 34 of the International Commercial Arbitration Act, from which it derived its jurisdiction, and concluded that any error by the tribunal in relation to its decision on the Ecological Decree was not 'patently unreasonable'.Consequently that part of the arbitral award was upheld. It should be noted, however, that the broad definition of expropriation applied by the *Metalclad* arbitral tribunal has not been utilised or adopted in other awards.

In *Methanex* v. *United States* (which is pending on the merits), a Canadian investor brought proceedings challenging Californian legislation restricting the use of MTBE, a methanol-based source of octane and oxygenate for gasoline, on the grounds that it 'presents a significant risk to the environment', by the possibility of contaminating drinking water. Methanex's claim, as amended, is that the Californian legislation was arbitrary and went beyond what was necessary to protect a legitimate public interest, and violated Articles 1105 and 1110 of NAFTA, as well as Article 1102 (prohibiting discrimination). In relation to Article 1110, Methanex claims that the legislation would end sales of methanol for use in MTBE in California and contribute to the extended closure of a plant, amounting to a substantial taking of Methanex's investment in two companies. Methanex claims that MTBE is safe and has not been prohibited in the European Union. The tribunal has ruled that it cannot make a final determination of whether it has jurisdiction until a fresh pleading is filed; it held that as the pleadings stood it would be likely to find that it did *not* have jurisdiction on the ground that the measures at issue did not 'relate to' Methanex in the sense of Article 1101 (Scope and Coverage) of NAFTA. It therefore gave Methanex another opportunity to file a pleading, together with all supporting evidence showing how the measures relate to Methanex such as to confer standing to commence the claim. It remains to be seen whether the tribunal will adopt a broad definition of expropriation, or follow other decisions which have taken a more traditional approach. The tribunal has already made a significant contribution to the participation rights of non-state actors: in January 2001, it ruled that it had the power pursuant to Article 15(1) of the UNCITRAL rules (governing the proceedings) to accept *amicus* written submissions from the International Institute of Sustainable Development. This appears to be the first time that the possibility of an *amicus* submission has been recognised in international arbitral proceedings.

Beyond the NAFTA system, in *Compania del Desarrollo de Santa Elena SA* v. *Costa Rica*, an ICSID tribunal applying a Costa Rica/

US bilateral investment treaty had to determine the amount of compensation to be paid to the investor for the expropriation of its property in Costa Rica. The property in question had been acquired in 1973 for the purpose of building a tourist resort, and comprised tropical dry forest which was 'home to a dazzling variety of flora and fauna' and located next to the Santa Rosa National Park. The property was expropriated in 1978 for the purpose of adding to the area of the Santa Rosa National Park and to conserve flora and fauna, including the protection of jaguars, pumas and sea turtles.

The parties were not in dispute that the object of the expropriation was lawful and for a public purpose, namely, to protect biodiversity; they disagreed as to the amount of compensation to be paid. In presenting its claim, Costa Rica invited the tribunal to have regard to the environmental objectives of the expropriation, and the concern that setting too high an amount would provide a disincentive for states, in particular developing states, to adopt legitimate environmental objectives such as the establishment and extension of national parks. Costa Rica also claimed that its expropriation was taken pursuant to and in accordance with its obligations under various international environmental agreements, including the 1940 Western Hemisphere Convention. The tribunal did not accept that the standard of compensation (applying the principle of full compensation for fair market value) could be affected by environmental considerations. It ruled: While an expropriation or taking for environmental reasons may be classified as a taking for a public purpose, and thus may be legitimate, the fact that the Property was taken for this reason does not affect either the nature or the measure of the compensation to be paid for the taking. That is, the purpose of protecting the environment for which the Property was taken does not alter the legal character of the taking for which adequate compensation must be paid. The international source of the obligation to protect the environment makes no difference. Expropriatory environmental measures – no matter how laudable and beneficial to society as a whole – are, in this respect, similar to any other expropriatory measures that a state may take in order to implement its policies: where property is expropriated, even for environmental purposes, whether domestic or international, the state's obligation to pay compensation remains.

Conclusions

This aspect of international environmental law has emerged since the publication of the first edition of this book, and it is clear from the not altogether consistent jurisprudence that it is yet to find its centre of gravity. A number of broad conclusions may be drawn. First, it has been confirmed that national environmental regulations (and their application) are susceptible to challenge on the grounds that they might interfere inappropriately with the property rights of foreign investors, either because they are expropriatory in character, or they fail to treat the foreign investor fairly, or they discriminate as between a domestic entity and a foreign investor. Secondly, it appears from the case law thus far that foreign investors may have a greater degree of protection than nationals, whose property is protected by human rights conventions. To o great a gulf between the two systems should be avoided. Thirdly, in the one decided case on point there has been a reluctance to have regard to international environmental obligations in determining the level of compensation to be paid for a lawful expropriation: the *Santa Elena* v. *Costa Rica* decision does not indicate a willingness to address environment and development in an integrated manner, as the requirements of sustainable development require and the jurisprudence of the WTO Appellate Body has done. Fourthly, the cases indicate that the relationship between the protection of investments and the protection of the environment touches upon the delicate issue of subsidiarity or federalism, namely, the level of government and decision-making at which environmental decisions (for example, on the siting of hazardous facilities) are to be taken. International adjudicators will need to be alert to the possibility of undermining support for foreign investment by inadvertently upsetting the delicate balance which many states have achieved, or are struggling with, in relation to this aspect.

These conclusions coalesce around a broad theme, which suggests the broad challenge for the next phase of this lively area of the law. There is a need for balance: between the domestic, the regional and the global; between the legitimate interests of investors and legitimate environmental and other social interests; and between the state and its constituent parts.

Bibliography

Bailey, Conner and Charles E. Faupel: *Environmentalism and Civil Rights in Sumter County*, Colorado, Westview Press, 1992.

Bryant, Bunyan: *Environmental Justice: Issues, Policies, and Solutions*, Washington, DC, Island Press, 1995.

Dasmann, R.F.: *Environmental Conservation*, New York, Wiley, 1972.

Erickson, Kai: *A New Species of Trouble: Explorations in Disaster, Trauma, and Community*, New York, W.W. Norton, 1994.

Gay, Kathlyn: *Saving the Environment: Debating the Costs*, New York, Franklin Watts, 1996.

Gelobter, Michael: *The Distribution of Air Pollution by Income and Race*, Berkeley, University of California, 1989.

Harrison, D.: *Who Pays for Clean Air: The Cost and Benefit Distribution of Automobile Emission Standards*, Cambridge, Ballinger, 1975.

Johnson, Rebecca L.: *The Greenhouse Effect: Life on a Warmer Planet*, Minn., Lerner Publications, 1993.

Mandelker, D.R.: *Environment and Equity: A Regulatory Challenge*, New York, McGraw Hill, 1981.

Sachs, Aaron: *Eco-Justice: Linking Human Rights and the Environment*, Washington, World Watch Institute, 1995.

Strahler, A. N., and Strahler, A. H.: *Introduction to Environmental Science: Santa Barbara*, New York, Hamilton Publishing Company; 1974.

Vallette, J.: *The International Trade in Wastes: A Greenpeace Inventory*, Washington, Greenpeace, 1989.

Wenz, Peter S.: *Environmental Justice*, Albany, State University of New York Press, 1988.

Zupan, J.M.: *The Distribution of Air Quality in the New York Region*, Baltimore, Johns Hopkins University Press, 1973.

Index

A

Associations, 183.

B

Binding Instruments, 1, 2, 3, 5, 40, 41, 70.
Border Environment, 204.

C

Climate Change Convention, 6, 31, 34, 35, 47, 51, 74, 97, 134, 138, 194, 206, 231, 232, 233, 239.
Communication, 34, 35, 51, 236.
Customary International Law, 13, 36, 38, 39, 71, 72, 84, 255, 256.

D

Developments, 2, 3, 7, 23, 27, 41, 52, 67, 82, 84, 89, 107, 124, 168, 169, 237, 245, 247, 249, 252, 253, 269.

E

Economic Instruments, 203.
Environmental Accounting, 60, 61, 62, 63, 76.

F

Financial Resources, 25, 35, 65, 135, 136, 217, 218, 219, 223, 227, 232, 233, 234, 236, 238, 239, 240, 251, 252.
Foreign Investment, 196, 219, 254, 255, 258, 269.

G

Global Environment Facility, 218, 230.
Governance, 230, 232.

H

Hazardous Materials, 51.
Human Environment, 91, 222.

I

Industry, 10, 106, 210, 235, 269.
Information Exchange, 27, 28, 29, 30, 31, 65, 228, 238.
International Agreements, 5, 6, 26, 37, 64, 94, 121, 166, 199, 244.
International Cooperation, 238.
International Courts, 37, 134, 141, 214.
International Crimes, 91.
International Enforcement, 138.
International Environmental Law, 136, 137, 141, 148, 160, 235.
International Relations, 52, 54.

J

Joint Protocol, 102, 108.
Jurisdiction, 2, 3, 7, 14, 15, 20, 36, 39, 40, 41, 42, 43, 44, 49, 54, 68, 71, 72, 79, 96, 99, 103, 104, 106, 107, 108,

117, 118, 119, 134, 148, 151, 153, 154, 155, 162, 163, 164, 183, 206, 242, 245, 262, 265, 266, 267.
Justice, 56, 66, 93, 122.

M

Management, 4, 7, 16, 17, 21, 22, 26, 31, 48, 49, 61, 63, 64, 195, 220, 224, 228, 237, 243, 254, 259.
Media, 6, 45.

N

Network, 46, 193.
Notification Convention, 27, 43, 45, 51.
Nuclear Accidents, 42.

O

Operations, 115, 155, 225, 232, 233.
Organisations, 4, 7, 20, 21, 24, 25, 30, 31, 32, 33, 37, 38, 39, 41, 45, 46, 48, 49, 51, 64, 65, 70, 87, 96, 130, 131, 141, 176, 198, 215, 216, 218, 224, 252.

P

Private Sector, 31, 37, 57, 223, 239.
Production, 11, 34, 60, 62, 67, 117, 138, 143, 145, 152, 154, 158, 168, 173, 183, 194, 195, 198, 199, 201, 208, 213, 244, 248, 249.
Projects, 3, 6, 8, 9, 10, 11, 12, 13, 20, 21, 22, 24, 25, 33, 47, 63, 204, 210, 219, 220, 223, 224, 225, 226, 227, 230, 231, 233, 234, 235, 237, 240, 255.

R

Risk Management, 21.

S

Scientific Community, 175.
Security, 17, 41, 52, 54, 75, 81, 87, 92, 102, 103, 105, 107, 110, 116, 121, 127, 128, 133, 145, 151, 186, 257, 259.
Society, 245, 246, 268.
Space Liability Convention, 78, 84, 93.
Strategic Environmental Assessment, 2, 12, 17, 20.
Sustainable Development, 29, 49, 58, 135, 146, 163, 164, 165, 181, 196, 203, 207, 208, 212, 216, 234, 240, 254, 255, 269.

T

Technology, 136, 144, 148, 161, 166, 211, 214, 217, 218, 229, 235, 236, 237, 238, 239, 240, 241, 242, 243, 244, 245, 247, 251, 252, 255.
Trade Associations, 183.
Trade Measures, 136, 137, 138, 139, 146, 154, 155, 156, 167, 168, 172, 206.
Trade Restrictions, 138, 139, 155, 182.
Treaty Arrangements, 46, 117, 241.
Treaty Provisions, 187, 235, 237.

W

World Bank, 12, 21, 22, 141, 142, 221, 222, 223, 224, 229, 230, 231.